A RINGSIDE SEAT TO HISTORY

Every Reader is an Author's Best Friend.

Bangalore, India
September 1, 2020

A RINGSIDE SEAT TO HISTORY

AN AUTOBIOGRAPHY

Pascal Alan Nazareth

KONARK

Konark Publishers Pvt Ltd

New Delhi

Konark Publishers Pvt Ltd
206, First Floor,
Peacock Lane, Shahpur Jat,
New Delhi - 110 049
Tel : +91-11-4105 5065
e-mail : india@konarkpublishers.com
e-mail : us@konarkpublishers.com
website : www.konarkpublishers.com

First Impression, 2026

Observer article on Isobel, Mix with the History-makers, dated 29 January 1978 is reprinted as an Annexure with permission.

Cataloging in Publication Data--DK
Courtesy: D.K. Agencies (P) Ltd. <docinfo@dkagencies.com>

Nazareth, Pascal Alan, author.
A ringside seat to history : an autobiography / Pascal Alan Nazareth.
pages cm
Includes index.
ISBN 9788194201878

1. Nazareth, Pascal Alan. 2. Diplomats--India--Biography. 3. India. Indian Foreign Service--Officials and employees--Biography. 4. Diplomatic and consular service, East Indian--History--20th century. 5. India--Foreign relations--20th century. I. Title. II. Title: History.

LCC DS481.N39A3 2020 | DDC 352.63092 23

Edited by Ranjana Narayan
Cover jacket by Misha Oberoi
Printed and bound at Thomson Press (India) Ltd

This autobiography is dedicated to all those who have inspired and supported me in my 35-year-IFS career and 25 post-retirement years, particularly former Foreign Secretary M.K. Rasgotra, High Commissioner B.K. Nehru, Justice M.N. Venkatachaliah, Mother Teresa and His Holiness The Dalai Lama.

It is also dedicated to daughter Premila, son Anand and grandson Kedar, who have persistently urged me to write this autobiography and keep writing it whenever the will to continue doing so slackened. And last, but not the least, to my very supportive wife Isobel who has painstakingly gone through and finessed it.

Contents

Foreword ix
Pre-Publication Praise xv
Preface xix
Acknowledgements xxi

1. Arrival on the 'Chess Board of History' 1
2. Metcalfe House, New Delhi,Charleville Hotel, Mussoorie and Snake-infested Dak Bungalows in Bihar 16
3. In the Land of The Rising Sun 26
4. Spiders, Tree Spirits and a 'Jewellery Crisis' in Golden Pagoda Land 42
5. An Up-in-the-Sky Apartment & a Sleek Jaguar for 'Our James Bond' in New York 58
6. In the Land of the Incas and Machu Picchu 74
7. Bangladesh and Europe on the Same Platter 99
8. VVIP Visits, 'Sun House' and a Virginity Test Crisis in London 113
9. Revolutions, Executions and Tata Buses in Ghana and Liberia 130
10. Theatre, Poetry, Ballet and NYPO in New Delhi 153
11. A Frozen Lake in Chicago and a Miracle in New York 171
12. In the Land of the Sphinx and Pyramids 184
13. 'La Magica de La India' in Mexico 201

14. Post Retirement Joys, Tragedies, Travels and Spiritual Awakening 218

Annexure 1: Mix with the History-makers (Observer article) 241
Annexure 2: Letter from Lord Mountbatten 242
Annexure 3: Letter from Mrs Zubin Mehta 243
Annexure 4: Message from US President Ronald Reagan 244
Annexure 5: My 'Egypt in Indian Eyes' article in Al-Ahram 245
Annexure 6: Letter from US President Barack Obama 246
Annexure 7: Prime Minister Manmohan Singh's Message for my Gandhi's Outstanding Leadership book (Mandarin Edition) 247
Annexure 8: President Pranab Mukherjee's Message for my Gandhi's Outstanding Leadership book (Russian Edition) 248
Annexure 9: Foreword by HH The Dalai Lama in my Gandhi: The Soul Force Warrior book 249
Annexure 10: Foreword by former Soviet President Mikhail Gorbachev in my Gandhi's Outstanding Leadership book (12 European language editions) 250
Index 253

Foreword

Diplomacy and history are integral to each other. *A Ringside Seat to History* is the prerogative of a diplomat's vocation. It is from that perch that he observes history being made by others; and plays his own role in making history, when age and experience, knowledge and wisdom have conferred on him the aura and authority necessary for the task.

Pascal Alan Nazareth secured his ringside seat to history on the very day he joined the Indian Foreign Service, on 31 March 1959, when he and nine of his IFS colleagues were received by Prime Minister Jawaharlal Nehru. Foreign Secretary Subimal Dutt suddenly came in and whispered something in his ear. It was, the Prime Minister revealed, about the Dalai Lama having crossed the border into India early that morning. Then turning to the Foreign Secretary, he said: 'These young officers will be dealing with the consequences of today!'

A year later, the Dalai Lama paid a three-week visit to Gaya to pray at the Bodhi Temple and preach at the monasteries there. Nazareth, then at Gaya for his 'district training', was appointed his liaison officer. He says he 'felt great exhilaration to meet His Holiness and was struck by his youth, good looks and humour. When asked by a reporter whether he knew Chinese, the Dalai Lama smiled broadly and said: "I know the Chinese".'

There are many more interesting accounts of Nazareth's encounters with renowned personalities and of historic events. There is the story, for example, of Mother Teresa arriving providentially at New York's Sloane Kettering Hospital to pray over his son Andy, then in critical condition after cancer surgery, and of his complete recovery thereafter. Of the historic events, the narration of two bloody coups in Ghana and an even more brutal one in Liberia, and of the devastating earthquake in Peru which buried an entire town of 30,000 residents within three minutes under an avalanche from the snow-capped Mount Huascaran, will arrest the reader's attention.

Nazareth's time as Deputy High Commissioner in London was marked by confrontations with corrupt arms dealers and arrogant senior bureaucrats, closely connected to VVIPs. For his vigorous and successful fight against virginity tests imposed on young Indian female migrants by British authorities he acquired the well-deserved sobriquet, 'Virginity Nazareth'.

An amusing tale describes Nazareth's dread of spiders, which drove him to make an offering of cakes and gin to appease 'Tree Spirits' in Rangoon whom he had enraged by pruning the branches of trees which were their abode. In their 'revenge' the spirits were said to have caused serious detriment to the health of his wife Isobel and her new born baby. The spirits were propitiated by the pagan offering and all was well thereafter.

Then there is the saga of Nazareth's chase, in US courts and subsequently in Costa Rica, of Jayanti Dharma Teja, a notorious fugitive from Indian justice. The details of his meeting with the Costa Rican President—his entering the Presidential Palace, though its kitchen entrance and inducing the President, over an early morning cup of tea, to have Teja extradited from Costa Rica—test credibility, but are true. His relentless pursuit of Teja ended when the criminal was delivered to Delhi's Tihar jail. All this is stuff of a James Bond movie!

Nazareth's efforts to strengthen India's economic and commercial relations with foreign countries were marked by noteworthy success.

As Chargé d'Affaires at the Embassy of India, Lima, he secured the largest order for Indian films (44), for release all over Latin America. In Ghana, he persuaded President Hilla Limann's elected government to purchase 400 Tata buses. This achievement, in the face of stiff opposition from British and German Embassies and the bus manufacturers of their countries, was so impressive that *The New York Times* carried a half-page article about it. Twelve years later *The Economic Times* recalled Nazareth's impact on India's relations with Mexico: 'For generations Mexicans have viewed India as an exotic destination that magically juxtaposes the wisdom of the Vedas, the beauty of Taj Mahal and the tragedy of abject poverty. They did not view it as a potential trade or investment partner, at least not until Pascal Alan Nazareth came to town.'

Nazareth's wife Isobel, with her abundant good looks, charm and elegance, her flair for diplomatic hospitality and her ability to handle all types of exigencies, has been a great asset to him. In the aftermath of the devastating Peruvian earthquake she contacted Peru's First Lady, Consuelo de Velasco, who was President of the National Disaster Relief Committee (NDRC), and offered to organize a fund-raising event in aid of the earthquake victims. The offer was accepted, and three screenings of the Indian film *Mera Naam Joker* in a reputed Lima theatre, the first of which was attended by Madame Velasco and many other VIPs, brought extensive publicity and many donations. The donations along with the screenings' collections made the Indian Embassy's contribution to NDRC larger than those of most other embassies, and Isobel's effort won her Lima's admiration. When President Velasco visited the modest Indian pavilion at the Lima International Trade Fair he spent more time there than at bigger pavilions, much of it chatting with Isobel.

In Ghana, soon after the first Rawlings coup when many Indian businessmen were arrested, Isobel visited their families. On one such occasion, when she was with a young, newly married woman whose husband had been arrested, the military police arrived to take her also for questioning. She clung to Isobel and pleaded for her protection. Isobel accompanied her, in a military truck, to the interrogation centre. When the Colonel in charge at the Interrogation Centre discovered who Isobel was, he courteously sent her back to India House in an official car. Isobel's courageous show of concern for the welfare of the Indian community had a good effect all around.

Soon after I joined the Ministry of External Affairs (MEA) as Foreign Secretary, Prime Minister Indira Gandhi had asked me to do something to revive and energise the Indian Council of Cultural Relations (ICCR) for its proper task of functioning as the cultural arm of Indian diplomacy. The Prime Minister agreed that the ICCR needed a new, experienced and senior IFS officer with a cultural bent of mind and appreciation of the arts and the cultural tradition not only of India but also of other major civilizations. I proposed Nazareth for the job, which she approved. Within a few months Nazareth transformed the ICCR into a powerful and dynamic organization for projecting the best of Indian culture to the world, and bringing the best of world culture to India. His dynamic and innovative leadership of the ICCR gave a new cultural dimension to Indian diplomacy. Nazareth carried his flair for cultural diplomacy to his ambassadorial assignments in Cairo and Mexico, breathing new life into India's interactions with those friendly countries with long cultural traditions.

The book's last chapter gives an account of Nazareth's praiseworthy post-retirement work to revive Gandhiji's ideals and highlight the unique quality of the Mahatma's leadership. He pursues this admirable activity through the Sarvodaya International Trust which he founded. His book titled *Gandhi's Outstanding Leadership* has received acclaim in India and abroad. As a part of this activity, recalling Gandhiji's keen desire for brotherly India-Pakistan relations, Nazareth organized, in collaboration with the highly-respected Pakistani leader, Dr Mubashir Hasan, Vice Chairman of PIPFPD (Pakistan-India Peoples' Forum for Peace and Democracy), a friendship visit by a group of five retired Indian diplomats to Pakistan which I agreed to lead at his request. This chapter also gives a touching account of the joys of Nazareth's family life, as also a heart-rending expression to their intense grief at the loss of a deeply loved child. The brief extract from Isobel's farewell message to her moved me to tears.

This long Foreword really does no more than give a few glimpses of the life and work of one of the most cultivated and dynamic couples in the Indian Foreign Service. There is much more in the book that will delight, inform, intrigue and enlighten readers about the ways in which Indian diplomacy engages with the world.

New Delhi
7 May 2020

Maharajakrishna Rasgotra
Former Foreign Secretary

Pre-Publication Praise

Ambassador Nazareth has written an engaging autobiography of his sojourns in various lands as a professional diplomat and brings out vividly the diverse situations that confronted him. He sheds much light on what to most of us are lesser known West Africa and Central America countries. Chapter 14 and the author's other writings shed light on the impact of Indian values, particularly Gandhian thought, on foreign audiences.

Mohammed Hamid Ansari
Former Vice President of India

Alan Nazareth's autobiography is a most welcome addition to autobiographical writing in India, much of which is a biography of oneself. Nazareth's is different. It is a finely crafted narrative of the personal and professional life of one of India's distinguished diplomats. It reveals an honest, self-critical, and intrepid person prepared to stand up for principles that define his moral identity. Nazareth has had achievements and frustrations, great joys, and intense sorrows, and has digested both into a coherent narrative.

Lord Bhikhu Parekh
Member of Parliament (UK); Emeritus Professor, Westminster & Hull Universities

Amazing life story of an upright and brave diplomat who served his country with honour and distinction for 35 years and in retirement strives to propagate the Gandhian ideals of communal harmony, non-violence and peace all over the world.

Margaret Alva
Former Union Minister & Governor of Uttarakhand and Rajasthan

Extremely well written, informative and provocative, this memoir provides invaluable insight into the foundation and evolution of India's diplomatic policies.

N.N. Vohra
Former Union Home Secretary and Jammu and Kashmir Governor

Ambassador Nazareth has written a memoir of his IFS days, when individual initiative and creativity marked Indian diplomacy. The cultural sensitivity and commitment to integrity evident in this book reflect what he stood for. His work in retirement to spread Gandhiji's ideals make for topical reading in our troubled days.

Shivshankar Menon
Former Foreign Secretary and National Security Adviser

A fascinating story of one who has been a diplomat, cultural czar, Gandhian scholar and raconteur; through his many lives runs a common thread — building friendship across continents in the best of Indian traditions.

Sujan Chinoy
Director General, Manohar Parrikar Institute for Defence Studies and Analyses, New Delhi

Ambassador Alan Nazareth modestly calls his autobiographical masterpiece *A Ringside Seat to History* but his narrative clearly indicates he was not merely a witness to history, but often its maker. He was very much the mover, a summiteer not a sherpa, as also a soft power warrior. His post retirement evangelism of Mahatma Gandhi is a continuation of his diplomacy, which stressed India's heritage of non-violence and universal brotherhood.

T.P. Sreenivasan
Former PR of India to UN & Governor for India at IAEA in Vienna

As skilled a story teller as a diplomat, Ambassador Nazareth has produced a page-turner. History unfolds from quite literally day one at work — Jawaharlal Nehru being informed of the Dalai Lama's arrival in India while meeting his batch of the IFS. Thereafter he takes his reader on a journey from Far East to Far West through coups, commerce and culture, and shares absolutely delightful anecdotes.

Ashok Malik
Former Press Secretary to President of India at New Delhi

Ambassador Nazareth's riveting narrative, extending over eight decades and spanning five continents, presents the reader with a deeply insightful tour d'horizon of tumultuous events in the second half of the twentieth century. Exercising the craft of diplomacy in masterly fashion, he is a 'man of all seasons', at home and in the world.

Gita Dharampal-Frick
Professor Emeritus (Modern History), Heidelberg University, Germany

Ambassador Nazareth has penned an autobiography that well serves as a guide, not just for diplomats but for all who seek the path of truth, as traced by Mahatma Gandhi. Perusing it, one is struck by the self-assurance and insights that mark his encounters with an array of VVIPS in diverse parts of the world. To me this book is less a narrative and more a spiritual introspection on life. It should be widely read.

Fr. Cyril Veliath S.J.
Professor Emeritus of Indian Philosophy Sophia University, Tokyo

This is a marvellous book. Alan Nazareth has recounted his diverse contributions to diplomacy and post-retirement efforts to promote Gandhian ideals through Sarvodaya International and his two acclaimed books on Gandhi. Many diplomats have had ringside seats to history, but few have made that seat, at times, as significant as the main action.

Joseph Prabhu
Emeritus Professor (Philosophy/Religion), California State University, Los Angeles

Of all the positions one serves his/her country, none is perhaps more honoured than being Ambassador or High Commissioner. Having served in these posts and lived through revolutions, executions and flying bullets in some countries, Ambassador Nazareth in retirement has taken up the most important task of promoting Gandhian values. This book about his life and work is remarkable and engrossing.

Rama Shankar Singh
Professor (Biology), McMaster University, Canada

Alan Nazareth's brilliant and engrossing autography is not confined to diplomacy alone. His horizon is broad spectrum and includes everything from politics, commerce and history to art, literature and spirituality in all of which he has vast knowledge and deep insights. When one commences reading his book it cannot be put down until all of it is read.

V. Mohini Giri
Chairperson, Guild of Service, New Delhi

Preface

I began writing my autobiography on my 80th birthday (7 April 2016), mainly because my son Anand kept nagging me about my having spent almost 20 years researching and writing about the already very well-known Mahatma Gandhi and not written my 'remarkable story which was far more interesting to GenNext'.

Having commenced writing it, I found little time for it because of frequent cruise lecture engagements, and travels for releases of the many language editions of my book, *Gandhi's Outstanding Leadership*. My daughter Premila and grandson Kedar urged me to keep writing as what they had read were 'fascinating and deeply moving'.

I decided to title my autobiography *A Ringside Seat to History* because in my 35-year IFS career I had witnessed numerous historical events, some inspiring and elevating and others brutal and shocking, at close proximity.

I was greatly encouraged when my revered mentor, former Foreign Secretary M.K. Rasgotra, kindly went through my manuscript, lauded it and made valuable suggestions for its improvement. Later he graciously agreed to write the Foreword and also to recommend it to his publisher. I am deeply grateful to him, particularly for the elegant Foreword he wrote for it. Sadly, his publisher retained my manuscript for seven long months and then responded, 'It is certainly interesting and made for a good read but unfortunately it does not really fit the profile of our current non-fiction list'.

My sister Margaret Alva then introduced me to her publisher. He, obviously interested primarily in spicy narratives of political party-hoppings and back-stabbings rather than in history and diplomacy, responded tersely in just two days: 'Thanks for sending this over. I had a chance to look at it over the weekend. Am afraid this wouldn't work for us'.

I anguished over these twice 'dashed hopes' for some weeks and then decided to make one final effort to get this manuscript published. I wrote to my much-published IFS colleague T.P. Sreenivasan. He kindly and promptly introduced me to his publisher, Konark Publishers. I am deeply grateful to him for this.

With Konark Publishers, the entire process—from initial contact to publication agreement signing—took only 33 days and was handled in a prompt, efficient and elegant manner. It was a sharp contrast to my experience with the two previous publishers.

I am deeply grateful to Mr K.P.R. Nair, Founder/Managing Director of Konark Publishers for publishing this book. I am also grateful to his editorial assistants Jiza Joy, Lekshmi Parameswaran and Ranjana Narayan for their efficient and courteous handling of the initial formalities and subsequent speedy and meticulous editing of my manuscript.

My many thanks to my very supportive wife Isobel for having stoically endured the many months of old diaries, letters and newspaper clippings strewn all over our home during the writing of this autobiography and for having patiently gone through the manuscript, and corrected typos and other errors.

Bengaluru **P.A. Nazareth**
22 March 2020

Acknowledgements

I am grateful to many persons for their guidance while I was in service and support after my retirement. Some of them I have already thanked in the main body of this book. Therefore, in this section I am thanking only the others.

In my IFS career, those I am deeply grateful to are Ambassadors Lalji Mehrotra (in Tokyo), R.D. Katari (in Rangoon), K.L. Mehta and G.J. Malik (in Lima) and Ambassador/High Commissioner B.K. Nehru in Washington/London for their valuable guidance.

Among IFS colleagues my grateful thanks to P.K. Banerjee, Eric Gonsalves, B.K. Sanyal, T.N. Kaul, Jagat Mehta, K.P.S. Menon (Jr), Ramesh Bhandari, A.P. Venkateswaran, N. Krishnan, Kris Srinivasan, Shashi Tripathi and Pripuran Singh Haer for their support while in service, and Kamalesh Sharma, Navrekha Sharma, Ajai Malhotra, P.S. Raghavan, Gurjit Singh, Ajay Bisaria, Ashok Sajjanhar, Sujan Chinoy, Navdeep Suri, Vikram Misri, Saurab Kumar, Dammu Ravi and Muktesh Pardeshi for their support in my post retirement years.

Among IAS colleagues my grateful thanks to P.C. Alexander, Narinder Nath Vohra, Surendra Singh, Madhav Godbole, Yashwant Sinha and N.K. Singh for their support both during my IFS career as also thereafter.

In my post retirement years I am deeply grateful to the following eminent persons who assisted me in setting up Sarvodaya International Trust in 1995 and nurturing it from a fledgling into a nationwide/

international organization: Justice M.N. Venkatachaliah, Princess Irene (President, World in Harmony, Madrid), Rajmohan Gandhi, Soli Sorabjee, Ustad Amjad Ali Khan, Bindeshwar Pathak, Vladimir Tolstoy. M.S. Swaminathan, N.N. Vohra, Tarjani Vakil, Julio Ribeiro, Lt Gen A.M. Zaki, Commodore R.S. Huja, Arun Mehta, Ismat Mehdi, Jeevan Kumar, Anita Reddy, D. Surendra Kumar, D.R. Mehta, Charan Dhillon, G.M. Bhat and Renu Nanda as also the following who are now deceased: IAF Marshal Arjan Singh, Mrinalini Sarabhai, Ibu Bago Oka, Abie Nathan, Glenn Paige, Justice Alladi Kuppuswamy, Dr A. Ramachandran, B.G. Verghese, B.R. Nanda, Alban Couto, Air Marshal Sarosh Dastur, Vice Admiral John D'Silva and John Zachariah.

My many thanks to the following persons who have assisted me in bringing out the 12 Indian and 23 foreign language editions of my *Gandhi's Outstanding Leadership* book: Sangeetha Malik and Madhu Pant (Hindi); Professor B.V. Sreekantan and S. Balachandra Rao (Kannada); Professor Talat Ahmad (Kashmiri); Melwyn Rodrigues (Konkani); Krishna Das Valsan (Malayalam); Madhav and Sujata Godbole (Marathi); Abasar Beuria (Oriya); Kapil Rawal (Gujarati); Professor Naresh Dadich (Rajasthani); Vinu Aram (Tamil); Professor Ismat Mehdi (Telugu); Professor Akhtarul Wasey (Urdu); Professor Zikrur Rahman (Arabic); Lubomir Svec (Czech); Sara Schmidt (Dutch); Sadeg Samii (Farsi); Shefali Sequeira (French); Manjula Nadia (German); Christoher Salole and Konstantin Kakuros (Greek); Professor Livia Szelpal (Hungarian); Inda Udayana (Indonesian); Sandro Zincarini (Italian); Professor Pema Gyalpo (Japanese); Mi Suk Lee (Korean); Professor Quanyu Shang (Mandarin); U. Myint Thu (Myanmarese); Rajeev Dhar Joshi (Nepali); Shaivya Rubczynska (Polish); Klaus Bruscke (Portuguese); Professor Ion Frunza (Romanian); Professor Marietta Stephaniants (Russian); Madhurima Knezevic (Serbian); Raul Obregon and Jose Porras (Spanish);

Professor David Stahl (Swedish) and Daniel Nazareth and Costa Sarioglu (Turkish).

My many thanks to Pragya Gerig/The Golden Shore in Nurenberg for having published 12 of the European language editions of my *Gandhi's Outstanding Leadership* book and to former Soviet President Mikhail Gorbachev for having written the Foreword for these editions.

I am deeply grateful to the following VIPs who released the following foreign language editions of my *Gandhi's Outstanding Leadership* book: HIH Princess Takamado (Japanese edition); H.E. Mr Made Mangku Pastika, Governor of Bali (Indonesian edition); Hon'ble Mr Gaber Asfour, Minister of Culture of Egypt (Arabic edition); Hon'ble Mr Lubomír Zaorálek, Chairman, Foreign Affairs Committee of Czech Parliament (Czech Edition); Mr Michael Moller, Director-General, UNOG, Geneva (French edition); Fr François-Xavier Dumortier, S.J., Rector, Pontifical Gregorian University in Rome (Italian Edition) and Professor A.A. Guseynov, Director, Institute of Philosophy, Russian Academy of Sciences, Moscow (Russian Edition).

I am also deeply grateful to the following VVIPs who sent congratulatory messages on the releases of the Mandarin, Russian and Japanese editions of my *Gandhi's Outstanding Leadership* book: Hon'ble Shri Pranab Mukherjee, Hon'ble Shri Manmohan Singh, Hon'ble Shri Narendra Modi and the late Smt Sushma Swaraj.

My many thanks to Shobit Arya/Wisdom Tree for having published my *Gandhi: The Soul Force Warrior* book and to His Holiness the Dalai Lama for having written the Foreword for it.

I am deeply grateful to Gandhiji's granddaughter Smt Tara Gandhi Bhattacharjee for having released my *Gandhi: The Soul Force Warrior* book at India International Centre, New Delhi on 4 December 2018 and to H.E. Shri Ram Nath Kovind for having personally received it from me at Rashtrapati Bhavan the following day.

My many thanks to *Business Standard* Editors T.N. Ninan, Sanjaya

Baru, Ashok Bhattacharya and Shyamal Majumdar for collaborating with me in setting up the annual Business Standard Seema Nazareth Award for Excellence in Print Journalism in 1999 and thereafter ensuring it is awarded every year without a break, and to the following VVIPs for presenting it: Former President K.R. Narayanan, former CJIs Justice M.N. Venkatachaliah and Justice R.S. Pathak, Leo Tolstoy Homestead Museum Director Vladimir Tolstoy, former Rajya Sabha Deputy Chairperson Najma Heptulla, IAF Marshal Arjan Singh, former Delhi Chief Minister Sheila Dikshit, former Prime Minister I.K. Gujral, former Vice President Hamid Ansari, former Lt Governor Tejendra Khanna, former HRD Minister Kapil Sibal, former Water Resources Minister Salman Khurshid, former I&B Ministers Ambika Soni and Manish Tewari, former West Bengal Governor Gopal Gandhi, Union Minister Prakash Javadekar, former I&B Minister of State R.S. Rathore, former and present Lt Governors of Delhi Najeeb Jung and Anil Baijal, Ashoka University Chancellor Professor Rudrangshu Mukherjee and Magsaysay Award Laureate TV Journalist Raveesh Kumar.

I am also grateful to Neil D'Souza, Vivian Peres and Raju Singh (Ventours Travels) for having recommended me as an onboard lecturer for Radisson Cruises and to Paul McEvoy (Radisson/Regent), Mary Thomas and Andrew Poulton (Silver Seas), Linda Raff (Seabourn), and Holly Johnsen (Holland America) for having invited me for onboard lectures on their respective cruise ships during the 1995-2017 period.

Last, but not the least, my many thanks to my reputed literary cousin Giselle Mehta for the moving poetic tributes she wrote to my daughter Seema and mother Elizabeth Lucy on their demises in 1999 and 2005.

1

Arrival on the 'Chess Board of History'
7 April 1936–11 May 1959

I arrived on the 'chess board of history' early on the morning of 7 April 1936 at Dr Lucy Lobo's Maternity Home on Light House Hill in Mangalore. This came to public notice in the Munsif's court at Kasaragod, 30 miles to the south, when a telegram was delivered to my father, while the court was in session. He opened it and smiled. A senior lawyer who was aware that my mother had gone to Mangalore to deliver her child, exclaimed: 'It must be a boy!' He and other lawyers then congratulated my father on the birth of his 'son and heir'.

My first 'historic role' was at the laying of the foundation stone of St Aloysius College in Mangalore by Sir Archibald Nye, then Governor of Madras, on 8 October 1946. Shortly before he and Lady Nye arrived, the college Rector Fr Jacques beckoned me to present the welcome bouquet to Lady Nye. For about three minutes I had the spotlight on me. I was just 10.

After this event, Sir Archibald and Lady Nye proceeded to my grand-uncle L.C. Pais' residence to attend a lunch in their honour.

On 23 June 1951, my grandfather Pascal D'Souza, a leading lawyer of Mangalore, passed away. Along with the family elders I was present at his bedside. This was the first time I witnessed death at the moment it occurred. A remarkable phenomenon occurred at that moment. All the approximately 50 fowls he had reared and fed every day cackled loudly and it seemed that they were seeing his soul depart and mourning over this. Since then I have felt that there is a close, though invisible link, between humans and other forms of life.

Those who made the deepest and most enduring impact on me in my youth were my Aunt Bryce and Asst Head Master Fr Stany Coelho.

Aunt Bryce, unmarried for seven of the eight years I spent in my grandparent's home in Mangalore, taught me to be always respectful and grateful to my elders and kind and generous to my companions. From her I also learnt the valuable maxim: 'It is always better to light a candle than curse the darkness.'

Fr. Stany reoriented my youthful views on studies, student life, hobbies, patriotism, religion and spirituality. For Christmas of 1949 he gifted me a bookmark with *A Boy's Prayer*. It reads as under:

'I pray whatever wrong I do,
I will never say what is not true;
Be willing at my task each day
And always honest in my play.

Make me unselfish with my joys,
And generous to the other boys;
And kind and helpful to the old,
And prompt to do what I am told.

Bless every one I love, and teach
Me how to help and comfort each;
Give me the strength right living brings,
And make me good in little things.'

I have made this bookmark my 'Mission Statement' since the day I received it. I still have it with me.

In May 1952, having completed my High School studies, I left Mangalore for Cuddapah, where my father was now District Judge. I did my two-year Intermediate course in the Government Arts College there.

When Prime Minister Jawaharlal Nehru visited Cuddapah in July 1952 I accompanied my father to the airport but stood about 500 feet away from him, District Collector P.C. James and Governor of Madras Sri Prakasa when they received him. This was the first time I saw him in person and I was thrilled.

During his years as District Judge at Cuddapah, Rajahmundry and Coimbatore, my father was greatly impressed by the young IAS officers he met there. This made him keen that I should be an IAS officer and he kept telling me so.

In 1954, while in Coimbatore as District Judge, my father learnt that two sons of a Mangalorean lawyer in Ooty, Eric and Alfred Gonsalves, had been selected for the IFS and that the former who had done the three-year Chemistry Honours course at Loyola College in Madras had secured a higher rank in the IAS/IFS exam than the latter. My father therefore decided that I should do the former course. I was happy about it as Chemistry was my favourite subject and I had scored 94 per cent in it in my Pre-University public exam.

I applied for Chemistry (Honours) in Loyola College but was admitted to its Economics Honours course. I was instructed to arrive at Loyola College on July 10, 1954 and report to Fr. Baznac, Dean of its Economics Department. Fr. Baznac seemed serious and stern when I first met him but subsequently warmed up to me.

In my first week at Loyola College I discovered that two of my classmates—R. Krishnan and Akbar Khaleeli—were renowned tennis stars. The former, soft spoken and quiet, was national champion; the latter, ebullient and witty, was national junior champion.

A good example of Khaleeli's wit was his response to Fr. Baznac, when asked who had enunciated the 'Multiplier Theory'. As he was inattentive to the latter's erudite lecture on this subject he was unaware of the answer, so thought a while and responded 'Adam and Eve'. The class roared with laughter. Even Fr. Baznac could not restrain a smile. He muttered 'Wrong answer Khaleeli, but a clever one. You are forgiven this time, but if you are inattentive to any of my lectures again, you will be expelled!'

In December 1955, when I came home for the Christmas vacation, two smart young men, who identified themselves as recently-arrived IAS Sub-Collectors residing in the neighbouring bungalow, came to the District Judge's Bungalow on Race Course Road and requested to meet my father. One of them, I. Mahadevan, informed my father that he was soon to marry a childhood friend who had been widowed a year ago. His parents were strongly opposed to this marriage. So he had decided to have it in Coimbatore and not his hometown. However, the bride and her mother, who would be arriving one day before the marriage, could not stay in his home before this ceremony took place; he would therefore be very grateful if Mr and Mrs Nazareth would kindly have them in their home for one day. They both gladly agreed to this request.

When the bride and her mother arrived, they were warmly received as family members. Early the following morning, my mother assisted in dressing the bride and at 8 a.m. the bridal procession, led by my parents and accompanied by my sisters Joan and Margaret, younger brother John and me, walked solemnly from our bungalow to the neighbouring one.

When the marriage ceremony began, the bridegroom's colleague, Sub-Collector S. Venkitaramanan, kindly explained to us the significance of every phase of it. This was the first time I was witnessing a Hindu marriage ceremony. I was deeply moved by it and struck by the thought that this elegant and meaningful ceremony must have been performed in the same format for many centuries.

Sub-Collector I. Mahadevan, his bride and her mother were very grateful to my parents for their hospitality and support prior to their marriage.

My father retired and left Coimbatore at the end of March 1956. Thereafter, neither he nor my mother had any contact with these two IAS officers. Thirty-one years later, in September 1987, when as Consul General of India in New York, I went to Kennedy Airport to assist Finance Minister V.P. Singh on his onward journey to Washington for that year's World Bank meeting, one of his accompanying officers asked me whether my father had been District Judge in Coimbatore. When I confirmed this, he smiled and said, 'We have met there some years ago'. He then revealed he was Sub-Collector S. Venkitaramanan, who had explained the Hindu marriage ceremony to me at his colleague I. Mahadevan's 'kalyanam' in December 1955, and was now Governor of Reserve Bank of India! I was amazed and delighted and enquired about Mahadevan and his wife. He told me they were still happily married but he had taken premature retirement and devoted himself to researching the Indus Valley Civilization and was now an internationally renowned scholar on it.

When I completed my Economics Honours course and returned to Bangalore in late April 1957, my father urged me to appear for that year's IAS/IFS exam in September. I would have preferred to take it the next year, but on his urging agreed to do so. Besides Economics, I decided to offer British and European History as my advanced study papers. As I had not studied these histories before, I bought and borrowed as many books on them as I could. One of the three bathrooms in our recently-purchased home on Ware Road in Fraser Town, was stripped of its sanitary fittings, furnished with wall-mounted bookshelves, a small table and chair and a low hanging light, and made into a cosy study for me. In it I spent 8-10 hours every day for the next four months with only short breaks for lunch and dinner, and attending church on Sundays.

In mid-September 1957, I travelled to Madras to appear for the IAS/IFS exam. It was held at Presidency College. On my return to Bangalore I learnt that my sister Joan's sister-in-law Stephanie's wedding to Xavier D'Souza (son of P.G. D'Souza, former Member of Mysore Maharaja's Privy Council and owner of Oorgaum House Mansion on Grant Road) was to take place in December and our home was to be the bridal residence. This caused me much concern as I would then be preparing myself for the IAS/IFS exam's 'Personality Test'.

As a member of the bridal retinue I had my first access to Oorgaum House. At a post-nuptial event I was seated in a corner of this mansion's spacious drawing-cum-dining room when 'Grandma Rose' (Mrs P.G. D'Souza) spotted and came to me. She asked me my name. When I gave it, she asked if I was 'Judge Nazareth's son'. On my confirming this, she asked what I was doing. I told her I had done my Economics Honours course and had recently appeared for the IAS/IFS exam. She promptly stated 'If you are Judge Nazareth's son you will definitely be selected.' Just then, an elegant and attractive young lady entered this room. Grandma Rose beckoned and told her, 'Isobel, come here. I have found a fine young man for you.' She demurely replied, 'Grandma, he is too young for me,' and swiftly moved away.

In the next three days of wedding festivities I saw Isobel more than once but had no opportunity to speak to her. On the fourth day, I heard her Aunt Louise asking her Bangalore-based cousins whether one of them could drop her and her sister Jeanette at the railway station that evening. As none of them could do this, I offered to do so. She initially hesitated but accepted my offer. So I picked up the two sisters at Oorgaum House in my father's Hillman car and drove them to the railway station. They greatly appreciated this and thanked me warmly. This was the first time I conversed with Isobel and Jeanette.

In mid-December that year I sent Isobel a Christmas card and to flaunt the little French I knew, addressed it to *La jolie y charmante Isobel.* I eagerly awaited her response but there was none, neither by Christmas nor New Year's Day, nor even by 10th January. Then to my great surprise and delight, on 14 January, not a card but a letter arrived in which she regretted the long delay in thanking me for my Christmas card and clarified that it was due to her accompanying her father, who was the Chief Commercial Superintendent of Western Railways, on a 10-day tour to Calcutta in the 'Cambay State' saloon! The letter was warm and considering her father's VIP status, remarkably modest.

In mid-January 1958, I was delighted to receive the Union Public Service Commission (UPSC) letter calling me for the 'Personality Interview' at Dholpur House, New Delhi on 2 February. As I had not travelled alone on such a long journey before, my father accompanied me. He had a friend named J.M. D'Souza at the *Times of India*, with whom we stayed. It was bitterly cold in New Delhi and we shivered most of the time despite wearing the warmest clothes we had. At the 'Personality Interview' the following day I felt even colder because of nervousness. However, I felt warmer thereafter as I thought I had done quite well at it. On all factual questions I had given prompt and accurate answers; on questions regarding national and international issues I presented their pros and cons without indicating which side

I supported, so as to ensure no member of the Board would be upset thereby.

We made our return journey via Bombay, where my father stayed for only one day but agreed to my staying on for a week for some relaxation after the recent high tension weeks, and visit my two uncles and three aunts there. I stayed at the home of Aunt Dot and Uncle Sonny at Byculla.

Isobel's elder sister Muriel's wedding was to take place on 8 February and I was keen to attend it as she had invited me to it. However, I did not want to go alone, so I induced my cousin Gerald D'Souza to accompany me by stating the Colaco's were good friends of our family and would be disappointed if none of us attended it. When we arrived at the venue of the reception Isobel's father T.L. (Tom) Colaco was receiving the guests. He had never met me or Gerald before. He coldly asked who we were. I gave my name and that of my parents, whom he knew and had been invited. After a moment's hesitation he allowed us to enter. Gerald then taunted me about being 'a close friend of the family!' My defence was that Mr Colaco was absent-minded and preoccupied and we would leave soon after the wedding cake was cut and the toast raised. We seated ourselves on the last row. About 30 minutes later, just as we got up to leave, Isobel, the bridesmaid, got off the stage, walked towards us, and came to sit next to me. I was stunned and exhilarated as it was a great triumph for me vis-a-vis Gerald. He too was struck by Isobel's action and her beauty and elegance. After chatting with us for a few minutes she took us to meet the bridal couple and her parents. Her father was quite warm to us this time!

That evening I decided that Isobel was the 'girl of my dreams' and if selected for the IAS, I would marry her.

The following morning Aunt Dot and Uncle Sonny told me we would be having lunch at The Volga restaurant. The lunch was sumptuous but when desert was served Uncle Sonny broke the news that the IAS/IFS exam results had been announced/carried in that morning's newspapers and my name was not among the successful candidates. This was a crushing disappointment, but I felt deeply grateful to Uncle Sonny for the discreet and elegant way in which he broke this unfortunate news to me.

The next day I left Bombay for Bangalore. When I arrived home my parents, despite their acute disappointment over my failure, encouraged me. My father, deeply religious, told me 'Alan, we can see only upto the horizon. God sees beyond it. He undoubtedly has something better for you next year.' He insisted that I take this exam again. I reluctantly agreed. However, to cover my personal expenses during the next 12 months, I accepted a job offer from St Joseph's College, as English tutor, on a salary of Rs 110 a month.

About a month thereafter, the marks sheet of my 1957 IAS/IFS exam arrived. I had scored 480/600 in the written tests but only 40 out of 400 in the Personality Interview! The latter amazed and depressed me. I had always assumed my personality was outstanding!

For my second attempt at this challenging exam, I worked even harder than for the first, read many new books, magazines and journals and met as many IAS officers in Bangalore as I could.

The 1958 IAS/IFS exam was also held in Bangalore for the first time, in the newly-constructed Vidhana Soudha building. I did quite well in the first three papers. For the fourth I had a bad cold, and more unfortunately, forgot to take a handkerchief with me. When the question papers were distributed little drops of 'cold' kept dripping on my answer sheets. One of the supervisors noticed this, came upto me and said 'Young man you are in trouble because of a cold and lack of a handkerchief. Here is mine. Use it.' I was very grateful to him for his gracious and timely help and much wanted to thank him, when I had finished writing my answers. Sadly he had left by then. So I asked one of the other supervisors for his name. He replied 'Mani Narayanswamy.

He is an IAS Deputy Secretary in Karnataka Government.' (I met him 17 years later at the Ministry of Commerce when I was posted there as Director (West Asia & North Africa). He was DG (Foreign Trade). When I thanked him for the mentioned kindness, he recalled this incident and jovially quipped 'I am still awaiting the return of my handkerchief!'

Having done well in all the written tests, I was fairly confident of being called for the Personality Interview. However, when the UPSC letter arrived on 18 January 1959, I was filled with great concern that my many months of strenuous effort might be decimated in just 20 minutes as had happened the previous year. So I mentally went through that interview many times over and tried to ascertain why I had fared so badly. I made the long train journey to New Delhi again via Madras. My father did not accompany me this time but arranged my stay at Constitution Club through his friend and Lok Sabha MP Joachim Alva.

When I went for breakfast the following morning, I saw a scholarly-looking man seated alone at a table, reading a book while having his breakfast. I asked one of the bearers who he was. He responded softly, 'Peter Sinai, IFS officer, stood first in 1957 IAS/IFS exam.' I promptly decided to avail of this golden opportunity to seek his advice. I walked up to him, timidly introduced myself and asked whether he would kindly spare a few minutes to advise me how to handle the interview I was going to that afternoon. He graciously agreed. So I sat at his table. His first advice was to be bold and self confident. He said he saw 'success written on your face'. He then gave me the following simple but vital advice: 'This interview is not a general knowledge test but an assessment of the candidate's mental maturity and the manner in which he formulates, presents and defends his opinions. If you are asked what is the diameter of the moon, or the population of Mongolia and you do not know the answer, boldly say so! But if asked for your opinion about GOI's agricultural, industrial or foreign policies, the merits of a presidential or parliamentary form of government or other such questions do not respond with 'It is difficult to say or it could be this or that'. You must quickly formulate an opinion, give it confidently and then defend it as best you can. You will be contradicted by one or more members of the interview board. Be prepared for it, do not be taken aback and defend your opinion boldly. This will impress the board members. But if you change your opinion and agree with the member who has contradicted you, you will imperil your chances.'

This was very valuable advice and I immediately saw why I had fared so poorly in the 1957 interview. I went into this one with a brand new 'batting technique'. The issues on which my opinions were sought were on Mrs Indira Gandhi's recent election as Congress President, the proposal for an alternate capital for India and China's territorial claims on India. On the first topic I disfavoured the Prime Minister's daughter being head of the ruling party; on the second topic I favoured the proposal in view of India's mammoth size, New Delhi's location in the far north and suggested Bangalore as the alternate capital; on China's territorial claims I stated they should be firmly resisted but India should ensure its documentation about its borders are accurate and up to date. As Peter Sinai had predicted, I was contradicted and taunted about being ill-informed but I firmly defended my opinions. Just when the Chairman (Mr V.S. Hejmadi) indicated I could leave, a board member (Mr Kanungo) who had not asked me a single question suddenly stated that as my bio indicated I was a Boy Scout I should recite the Scout Promise. I was terrified. I had not recited it for many years. I made a frantic effort to recall it and recited it thus. 'On my honour I promise that I will do my duty to God and my country, to obey the scout law, to keep myself physically strong, mentally alert and morally straight and will do my best to help everyone some day.' There was a loud guffaw of laughter when the last three words were uttered.

Instead of promising to help 'someone every day' I had promised to help 'everyone someday'! The Chairman jovially commented it was a remarkably innovative and convenient Scout promise! I left the interview hall quite disheartened and felt I had been 'shipwrecked in port'. I made the long journey back to Bangalore in this frame of mind. On arrival home, I recounted this episode to my father and my fears that it might be the tragic 'coup de grace' to my second attempt to be selected for the IAS. My father, in his usual deeply religious way responded 'Our destinies are in the hands of God and not in the words of men!'

Two weeks later, when my father was listening to the 9 p.m. AIR news he heard that the IAS/IFS results had been announced. He excitedly called out to me. When I got there, the names of the top 15 on the selected list were being read out. Since my brilliant Eco (Hons) classmate A. Ramji was not among them I feared mine might not be even in the top 50! However, my father, full of excitement and hope, proposed we have an early dinner and go to the *Deccan Herald* office, where he had a friend among the editors. It was 10.45 p.m. when we reached there. My father's editor friend invited us into the 'newsroom' and had two chairs placed for us next to the telex machine on which the New Delhi newsfeed would come in. It finally began to come in at 12.35 a.m. Initially it was political, economic, crime and sports news, and then finally, at 12.50 a.m. the names of the successful candidates in the 1958 IAS/IFS exam began to come in. My father and I already knew the first 15 names as we had heard them on the AIR 9 p.m. news. After the 15th name was printed, the telex machine began to print **P A S C A L A L A N NA Z A R E T H**. As each of these alphabets were printed my heart kept pounding faster. An 'Unseen Hand' was writing my name, and destiny, alphabet by alphabet and I was witnessing this with my own eyes. This was the most thrilling moment for me until then and most likely for my father too. He began weeping and exclaiming 'Thank you Lord Jesus.' I too was shedding tears and thanking the Almighty but in a more subdued way. The DH editors congratulated us on my success and the high place I had secured among the selected candidates and put bits of sugar candy into our mouths.

Three weeks later my marksheet arrived. I had secured 490/600 in the written test and 340/400 (300 more than the previous year!) in the Personality Interview. The latter was entirely due to Peter Sinai's vital advice on the morning of this interview. (I have conveyed my deep gratitude to him many times after we became colleagues in the IFS.)

In early March, an MEA letter arrived inviting me for the IFS interview. My father, who was keen on my being in the IAS and unenamoured with the IFS (which he thought was mainly 'cocktail parties and golf!') opposed my going for this interview. He reluctantly agreed to this when I pointed out that as only a third of those invited for this interview would be selected, my chances of being selected for the IFS were marginal.

This interview was held at the Ministry of External Affairs in the majestic South Block of the GOI secretariat, on 30 March 1959, 9 a.m. onwards. It was chaired by an MEA Secretary and had an Additional and a Joint Secretary as other members of the Board. Each interview lasted about 20 minutes and we were instructed to come back at 12 noon the following day to know the outcome of this interview.

When I returned to MEA the next morning, I was greatly surprised to learn that I had been selected and placed fourth among the selected candidates, and if I decided to accept the IFS and signed its acceptance letter, I and the others who did so would be taken to meet Shri Jawaharlal Nehru 'not as Prime Minister but as Foreign Minister' at 5 p.m. that evening. The prospect of meeting this much-loved, world-renowned leader was so exhilarating that I decided to sign the acceptance letter despite my father's strong opposition to the IFS.

The officer who escorted us to Jawaharlal Nehru's elegant office that evening was Under Secretary (Personnel) Natwar Singh. (Twenty years later I succeeded him as Deputy High Commissioner in London!). Jawaharlal Nehru received us with his usual warm and captivating smile. He spoke to each of the 10 of us for about five minutes. Surjit Mansingh, the only woman in our batch, was spoken to first. We were all asked what and where we had studied and why we had joined the IFS. Then he stated 'My young officers, you will often be told that diplomacy is all about going abroad to lie on behalf of your country. I want to assure you that India does not expect you to lie on its behalf. Never tell a lie but always remember you have no obligation to reveal the truth! The less said the better; the best is to listen.' He had just finished saying this when Foreign Secretary Subimal Dutt came into his office and whispered something in his ear. It obviously was vital information for his relaxed demeanour suddenly changed and he became grave. He eagerly but softly asked, 'When did this happen? Has it been confirmed? If so, by whom?' Then he said to the Foreign Secretary 'Why are we speaking in whispers? These young officers will have to deal with the consequences of today.' Prophetic words! The vital news the Foreign Secretary had whispered to him and he now shared with us, was that His Holiness the Dalai Lama had crossed the Tibet border into India early that morning. For all of us it was a stunning revelation. We must have been among the very first few in India, or the world, to learn of this historic event!

For me, my 'ringside seat to history' began on my very first day in the IFS.

When I arrived home three days later and informed my parents about my selection for/acceptance of the IFS, our home became like a house of mourning. In view of this I offered to reconsider my decision if a mutually agreed arbiter agreed with them that my choice of the IFS was an error of judgment. The mutually agreed arbiter was Praxy

Fernandes, a 1952 IAS officer, then chairman of Karnataka State Road Transport Corporation (KSRTC). My father secured an appointment with him. At his office, my father made an eloquent lament about my choice of the IFS. My mother did likewise but less emphatically. To their dismay, Mr Fernandes congratulated me heartily on my selection for/acceptance of the IFS and stated that if he had this choice he would have done likewise.

On 21 April, I received official notification from MEA instructing me to report at Metcalfe House, New Delhi on 11 May, 1959 for the 'Foundational Training Course'.

I left Bangalore on the morning of 9 May, again by train via Madras, but by First AC this time, and arrived at the impressive and historic Metcalfe House in Civil Lines, New Delhi on 11 May at 8.30 a.m.

2

Metcalfe House, New Delhi, Charleville Hotel, Mussoorie and Snake-infested Dak Bungalows in Bihar

(May 1959–July 1960)

Metcalfe House was a transformational experience for me. From a modest middle-class home in Bangalore I was suddenly transported into a palatial mansion, with spacious reception and dining halls, billiard and card rooms, and located on the south bank of the Yamuna River. More importantly Metcalfe House was a historic mansion occupied by Sir Thomas Metcalfe, the last British Resident at the court of the Mughal Emperor Bahadur Shah Zafar II. Captured by warriors of India's first War of Independence in 1857 they made it their forward defence outpost against British troops advancing towards Delhi from the west. William Dalrymple has written about this in his '*The Last Mughal*'.

In the extensive grounds of Metcalfe House, then known as the IAS Training School, each 'probationary officer (PO)' was allotted a fully furnished barrack type 'bungalow' and a valet who attended to the needs of five of us. The breakfast, lunch and dinner served each day in the elegant dining room were sumptuous and served by uniformed staff. Besides, our soiled clothes were washed/ironed and our shoes polished every morning. At the end of every month we received Rs 390 for merely listening to lectures, doing the prescribed reading and undergoing horse riding training.

Initially, we were 90 probationers belonging only to IAS/IFS. In early July 60 more from the IPS. IAAS, IRS and IPTS (Posts/Telegraphs) joined us in keeping with Home Minister Govind Ballabh Pant's administrative reform for making India's top civil services less elitist, and more cohesive. The IFS officers' one-year post Metcalfe House training at Oxford/Cambridge was therefore terminated and replaced with a four-month 'district training' in one of the states. Besides, the IAS Training School was replaced with a National Academy of Administration in Mussoorie.

The 150 probationers were from all over India, but three of them had come from abroad. Kris Srinivasan, an 'Oxford Blue in Boxing' as he proudly revealed soon after his arrival, came from London. Omi Marwah and Saurabh Gupta had studied at the London School of Economics and hitch-hiked through Sweden before arriving at Metcalfe House. I was among the few self-effacing and timid ones. Yet, when the election for the 'Mess Committee' was held in early June, my IFS colleagues Surjit Mansingh and Akbar Khaleeli proposed my name as Secretary and I was elected to this post. Those elected President and Vice President were N. Raghunathan and R. Rajamani, both of whom were from the IAS.

The first VIP whom our Training Course Director K. M.

Radhakrishna ICS invited to address us was Mr V.S. Hejmadi, UPSC Chairman. As Mess Secretary, I had the honour of receiving him along with the Mess President. It was an exhilarating experience as the last time I had met him was at the IAS/IFS interview when I was trembling in my shoes in his presence! In his cordial address to us that evening he greatly deflated our egos. After congratulating us on being appointed to our respective services he told us to discard the idea that we are the most brilliant young men/women in the country because we had been successful in the highly competitive IAS/IFS/IPS/Central Services examination. He said the most brilliant students go into research institutions and win Nobel and other such prestigious awards. We had been selected only because we were the best equipped to be trained as administrators/policy formulators for our respective services. I have always kept this in mind thereafter and advised younger colleagues accordingly.

Among the other VIPs who subsequently addressed us were Mr Tarlok Singh ICS, author of India's First Five Year Plan, Mr A.K. Chanda, Comptroller and Auditor General of India, Professor S.R. Maheshwari, Chairman, Indian Institute of Public Administration, Mr Amalananda Ghosh, Director, Archaeological Survey of India, and the renowned mountaineer Gurdial Singh (who had climbed Nanda Devi and was the first Indian to be admitted to the Alpine Club).

Our curriculum included Indian history/civilization, India's Constitution, Economic History and Sociology, Indian Civil/Criminal Codes, Hindi, First Aid and horse riding. When some of us in the IFS asked why we had to undergo training in First Aid and horse riding, Deputy Director R.K. Trivedi (who 25 years later became the Chief Election Commissioner/Governor of Gujarat) pointed out that medical emergencies occur even in embassies abroad and learning to control a horse is the best way to acquire the ability/self-confidence to handle all situations. Besides, in countries like Afghanistan, Nepal and Mongolia travel on horseback is the only option in some remote areas.

Surjit Mansingh was the best and Kris Srinivasan the most timid of horse riders in our entire group of 150 probationers. Though an 'Oxford Blue in Boxing', Kris was terrified of horses. Our riding instructor had cautioned us more than once never to approach a horse from behind as it would kick anyone who did so. One morning Kris was allotted a horse bigger and more restive than the others. So he cautiously approached it from behind and got such a strong kick from its left hind leg that the watch on his left hand was smashed and his wrist severely injured. Thereafter, with a five-day exemption from riding, he was always allotted an old/docile horse. Though poor in riding he excelled in his studies and was a fine billiards and trombone player (Thirty-six years later he retired as Foreign Secretary and seven years thereafter as Deputy Secretary General of the Commonwealth!)

In early August, our Director announced that the Government of India had decided to move all of us from Metcalfe House to Charleville Hotel in Mussoorie in early September as the new National Academy of Administration (NAA) was being established there. N. Raghunathan, R. Rajamani and I, being President, Vice President and Secretary of the mess committee respectively, were instructed to go ahead with five of the kitchen/dining room staff to identify/appoint food stuff suppliers and clean up/allot rooms to 150 POs who, unlike at Metcalfe House, would have to be accommodated on a two per room basis.

The three of us, accompanied by the mentioned staff, travelled to Mussoorie by mini bus on 23 August 1959. We arrived at Charleville Hotel (CH) a little before sunset. When I woke up the next morning and looked out of my window I saw a stunningly beautiful sight; a whole range of snow-capped Himalayan peaks bathed in pink as the sun slowly ascended the eastern sky. All the disappointment I had earlier felt about being moved from Metcalfe House to Charleville Hotel in Mussoorie evaporated. While Raghunathan and Rajamani undertook to handle the 'big' issues concerning the selection of/ contracting food and other suppliers I undertook the lighter task of examining the rooms/making the room allotments.

On 10 September the distinguished Mr A.N. Jha ICS arrived and took charge as NAA Director. His ample physical girth, cigar smoking and measured gait made him resemble Winston Churchill! Though initially he appeared formal and stern we soon discovered he was friendly and jovial. A good example of this was the way he dealt with Surjit Mansingh's complaint that the riding instructor abused everyone, including women officers, even for minor errors. The Director stated that this instructor should be suitably punished and offered a Rs 100 prize to anyone who would bring his topee to him. Considering his height, strength and vile temper this seemed an impossible task to all of us, but to everyone's amazement, including Director Jha's, Akbar brought it to him three days later and claimed the Rs 100 prize. The Director gave it to him promptly and asked how he had achieved this incredible feat. Akbar revealed that he had engaged this instructor in friendly conversation, praised his turban, enquired when and where he had bought it and how much he had paid for it. When the latter revealed that he had bought it five years earlier and paid Rs 70 for it, Akbar gave him Rs 70, took his topee and told him to buy a new one. Director Jha had a hearty laugh, congratulated him on his clever strategy and told him he would make an excellent diplomat. He recounted a definition of diplomacy by Winston Churchill: 'The art of telling a man to go to hell in such a way that he asks for directions to it!'

Narinder Nath Vohra was another colleague who often created mirth. He was a great tease. Rajamani, the tallest among us (6'6") he nicknamed 'Bamboo Raja', and me, when he discovered I loved

South Indian food, as 'Idli dosa Alan'. However, the person he teased the most, was our tall and elegant colleague Usha Gautam. She had got into the Indian Audit and Accounts Service (IAAS) that year but keen on the IFS had decided to reappear for its exam the next year. She therefore spent most of her spare time in the library or her room, preparing for it. Narinder railed against her. 'Punjabi women are always friendly, lively and outgoing; Usha is the only sad exception. She is our "Mater Dolorosa".' Amazingly five years later he married her! It then became clear to me that all his remarks about Usha were made because she was resisting his efforts to befriend her! She was selected for the IFS in 1960 but because of parental insistence chose the IAS. (Isobel and I spent three memorable days with Narinder and Usha at Srinagar Raj Bhavan in September 2014. He was then Governor of J & K and served in that post longer than any of his predecessors).

In mid-September, Louis Menezes and I had met a Goan pianist named Gloria at the Mussoorie Catholic Church. As there was a piano in the ballroom of Charleville Hotel we asked her whether she would give us piano classes. She readily agreed and quoted Rs 50 per month for two classes a week for each of us. Mohandas Moses also joined these classes. These were given from 6-7 p.m. on Mondays and Fridays. However, we were required to practice piano playing for half an hour every day, by rotation from 9.30-11.p.m. As there was a rumour about the ghost of an English woman, who had been pushed off the ballroom balcony by her British husband, appearing on it now and again, I dreaded the 10.30-11 p.m. slot. One night I was terrified when I saw a white dress fluttering outside the glass door next to the piano. I fled from there to Louis' room and recounted this eerie incident to him. He summoned his intrepid *pahadi* valet Nar Bahadur to investigate this 'ghost'. He came back smiling. The 'white dress' was actually the lower part of the nylon curtain of the balcony door, which had got left out when the door was shut!

On 1 December 1959 I along with my nine IFS colleagues left Mussoorie for New Delhi. We spent one week at MEA, submitted reports on what each of us had gained from our six-month 'foundational training' as also our options for our 'District Training' states. I opted for Tamil Nadu so as to be close to my parents in Bangalore.

On 10 December, we left New Delhi by rail for Dhanbad, the first halt on our two-week 'Bharat Darshan' tour. Here we visited the Central Institute of Mining and Fuel Research and the Kosi river project. We then proceeded to Calcutta and visited the Chittaranjan Locomotive Works and Naval dockyard there; then went to Sambalpur in Orissa to view the newly built Hirakud Dam and to Visakhapatam to visit the naval shipyard.

From Vizag we went to Bangalore to visit the Hindustan Aircraft and Hindustan Machine Tool factories. I managed to find a two-hour slot to visit my parents with Surjit Mansingh and Akbar Khaleeli. They were delighted to meet both of them. They had met Akbar before but were meeting Surjit for the first time and were greatly impressed with her elegance, poise and self-confidence.

On conclusion of our two-week Bharat Darshan tour we returned to MEA and submitted our reports about it. We were briefed about our impending four-month 'District Training' (DT). To ensure that Japanese would be allotted to me as my foreign language I stayed on at MEA one evening to meet Under Secretary Natwar Singh and requested him to allot it to me. He chuckled and assured me it would be allotted to me 'on a silver platter'! He complimented me on choosing this language and pointed out that probationers generally ask for easy languages like French and Spanish rather than tougher ones like Chinese, Japanese and Russian. The latter are far more important for the IFS than the former.

On 2 January 1960 each of us left for our respective 'District Training'. Mine was Gaya in Bihar and I was to report to District

Collector Alban Couto. He was a handsome Goan bachelor who had his devout Catholic mother managing his home for him.

In welcoming me Mr Couto stated that my arrival was perfectly timed as His Holiness the Dalai Lama was arriving in Gaya later that week for a two-week stay at Bodh Gaya. He had therefore decided to appoint me as his Liaison Officer. My duties would be to ensure that the food, medical, transport and PR requirements of His Holiness and his retinue were promptly met.

When His Holiness arrived in Gaya and I was introduced to him by Mr Couto as his Liaison Officer. I felt a great exhilaration and was struck by his self-confidence despite his youth, and his humorous repartee notwithstanding his minimal knowledge of English. At his first press conference, which I arranged, when a reporter asked him whether he knew Chinese, he smiled and responded, 'I know the Chinese!'

My 'District Training' commenced soon after His Holiness' departure. An extensive tour programme was drawn up for me by Mr Couto so that I could observe and study how India's administrative structure is constructed and functions from village to district to state government levels; how agricultural, education, health and rural development programmes are implemented and impact on people's lives.

On these tours, nearly all done by jeep, I was wonderstruck by the sharp contrast between Bihar's extremely fertile northern part and its arid but mineral rich southern part; and its many historic and religious sites in both parts. Some of the dak bungalows I spent nights in were in remote, wild animal- and dacoit-infested areas. In the bathroom of one of them there was a noticeboard which cautioned guests about poisonous snakes, and mentioned two guests who had died—one stung by a cobra coiled under the pillow and the other by a viper nestled under the toilet seat!

Back at MEA in early May, I learnt with much pleasure that Japanese had been allotted to me as my Foreign Language and my Bombay to Yokohama passage was being booked on the *S.S. Vietnam* in mid July 1960. Those days only Ambassadors and High Commissioners were entitled to travel by air. I was also informed that I could avail of four weeks leave before leaving for Japan and should I decide to get married during the period my wife could travel with me at GOI cost. I was delighted about this.

On arrival in Bangalore I conveyed the above information to my parents and informed them of my intention to marry Isobel before leaving for Japan. My father expressed surprise and firmly opposed this proposal. He stated that studying Japanese was a big challenge and I would be confirmed in the IFS only when I passed it. If I got married now the first child would most likely arrive within the first 12 months and I would be burdened with fatherhood responsibilities and unable to focus on my Japanese study. I timidly argued that even language officers are required to handle some official hospitality which a wife could assist me with. My father trumped me on this by offering to send his wife to assist me! This dashed my fond hopes of arriving in exotic Japan with a much loved, newly married wife!

I visited Isobel a few days later and conveyed the above to her. She and I were already strongly bonded emotionally. So when I requested her to await my return two years later she tearfully agreed but made the point that my father and I were being quite unfair to her.

Neither she nor any members of her family came to the railway station to see me and my mother off to Bombay on 20 July 1960. We were accompanied upto Bombay by my father, sister Margaret and Don.

My mother's and my departure for Japan triggered a great family reunion at Bombay. For the first time, two of my mother's brothers and her four sisters, their spouses and their children attended the pre-departure dinner hosted by her elder brother. The next day all of them came to the Bombay port to see us off. As port security was quite lax those days, all of them were permitted to board the ship along with us.

Compared to our simple life and food at home, the three-week voyage on the *S.S. Vietnam* with large buffets of Indian and French food items at every meal and even wines being served free of cost during dinner, was ultra-luxurious for us. The ship made two-day stops at Colombo, Singapore, Saigon, Hong Kong and Kobe. Each of these ports was fascinating in its own way, Hong Kong particularly so after sunset, when the myriad lights of the city, which spread upwards from the port to the top of the surrounding hills, shimmered in the bay. It was a great joy for me to see my mother's exultation over these new sights and experiences. At every port she purchased three picture post cards. Forty-six years later, when she passed away and I went through her belongings, I found thesc postcards all neatly pasted in an album with the names of the ports they pertained to, neatly written on the top of that page.

3

In the Land of The Rising Sun
(August 1960 – July 1963)

We arrived in Yokohama at 8 a.m. on 14 August. By 10 a.m., we were at the renowned Imperial Hotel (IH). This was a big surprise. The Indian Embassy attaché who had escorted us here informed me that a room had been booked for two nights at this hotel for a senior GOI official. As his visit was suddenly cancelled and the room had already been paid for we were being accommodated in it.

Staying at this hotel was a stunning experience. It was Tokyo's most renowned because its architect was the famed Frank Lloyd Wright. Besides, it was the only building in Tokyo to withstand Japan's devastating 1 September 1923 earthquake which killed 143,000 people. Its promotional slogan therefore was 'The Imperial Hotel is Alright because it is All Wright'.

The elegance and opulence of this hotel made me and my mother feel like country bumpkins suddenly thrust into imperial grandeur.

When we looked at the room service menu and prices therein we were dumbfounded!

Before leaving, the attaché gave me an invitation for the Independence Day flag hoisting at the Ambassador's residence the following morning. The invitation included my mother's name. The attaché informed me that the Embassy of India (EI) staff car would come to take us to this event and bring us back to the hotel thereafter.

At the flag hoisting and subsequent reception I met most of the EI diplomatic officers. I was particularly happy to meet the two Third Secretary language officers Arjun Asrani and Hardev Bhalla. My mother was happy to meet First Secretary (Info) Joy Jacob and his wife Molly, whose brother Mathew was married to Isobel's aunt Louise, who was well known to her. Ambassador Lalji Mehrotra and Mrs Mehrotra welcomed us warmly.

The following day we werc moved to the far less expensive Azabu Prince Hotel. Three of the EI officers, including the Jacobs, lived close to it and kindly took turns to invite us to lunch, or dinner almost every day. We greatly appreciated this.

My next two weeks were spent in house hunting. Almost all the houses I liked had rents higher than my rental ceiling of US$ 45. I finally found one within this ceiling. It was newly constructed, had a fair sized sitting room, two 'tatami' bedrooms and had only one bathroom. The dining room faced a mini garden and had a covered driveway as a garage. The lease was signed the following day and we moved into it three days later when EI had furnished it.

The next challenge was to find a housemaid. We were advised to insert an ad in the neighbourhood bulletin indicating she was needed to work in an Indian diplomat's house. That weekend a taxi stopped outside our home, and an attractive, well-dressed young woman alighted and came to our door. She said in rudimentary English that she had seen my ad and would be glad to work in my home. She added that she was aware Indians spoke good English and wished to improve her knowledge of it before going to England for higher studies later that year. If decision-making in this matter was left to me she would have got the job but my mother, who had the last word in household matters, courteously and firmly told her that she was 'over qualified' to work in our modest home. Quite disappointed, she left soon after.

Three days later, another applicant arrived. She was plump, middle-aged, and unattractive but a sturdy woman named Masuko. She was employed and worked, first for my mother and me, and then for Isobel and me for the next three years.

My Japanese classes commenced the following week. A teacher certified by the reputed Naganuma Japanese Language School, and appointed by EI arrived at my home to give me the first of my classes. These would be given twice every week for the next 18 months.

I will never forget my first Japanese language lesson. The teacher, a soft spoken, middle aged woman, arrived at 4 p.m. with a bunch of flowers in her hand. She introduced herself thus. 'I am your Japanese teacher. My name is Sachiko Kimura. My English is only little, so I speak only in Japanese. You listen me carefully. Japanese must be learnt, like a child, through the ear and not the head.' She then picked a red flower from the bunch in her hand and said '*Kore wa nan des ka? Kore wa hana des*'. She made me repeat these sentences five times and then asked what they meant. This was fairly obvious and I replied 'What is this? This is a flower'. She smiled and exclaimed 'Ojozu' (excellent). She then held up the same flower and said '*Kore wa akai hana des*', made me repeat it five times and then asked what it meant. It was quite obvious again and I replied 'This is a red flower'. Next she picked a white flower, and said '*Kore wa shiroi hana des*', made me repeat it five times and then asked what it meant. I replied 'This is a white flower'. Each time I repeated a sentence she ensured it was pronounced and intoned exactly as she had done. By the end of my very first two-hour lesson I had learnt, and have never forgotten, basic sentence construction and the Japanese words for flower and its many colours (*sakurairo*: pink; *kakiiro*: orange; *chairo*: brown; *sorairo*: blue; *midori*: green; *murasaki*: purple and *makkuro*: black). Subsequent classes followed the same pattern but the sentences became longer and more complicated. One such was the following '*Hashi no hashi no hashi o aruku*' (to walk on the edge of a chopstick on a bridge).

I was not taught the Japanese Kanji (ideographs) and phonetic scripts (Katakana/Hiragana) for the first four months. When these lessons began I was fascinated by the way more and more meaningful ideographs were constructed from simpler ones, e.g. two trees together was a grove, three trees together was a forest; three women together was noise! Fire and water together was steam; horse and carriage together was a horse carriage; fire, water and carriage together means steam locomotive!

Along with my twice-a-week Japanese classes I also had to handle student welfare work (there were a few Indian students in Japan even in 1960) and prepare the first draft of the monthly political report.

In the latter connection I was now and again deputed to attend public political meetings. One such was a pre-election political rally at Tokyo's Hibiya Hall on 12 October 1960 in which Inejiro Asanuma, leader of Japan Socialist Party, was to speak. He was controversial because he often praised Communist China's achievements. About 10 minutes after he started speaking, a youth rushed onto the stage and stabbed him in the chest. He was rushed to the closest hospital but died later that evening. The assassin, Otoya Yamaguchi, was a 17-year-old member of one of Japan's right-wing groups. As this debate was nationally telecast by NHK (Japan's broadcaster), the Asanuma assassination was seen by thousands of people all over Japan on their TV screens. I witnessed it in Hibiya Hall, as and when it happened!

The following month another sensational death occurred in

Tokyo. Air Chief Marshal Subroto Mukherjee, accompanied by Air Commodore (later Air Chief Marshal) P.C. Lal arrived in Tokyo at 3 p.m. on 8 November 1960, as VVIP invitees on Air India's inaugural Jet service to Tokyo. The former was received at the airport by Japan's Air Force Chief. His motorcade into the city was given a ceremonial motorcycle escort.

The same evening Ambassador Mehrotra hosted a reception in Air Chief Marshal Mukherjee's honour. It was attended by all the three chiefs of Japan's Defence Services and was an impressive event. We all left the Ambassador's residence elated by the impactful events of that day.

I was woken up at about 5 a.m. by a telephone call from Jacob. He told me to be in office by 8 a.m. as we had a crisis to handle—Air Chief Marshal Mukherjee had died. Jacob was informed of this by our Military Attaché Col. C.S. Mehta, who had learnt of it from Commodore Biren Ghosh, the Tokyo-based naval officer who handled the Indian Navy's hi-tech electronic purchases from Japan.

We subsequently learnt that after Air Chief Marshal Mukherjee returned to his hotel from the Ambassador's reception Commodore Ghosh, who was his long-time friend, called on him and suggested a 'Japanese dinner at a traditional Japanese inn'. The former agreed to this. Among the items served at this dinner was sashimi (marinated raw fish). When the Air Chief Marshal put one of these sticky rice and tuna morsels into his mouth; he not relishing it tried to gulp it down but it got stuck in his throat and he died before any medical aid could reach him.

By the time Jacob and I arrived at EI (which is located on the Imperial Palace Moat close to the British Embassy) telephone calls were already coming in from newspaper offices enquiring whether the shocking news about the Indian VIP's death was true and if so, how and where it occurred. As most of these calls were in Japanese I had to handle them with the little Japanese I knew, until our Japanese staff arrived 9 a.m onwards. By 11 a.m., this news had spread to diplomatic missions, the Foreign Office, Defence Ministry and Indian community. The Ministry of Defence (MoD) in New Delhi had been informed of this tragedy by our Military attaché soon after he learnt about it from Commodore Ghosh a little before midnight of the previous day. By 9 a.m. MoD's instructions were received that the Air Chief Marshal's body should be embalmed and sent to New Delhi in an airtight coffin by Air India's return flight. The embalmed body, in an airtight, elegant Japanese coffin was taken to Tokyo's Haneda airport, escorted by the same motorcycle riders who had brought the Air Chief Marshal into Tokyo the previous day. It was carefully raised into the belly of the Air India plane with thick nylon ropes wrapped in silk, to give the coffin the elegance and solemnity it deserved. For me, it was a deeply moving experiencc and a stark reminder of the following lines of Thomas Gray's *Elegy in a Country Graveyard*:

> 'The boast of heraldry, the pomp of pow'r,
> And all that beauty, all that wealth e'er gave,
> Await alike th' inevitable hour.
> The paths of glory lead but to the grave'.

(Three hours after the coffin arrived at the Palam Airport on 10 November, the late Air Chief Marshal's body was cremated with full military honours. It was an impressive ceremony with a fly-past of 49 aircraft, (one for each of his 49 years), each aircraft dipping its wings in a last salute to the 'Father Figure' of the Indian Air Force. He was its first, much loved Chief of Air Staff. His wife Sharada Mukherjee (niece of Mrs Vijaya Lakshmi Pandit) was some years later appointed the Governor of Andhra Pradesh (1977-78) and then of Gujarat (1978-83).

In early November 1960, I was put in charge of the visa section. This gave me the privilege of signing the visas of Crown Prince Akihito and Princess Michiko for their 10-day visit to India from 27 November–6 December. This was the first visit to India by a member of Japan's Imperial family. They got a warm, high-level welcome, being received at the airport by President Rajendra Prasad, Vice President S. Radhakrishnan and Prime Minister Jawaharlal Nehru. The last mentioned described Princess Michiko as a 'vision of grace and beauty'.

Ten days after the Imperial couple returned from India, the Imperial Chancellor requested a call on Ambassador Mehrotra. On the day of his call on the Ambassador, all officers were told to come to his office a little before he arrived. The Chancellor came carrying an elegantly packed, Imperial crested silver frame with an autographed photo of the Crown Prince and Princess at the Taj Mahal, as a token of their appreciation for the excellent arrangements made for their visit to India. The Ambassador proudly held it up for all of us to see and then suddenly told me to identify which was the Crown Prince's signature. I froze in my shoes. My study of Japanese Kanji had not yet commenced and my Japanese was only the spoken language. Fortunately, among the few Kanji (9 or 10) I could identify was *Ko*, an adjunct to most female names. I noticed it in one of the signatures. That obviously was Princess Michiko's. So I pointed to the other as that of the Crown Prince. The Chancellor was very impressed. He stated that both signatures were highly stylized and therefore not easy for any foreigner to identify. He said my ability to do so was '*rippa*' (excellent). The Ambassador gave me a pat on the back and my colleagues clapped. None of them knew I had come through this ordeal by 'the skin of my teeth'. (Fifty-eight years later Princess Michiko's daughter-in-law Princess Takamado released the Japanese edition of my *Gandhi's Outstanding Leadership* book at the EI Vivekananda Cultural Centre! A photo of it is among those in this book).

In early June 1961, P.K. Banerjee, who was Deputy Chief of Mission (DCM) and my principal mentor, left Tokyo for Beijing to take over as Chargé D'Affaires (CDA) when Ambassador G.K. Parthasarathy departed and until his successor, who had not yet been named, arrived. Three weeks later Ambassador and Mrs Parthasarathy came to Tokyo en route to India. Ambassador and Mrs Mehrotra hosted an informal dinner for them to which all the EI diplomatic officers were invited. They graciously invited my mother also.

In his briefing to us Ambassador Parthasarathy spoke of the disastrous consequences of Chairman Mao Zedong's 'Great Leap Forward'; over 20 million starvation deaths had occurred in the previous three years. The economy was in shambles. Senior party leaders were, for the first time, criticizing the 'leap'. This had made Mao more authoritarian and bellicose than before. The strained India–China relationship, could become more so hereafter. Therefore, India needed to deepen its relations with Japan and the US. (As a follow-up on this suggestion Ambassador Mehrotra proposed to MEA that Japanese Prime Minister Hayato Ikeda be invited to India. This visit took place in November that year).

Ambassador Parthasarathy's briefing on recent developments in China was absorbing but Mrs Parthasarathy and my mother got engrossed in recalling their days together in St Agnes High School in Mangalore where they had spent six years in the 1920s!

In July (1961), Arjun Asrani and Hardev Bhalla completed their language studies and left Tokyo, the former to MEA (East Asia Division) and the latter as CDA, EI, Prague. Of the three of us, who had so painstakingly studied Japanese, only Arjun Asrani went back to Japan, first as Counsellor and later as Ambassador (1988-1992).

On Hardev's departure I moved into the house he vacated. It was larger and better furnished, and was located just a five-minute walk from a Benedictine Catholic Church. My mother and I therefore liked this home much more than the previous one. However, my mother spent only three months in it as she returned to India in mid-October.

In January 1962, I passed my Japanese language exam with distinction, was confirmed in service and promoted to Second Secretary. My prime concern now was to return to India and marry Isobel. The only way I could travel to India and back within a month was by air but this was far too expensive. So I wrote a personal letter to then US (PA) Mrs Soonu Kochar requesting her advice. Her response was a wonderful surprise. She wrote that the IFS rules had recently been amended and officers were entitled to home leave after two years abroad. She advised me to apply for home leave and state that my promotion to Second Secretary had increased my 'representational responsibilities' which having a wife would facilitate. This is what I did. Within a month thereafter, seven weeks home leave with a two-way passage for me and one-way passage for my wife were sanctioned.

I arrived in Bombay by the P&O ship *Orsova* on 7 August and proceeded to Bangalore by rail the following day. It was a great joy to meet my parents again, particularly my father, who kept shedding tears of joy and pride every time anyone complimented me on completing my Japanese language study so quickly. But the greater joy was to be with Isobel who had waited patiently, and trustfully, for my return for two long years.

Our wedding took place at St Francis Xavier Cathedral on the morning of 1 September 1962. My IAS batchmate Louis Menezes, then Sub-Collector at Dindigul, kindly agreed to be Best Man and became the cynosure of many young women and their mothers! At the reception, held at the Lal Bagh Glass House that evening, Mr Vaikunta Baliga, Speaker of Karnataka Legislative Assembly, proposed the toast. Other VIPs present were Justice Nittoor Sreenivasa Rao and Justice Hombe Gowda, Chief Justice and Puisne Judge of Karnataka High Court respectively, whom I had taken for sight-seeing to Mt.

Fuji when they visited Tokyo the previous year.

We spent our first night at the Taj West End. The following day we set off in a Chevrolet station wagon, kindly lent to us by a friend of my sister Joan, on a 10-day honeymoon to Mysore, Bandipur Wildlife Sanctuary and Ooty. It was as enjoyable as it was adventurous! We spent the next two weeks calling on family elders and shopping for winter clothing for Isobel and left for Bombay by rail. On 27 September afternoon we boarded the *SS Cambodge* for the three-week voyage to Yokohama, via Colombo, Singapore, Saigon, Hong Kong and Kobe. It was smooth sailing all the way to Hong Kong. By the time we got to that port I was convinced that travel by ship was the best for IFS honeymooners as travel time is treated as 'duty period'! This two-week voyage from Bombay to Hong Kong was the most enjoyable 'duty period' in my entire 35-year-IFS career!

The *SS Cambodge* was scheduled to stay in Hong Kong for three days but on the afternoon of the second day its Captain announced that it would be departing at 9 p.m. that night in order to avoid a typhoon that was expected to strike Hong Kong at about midnight. Unfortunately, it changed course, headed northwards and caught up with us at around 3 a.m. the following morning. Its shrieking winds and enormous waves were terrifying. Each of these waves raised our ship by about 30° to its crest and then dropped it into its trough with a terrifying bang, which sounded almost like a cannon ball fired into it. The entire ship would shudder each time this happened. I got the cold feeling that this ship would not survive the terrible battering and would soon split into two or more bits and sink to the bottom of the ocean with Isobel and me and all others on board. Fortunately, this did not happen and by 9 a.m. the sea was calm again. At 8 a.m. the captain spoke on the ship's sound system and informed us that it was only the 'outer winds' of the typhoon that the ship had encountered.

On arrival in Yokohama on 19 October we had a pleasant surprise.

The EI attaché who received us informed me that Ambassador and Mrs Mehrotra had invited us to spend our first day with them at India House. I had been in this elegant and historic residence many times but never in any of its upstairs bedrooms. We were given the one closest to the stairs, usually given to VIP guests. This was Ambassador and Mrs Mehrotra's gracious kindness to us. We had a homely lunch with Mrs Mehrotra and an informal dinner with the Ambassador and her that night during which they enquired about our wedding and voyage from Bombay to Yokohama and complimented me for bringing a lovely and graceful bride into the 'Embassy Family'.

When we came down for breakfast at 8 a.m. the next morning, the ground floor scenario was a stark contrast to its quiet elegance of the previous day. The Ambassador was greatly agitated. All the senior EI officers were there. The telephones were ringing constantly. We soon learnt that all this agitation was because China had invaded India in Ladakh and across the McMahon Line early that morning! We were stunned! I had a hurried breakfast and rushed off with the others to EI soon thereafter. I returned to the Ambassador's Residence only at about 7 p.m. to pick up Isobel and our baggage and go to our own Japanese-style home at Kamimeguro 8 Chome (8th Cross). Isobel loved it at first sight.

For many weeks after 20 October all EI officers and India-based staff worked until late every day. It was a very tense period not only in India–China but also in US–Soviet relations in view of the Cuban missile crisis.

In early January 1963, Japan's revered painter Saburo Miyamoto came to EI with his secretary. His request was simple but unusual. He wanted an Indian woman to model for him, on her knees, for his new series of *'An Indian Woman at Prayer'* paintings. Flummoxed by his request, the EI receptionist sent him to me as Japanese language officer. When his secretary conveyed his request I responded that the only Indian woman in Tokyo who might agree to this request was my wife as she is newly married! I spoke to Isobel on telephone. She meekly agreed. She was amply rewarded with temporary fame when these oil paintings were presented at a leading Tokyo art gallery some weeks later and the gift of a pastel painting of herself she got from this artist.

During the April–May 1963 period I was put in charge of the commercial section, as FS (Com) R.K. Jerath went to India for consultations and the much delayed six-weeks' home leave. This was the first time I met the famed (subsequently ill-famed!) Dharma Teja, founder of Jayanti Shipping Company. With his 6.4 feet height, Savile Row suits and suave manner he was an imposing figure. He was a budding shipping magnate then, and more importantly, known to be a close friend of Prime Minister Nehru. He had been trained as a nuclear scientist by the renowned Enrico Fermi at University of Chicago and had subsequently worked as a research scientist at Centre for Nuclear Energy Research (CERN) at Geneva. However, having met Prime Minister Nehru in 1958 and learnt from him about India's pressing need for a modern shipping fleet he decided to give up the nuclear field for shipping. He founded Jayanti Shipping Company (JSC) in 1959 and within a few months thereafter secured a Rs 20-crore loan from India's Shipping Development Fund (SDF). This is miniscule today but in 1959 was a mammoth amount. Besides SDF was authorized to give loans only to public sector shipping companies which were permitted to acquire bulk carriers! JSC, a completely private shipping company, not only secured the mentioned loan but also used it to acquire bulk carriers!

Having travelled the world extensively and established high-level contacts in diverse fields, including shipping, Dharma Teja was aware that in the late 1950s there was a slump in the Japanese shipping industry. So he contacted its leading shipbuilders and indicated JSC interest in acquiring 20 bulk carriers in the next 10 years and invited offers. Initially, no one took him seriously but when they learnt that JSC had secured a US$40-million (equivalent of Rs 20 crore) loan from SDF, Mitsubishi made an offer of eight bulk carriers, with one delivered every six months, one down payment on each and the balance in instalments. This was an amazingly attractive offer.

The first of these Mitsubishi bulk carriers, named *Adi Jayanti*, was launched on 11 May 1961 by then Shipping Minister S.K. Patil. The fifth ship, the 35,000-ton *Chandragupta Maurya* was launched by then Finance Minister Morarji Desai on 11 May 1963. On this occasion Mr Teja was not only accompanied by his attractive and elegant wife Ranjit but also by Gen B.M. Kaul, former Chief of General Staff in the eastern sector who had disgraced himself when the Indian defence there collapsed and Chinese troops almost reached Tezpur. It was pathetic to see this General, who had been decorated with the PVSM in 1960, being treated like a valet by Mr and Mrs Teja, making him carry the former's briefcase and the latter's fur coat.

On the day after the *Chandragupta Maurya* was launched, Ambassador Mehrotra hosted a reception in honour of Finance Minister Morarji Desai. His Japanese counterpart and senior officials of his ministry and of the Foreign Office, Shipping and Commerce ministries attended this reception. So did Mr and Mrs Teja and Gen B.M. Kaul. After this reception Mr Teja invited officers of our Finance Minister's delegation, and me (as the officer then in charge of the EI Commerce Wing and Japanese language officer) for 'an appropriate celebration' of his latest launch. He took us to an elite nightclub. We were 10 in all, including Mr and Mrs Teja and Gen Kaul. We stayed just about an hour to watch the spectacular cabaret and only had drinks and snacks and no dinner. When Mr Teja asked for the bill and the waitress brought it to him, he gave it to me and asked how much it was. I looked at it and was stunned. It was a little over a million yen, equivalent to about US$310! When I told him this, he did not bat an eyelid, just pulled out a wad of US$100 notes, gave me four of them, told me to settle the bill, and give the rest to the waitress as a tip for herself and the two others who had served us. On a US$310 bill he gave a US$90 tip! Those were Mr Teja's days of glory. He was widely respected, had friends in high places in many countries, and was 'rolling in wealth'. I was to meet him again five years later in New York in quite different circumstances.

In early March 1963, Ambassador and Mrs Mehrotra, EI diplomatic officers and their spouses had the thrilling experience of a test run of Japan's superfast Shinkansen (bullet train) from Tokyo to Nagoya. This was arranged by our FS (Railways) P.C. Luther. The train moved so fast that the verdant countryside looked like a blurred mass of green but we could see beautiful Mount Fuji quite clearly. We were served a sumptuous lunch on the outward and high tea on the return journey.

The two enduring friendships which Isobel and I made with fellow diplomats in Tokyo were with David and Dominique Waterstone of the British Embassy and Wilhelm (Bill) and Sylvia Hass of the German Embassy.

David was an ebullient outgoing type who drove around in a bright red MG sports car. He and his French wife Dominique often invited us to their home, and on one occasion for a weekend drive to the scenic Izu Peninsula (about 100 miles south of Tokyo) and trek to a nearby mountain. It was an exciting and memorable experience though at times both Isobel and I had our hearts in our mouths because of the speed at which David drove his MG on the winding, cliff edge roads and also because we lost our way in the latter part of the trek which was unmapped. Fortunately, we both could speak and read Japanese and this enabled us to get back to our inn before nightfall.

About 10 years later, David resigned from the British Foreign Service to take up the post of Special Assistant to the Chairman of

British Steel. This was an important/highly paid job at which I met him when I was Deputy High Commissioner in London. However, he had to demit this office when Margaret Thatcher assumed office. The years thereafter were rather difficult for him professionally. Besides, his marriage to Dominique broke up. Nonetheless he stayed in touch with us until his death in early 2015.

Bill and Sylvia Hass were also recently married, like Isobel and me. Bill's father was the Federal Republic of Germany's Ambassador to Japan and Sylvia belonged to one of Germany's top industrial families. Bill and Sylvia's home was like a mini Ambassadorial residence. Our modest home was about a third of its size and sparsely furnished compared to theirs. But they never allowed this vast difference in our lifestyles to affect the warm friendship between us. They often invited Isobel and me to their home for formal dinners and informal gatherings. We have been in touch with each other ever since and met again after many years in Berlin in October 2015 when the German edition of my *Gandhi's Outstanding Leadership* book was launched at Humboldt University. It was Bill Hass who introduced me to the distinguished gathering on this occasion.

In the third week of May 1963, I received an unexpected transfer order to EI, Rangoon. It was a big surprise as I was then the only Japanese language officer at EI Tokyo. Ambassador Mehrotra wrote to Foreign Secretary urging reversal of this order but was informed this was not possible as my post was a 'language officer's post' which was now needed elsewhere. So, with Isobel, our cook Joseph and our few belongings, we boarded the P&O *Orsova* on 8 July for the travel from Yokohama to Singapore where we were to transfer to the Norwegian cargo-cum-passenger ship *Hailee*, for the onward travel to Rangoon. The former ship was 30,000 tons; the latter only 3,000 tons!

The normal Singapore–Rangoon travel time is only four days, but as the *Hailee* was a cargo-cum-passenger ship, it made three day stops in Malacca and Port Swettenham, because of which we spent 10 days on it. We became friends with our Burmese fellow passengers, two of whom had just completed their postgraduate studies in Japan and were returning home. From them we learnt that though the *Hailee* ship was a tiny and nondescript vessel it was 'historic' for the Burmese as General Aung San had secretly fled Burma in it, in 1939 to seek Japan's assistance for its liberation from British yoke.

4

Spiders, Tree Spirits and a 'Jewellery Crisis' in Golden Pagoda Land

(August 1963 -December 1966)

Our ship arrived in Rangoon on 2 August morning. We received a much warmer welcome than expected. I had met/assisted Ambassador R.S. Mani's wife when she had visited Tokyo in April that year. Besides, at his request, I had brought some photographic material for him. He, therefore, sent his PS to receive us at the port and bring us to India House for lunch.

The stately and spacious India House at Rangoon was the residence of the Imperial Bank of India Manager in pre-independence days. It had a large compound with many trees, a sizable lawn and a tennis court. Mrs Mani served us a sumptuous Indian lunch, which was particularly delicious in view of our previous 10 days of bland Norwegian food on the *Hailee*.

The home that awaited us was the central one of five EI-owned bungalows on Budd Road. It was spacious and well-furnished and also had a large lawn. But it had one major, unsightly defect. It was populated by many large black spiders, some heavily pregnant with white underbellies. There were about three or four of them in every room. So I induced Isobel to come with me for a drive through Rangoon while the EI staff 'laid to rest' all of them. They had done this by the time we got back at 5 p.m. and showed us a box full of them as proof of their arduous efforts. They were rewarded handsomely for this. Arachnophobia is my greatest handicap!

When I arrived in Rangoon, Burma was in the throes of radical changes and was being dragged onto the 'Burmese Way to Socialism' by General Ne Win and his Revolutionary Council. He had first appeared on Burma's political stage in October 1958, when Prime Minister U Nu's AFPFL party had split into two factions and his government was on the verge of collapse. U Nu had requested him to form an interim Caretaker Government, restore law and order in the country and then have national elections. He had agreed to this and ruled Burma for 16 months, during which he dealt firmly with ethnic secessionist groups, and in February 1960 organized a free fair general election. U Nu's AFPFL faction won it with a large majority and the previous political impasse was ended. General Ne Win then handed over power to him. But on 2 March 1962 he staged a coup. It was as much of a surprise as it was innovative. Prime Minister U Nu and all his ministers as also Burma's Chief Justice were invited to an Army Day banquet. While they were all enjoying the dinner and cordiality, Ne Win's 28 co-conspirator generals 'bloodlessly' took over Rangoon and most of the rest of the country. U Nu, his ministers and the Chief Justice were escorted to their homes and placed under house arrest for some weeks and released thereafter.

A Revolutionary Council (RC) of 16 Generals, chaired by General

Ne Win was set up. It justified the coup on grounds that Burma, plagued with multiple political parties and a constitution which gave its ethnic minorities the right to secede posed great dangers to Burma, of disintegration and foreign intervention. It then imposed martial law, banned all political parties, abolished both Hluttaw (parliament) houses, the Supreme and High Courts and the regional councils of the ethnic minorities. All the executive, legislative and judicial powers of these bodies were taken over by the RC.

On 7 May 1962, the 'Burmese Way to Socialism' (BWS) was promulgated and on 4 July that year, the Burma Socialist Programme Party was launched to promote the BWS ideology and mobilize support for it. Its stated objectives were to ensure Burma's national unity, state control of its national resources, promotion of agricultural development, peasant welfare, Burmese language and culture and prevention of foreign interference in its internal affairs.

Soon thereafter, Burmese was made the official language; all streets with names of colonial administrators were renamed with those of Burma's national heroes. All foreign scholarships, except those for studies in the Soviet Union and East European Countries were terminated. Visas for foreigners were restricted to 24 hours.

The Enterprise Nationalization Law, passed on 1 June 1963, was in the initial stage of implementation when I arrived in Rangoon. All major enterprises, including petroleum, mining, teak, rubber, banking and import-export trade of rice, had just been taken over. All these industries were put in charge of middle-level military officers with hardly any knowledge of them. A few weeks later, almost 15,000 private firms, including supermarkets, pharmacies and transport companies, were taken over, grouped and put in charge of captains and other low-level military officers. Thus, in some cases, a captain was in charge of 10 supermarkets or 20 pharmacies, all of which were now called People's Stores or People's Pharmacies, each with a separate number!

It was my dubious privilege to witness the disastrous effect these radical, ill-conceived and peremptorily-imposed changes were having on the lives of Burma's happy, well-educated (by South Asian standards) people and on its richly-endowed/flourishing economy.

As most of the nationalized small business firms were owned by Indians and Chinese they were the ones severely affected. However, the latter suffered less as most of them had Burmese wives and were well integrated into the local social network. Very few Indians had Burmese wives, and were therefore constrained to leave for India.

By early October 1963, about 5,000 Indians were leaving Rangoon every alternate week by Mogul Line ships which GOI, as urged by EI Rangoon, had arranged for their evacuation. As most of them did not have Indian passports special arrangements had to be made to issue these to them. I was the Second Secretary in charge of this section. We initially worked from 9 a.m. to 7 p.m. and later to 9 p.m, issuing about 500 new passports per day, all handwritten!

In late October 1963, Ambassador R.S. Mani left Rangoon. He had hoped to be appointed as Secretary (West) at MEA but was posted instead as Ambassador to Yugoslavia. Mr S.N. Mishra was appointed as his successor but managed to get this changed. Eric Gonsalves (EG), just a First Secretary then who had taken over as Chargé D'Affaires (CDA) when Ambassador Mani left held that office until mid-June 1964, when Admiral R.D. Katari finally arrived as India's new Ambassador to Burma.

In early March 1964, the Revolutionary Council forbade departing Indians from taking their jewellery, including *mangalsutras*, with them, on grounds that the gold with which they were made was Burmese. Any jewellery item found on them or in their baggage was confiscated. So the only option these Indians now had was to leave all such items with Indian friends still in Burma. More and more jewellery thus got accumulated in fewer Indian hands, exposing them to the mounting risk of being burgled or raided by the police. CDA Gonsalves took up this matter with the Burmese authorities energetically but they were unrelenting. He, therefore, sought and received MEA clearance to receive this jewellery for safe keeping in EI. The Indian community was greatly relieved but the Burmese authorities were outraged.

The jewellery collection was made by the Consular Section, which was headed by First Secretary S.E. Joshi (who 25 years later retired as RAW Chairman) but I was asked to assist in this. It was an onerous task, in which every piece of jewellery had to be separately listed, then packed with other items belonging to that person and sealed with red wax in the owner's presence and then deposited in the Embassy's steel vaulted strong-room.

The Burmese authorities demonstrated their outrage over this 'jewellery collection' by organizing daily anti-India slogan-shouting outside our Chancery on Merchant Street. As this four-floor building had only one entry/exit we all faced the great risk of being burnt alive if anyone from the angry mob outside hurled a lighted straw torch into any of these floors. Most of us feared this contingency but CDA Gonsalves remained as 'cool as a cucumber'. He kept assuring us that nothing untoward would happen because any anti-India crowd that became riotous would soon become anti-RC because of the great anger among the people against it! He was proved right on this. Though the anti-India sloganeering continued for three more weeks we were not harmed.

In the midst of this 'jewellery crisis' my family kept pressing me to come for my sister Margaret's wedding to Niranjan Alva, son of the renowned parliamentarian couple Joachim and Violet Alva. The former had even written to Foreign Minister Swaran Singh to permit me to attend this event. Soon thereafter CDA Gonsalves received a telegram from Foreign Secretary Y.D. Gundevia to permit me to leave Rangoon for a few days. In conveying this to me, CDA Gonsalves said, 'Please go if you feel that attending your sister's wedding is more important than standing on the burning deck with your colleagues.' I asked him what he would have done in my place. He replied that he would have stayed. So this is what I did, much to the chagrin of Mr Joachim Alva and my parents' great disappointment.

On 24 May (1964), because of heightening tensions with the Burmese over the jewellery issue, Foreign Secretary Gundevia came to Rangoon. The outcome of these strenuous and strained two-day discussions with his Burmese counterpart was the decision that EI would cease the jewellery collection and transfer the collection already made, along with lists of contents/names of their owners to National Bank of Burma for safe keeping until the issue of their final disposal was decided upon at a political level. This greatly disappointed the Indian community which openly rued their trust in the EI promise to protect their interests.

On the morning of 27 May, when all EI diplomatic officers were at Rangoon airport to see off Foreign Secretary Gundevia, news was received that Prime Minister Jawaharlal Nehru had passed away that morning. We were all stunned. Mr Gundevia slumped into a chair and wept into his hands. There was much sadness among the Burmese also. All their flags were promptly lowered to half-mast. The next day CDA Gonsalves was informed that as General and Mrs Ne Win were unfortunately unable to attend the Prime Minister's funeral, they would be making a condolence visit to New Delhi in the near future. This was immediately conveyed by him to MEA.

This visit took place three weeks later. They made condolence calls on the President of India Dr S. Radhakrishnan and Mrs Indira Gandhi. During the latter call, they invited her to Burma for a 'quiet, recuperative holiday as their personal guest'. In her deep bereavement Mrs Gandhi quite likely paid no heed to this invitation but Foreign Secretary Gundevia who was present during this call recorded it and some weeks later induced her to accept it so as to ease the strained India–Burma relationship. I shall come back to this fascinating visit later in this chapter.

In early July 1964 Admiral R.D. Katari arrived in Rangoon as India's new Ambassador to Burma. This had an electrifying effect on the Indian community in Burma. Many of them naively believed the Admiral had been sent to 'teach the Burmese a lesson' and that Indian Naval ships would soon follow! Every morning, sizeable crowds would gather outside the EI building and shout '*Ambassador Saheb ki Jai*' whenever he came into or out of it. One day, the Ambassador's departure for lunch was delayed by about 15 minutes and the military attaché Col. Mitra came out before the Ambassador. The crowd as usual shouted '*Ambassador Saheb ki Jai*'. Rather elated by this Col. Mitra happily recounted this at that afternoon's officers' meeting. The Ambassador smiled and made the following piquant response: 'Col. Mitra, I do not mind in the least people mistaking the Military attaché for the Ambassador, but that they should mistake an army officer for a naval officer is grave and it hurts!!' The Colonel had not expected this jibe and was tongue-tied for the rest of the meeting.

The Admiral had an amazing effect on the Embassy's functioning. He would arrive at his office every morning at 9.15 a.m. and at his first meeting with all the EI officers/staff on the third day after his arrival stated that he came to office at 9.15 a.m. only to give all of us a 15-minute 'grace period'. If anyone arrived after that he would have to report to his PS and explain why he had arrived late. He also made the point that he was a stickler for discipline and team work, and detested laxity at work and gossip-mongering. He called upon senior officers to have humane concern for all those who worked under them, particularly the Class IV staff, 'as the strength of every chain lies in its weakest link'. Within two months of his assuming charge of EI Rangoon, he had transformed it into a disciplined, efficient, hard-working and productive organization with a strong team spirit.

It is from Ambassador Katari that I learnt, for the first time, the great importance of morale and team work in the smooth and efficient functioning of a large embassy. I shall always be deeply grateful to him for this.

In early September 1964 Foreign Minister Sardar Swaran Singh came to Rangoon to ameliorate the strained India–Burma relationship. Some amelioration took place but no progress was made on the sensitive Indian jewellery issue on which our side made some suggestions for its solution and the Burmese side promised to consider and revert before long.

In mid-December 1964 Eric Gonsalves and Rose left Rangoon for Madras by one of the Mogul Line ships on which over 100,000 Indians had left Burma already, from where after a family reunion at Christmas, he was to proceed to London. He had been promoted and posted as Counsellor to High Commission of India, London and instructed to arrive there by early January 1965. His diplomatic efforts and leadership role at EI Rangoon, during the nine months he was CDA were verily outstanding and heroic. In my 35-year IFS career I have not come across any other colleague so cool, considerate, clear-headed, dedicated, deeply religious and inspiring as him.

In early January 1965 Mrs Indira Gandhi came to Rangoon for the 'relaxed, recuperative holiday' which General and Mrs Ne Win had invited her in June the previous year. She was then Minister of Information & Broadcasting in Prime Minister Lal Bahadur Shastri's Cabinet.

As pre-arranged with Gen Ne Win's office, she was received at the airport by Ambassador and Mrs Katari, (accompanied by me as DCM) and brought to India House, where she was served tea while she awaited General and Mrs Ne Win. They arrived at 5 p.m. in a Rolls Royce car. He was driving it himself! They both came into India

House and after the usual pleasantries with Ambassador and Mrs Katari escorted Mrs Gandhi to their elegant car. General Ne Win opened the rear door for the two ladies, closed it, then got into the driver's seat and drove away with one pilot car in front and another behind his Rolls Royce. For Ambassador and Mrs Katari and me, the General's gracious gentlemanliness on this evening was a big and pleasant surprise.

Six days later Mrs Gandhi returned to India House, but this time in a chauffeur-driven Rolls Royce with the two pilot cars. Ambassador and Mrs Katari hosted a lunch for her to which the EI senior Diplomatic officers and their wives were invited. After lunch the Ambassador requested Mrs Gandhi for a briefing about her 'recuperative holiday' with General and Mrs Ne Win. The gist of what she narrated was as follows:

The first night was spent at General Ne Win's official mansion in Rangoon. She was treated not only as an honoured guest but also as a revered family member, introduced to children, grandchildren and the General's and Mrs Ne Win's parents. A sumptuous dinner was served thereafter and some Burmese music and dance items in which the children and grandchildren participated. The following morning, after breakfast she was taken for a drive through Rangoon with short stops at the Aung San memorial and the Shwedagon pagoda. She availed of this drive to tell General and Mrs Ne Win how much her father loved Burma and its people, his close friendship with Prime Minister U Nu, and concern for Indians in Burma. She then spoke of her sadness about news reports of harsh treatment being meted out to departing Indians and requested them to ensure that they were treated 'like her sisters and brothers'. The General responded that most of these reports were untrue or exaggerated but he had taken note of her request and would follow up on it to the extent possible in Burma's present difficult 'move to Socialism' phase.

After an early lunch, they flew, in the presidential aircraft, to Ngapali, a beach resort on Burma's west coast. They stayed at the luxurious State Guest House, located on a hill with a panoramic view of Ngapali Bay, for three days and nights. Every morning she was driven to a nearby sacred or scenic site and after dinner every night entertained with Burmese music or dance. She enjoyed all of this but most of all just gazing out on the beautiful blue waters of Ngapali Bay, and the movement of fishing boats on it.

She then recounted what transpired on her last evening there. The sky, with a few clouds on it, and the bay were tinged with crimson gold as the sun was beginning to set, and presented an incredibly beautiful sight. She felt a strong urge to have a swim in the bay. She asked whether this secluded part of the bay was quite private and Mrs Ne Win assured her it was so and offered to accompany her on her swim. So both of them quickly got into swimsuits and walked down to the beach and into the water. Mrs Gandhi was enjoying her swim greatly when she spied a man peering at her from behind a tree on the cliff overlooking the beach. She quickly turned away from his gaze when she spied another man doing the same from behind a tree further away. When she expressed amazement at this, Mrs Ne Win promptly assured her not to be concerned as they were all her husband's trusted bodyguards who had been deployed there to ensure this beach was 'completely private and secure'. I still vividly remember Mrs Gandhi's coy smile and soft chuckle as she recounted this incident. None of us who heard her recount it ever imagined that this shy, soft spoken, graceful lady would, just six years later become the bold and intrepid Prime Minister of India who would midwife the birth of Bangladesh, despite an ominous US nuclear blackmail.

Until end December 1964 there was no indication of any baby in the offing for Isobel. Her mother and mine made regular enquiries about this 'good news' but we had to disappoint them each time and convey we both had so many official and social responsibilities to shoulder that we were in no particular hurry to have the additional ones of parenthood. But on 7 April 1965 (my 29th birthday) Isobel in her birthday card wrote that her gift to me on this birthday was our first child which her gynaecologist Dr (Sr) Barton of Holy Family Hospital, had told her the previous day, was due in mid-November. This happy news was promptly conveyed by me to her and my parents.

Isobel's pregnancy was progressing well with regular monitoring by Dr Barton. Sadly, on 1 July 1965 the RC nationalized all private hospitals in Burma, including the Holy Family, Ramakrishna and Seventh Day Hospitals in Rangoon, and the renowned Dr Gordon Seagrave's Hospital at Namkhan in Northern Burma. This was a big blow to the thousands of Burmese and foreign nationals in Burma who depended on these fine hospitals for healthcare. Soon after this nationalization was announced Dr Barton left Rangoon for Moulmein to assist her fellow nuns there in handling the procedures for handing over their hospital to the Burmese authorities. Isobel's pregnancy monitoring now had to be made by Dr Daw Khin Kyi at the big, British-era Dufferin Hospital (DH). She was well qualified but had to attend to the hundreds who came to her every day. Everyone had to take their turn to be seen by her. This was quite a harrowing and exhausting exercise for Isobel each time she went to see this doctor. This was also the rainy season and getting out of and into the car at the hospital was quite a task. All this depressed her and the dampness and darkness inside the house made it worse. So I decided to have the branches of the trees close to our home chopped off and instructed our gardener to do this. He made various excuses and did not do this. So I got our Indo-Burmese staff car driver Manickam to do it. This brightened the interior of our home but Isobel's condition worsened. By an eerie coincidence two or three spiders reappeared in our home after almost two years!

Soon thereafter swelling was noticed on her hands and feet. So I took her to the mentioned DH doctor. On examining Isobel she found that her blood pressure (BP) had also risen and therefore advised that Isobel be admitted to this hospital for observation and treatment. She was there for five days. When she returned home the swelling on her hands and feet and her BP had reduced but she had lost her appetite, and was unable to sleep. When I telephoned the doctor she told me to come and collect a prescription which she would write, buy that medicine and give it to Isobel in the indicated dosage. Having collected this prescription I had to go to seven 'People's Pharmacies' before I found and bought the prescribed pills. After Isobel began to take them she became listless and began to have tremors in her hands and feet, initially every alternate day but subsequently once or twice every day. I felt greatly alarmed. My one ray of hope now was Dr Barton who I learnt had just returned to Rangoon from Moulmein. So I telephoned and pleaded that she come to examine Isobel. She kindly agreed. So I went to pick her up. I had just left our home when it began to rain heavily. Soon thereafter one of the windscreen wipers fell off. So I could drive the car only at snail's pace. When I reached the gate of the Holy Family Hospital the brakes of the car got jammed and I had to press the accelerator quite hard to get it to the hospital porch. When Dr Barton came out to meet me I could not utter a word and wept profusely. Seeing how emotionally stricken I was she kindly led me to my car (which she knew quite well) and offered to drive it, which I was very grateful for. Amazingly, when she switched on the engine the jammed brakes were released, the rain ceased and we reached our home in just 15 minutes.

I had much hoped she would assure me that Isobel was not as ill as I had feared. Instead, on first sight of Isobel she exclaimed 'This dear girl is very sick and must be rushed to hospital immediately'. She spoke to Dr Daw Khin Kyi, informed her that Isobel who was her patient, was presently showing symptoms of eclampsia, needed an emergency Caesarean section and that an ambulance should be sent to our home immediately. I was stunned. Fortunately, Isobel's mother Matilda ('Tilly') had arrived at our home three days earlier and provided the much-needed mental and emotional support to Isobel and me at this critical juncture.

The DH ambulance arrived soon thereafter and Isobel, her mother, Dr Barton and I arrived at DH 20 minutes later. Her surgery was scheduled for 9 p.m. that day and preparations for it began immediately after her admission. The move to the operation theatre, which was at the far end of the hospital, at about 8.30 p.m., in a wheeled stretcher along a dimly lit corridor was quite eerie and tedious for Isobel's mother and me. However, when we got there, we were very glad and relieved to learn that Dr Daw Khin Kyi had permitted Dr Barton to be with Isobel during the surgery.

At 9.40 p.m., after what seemed like an age of intense anxiety, Dr. Barton came out holding the tiniest and loveliest little baby girl I had ever seen. I burst into tears, more out of relief than joy for I had greatly feared that neither Isobel nor the baby would come through the terrible ordeal of the preceding 10 days. Both of them were brought back to Isobel's room at about 11 p.m. Her mother Tilly, Dr Barton and I stayed with her an hour longer and returned to our respective homes thereafter.

That day of intense anxiety and great relief and joy, 23 October1965, was Tilly's 54th birthday.

Though Isobel's surgery was successful, her travails continued. On the third day she developed a stitch abscess and as she was nursing the baby, the latter was also infected. A pinkish inflammation appeared on her left nipple and soon spread sidewards and swelled up to look like an inch-long centipede. Dr Daw Kin Kyi indicated it needed to be lanced and the only surgeon qualified to do so was an Israeli paediatric surgeon at the WHO office in Rangoon. I had never met him but had informally met the Israeli CDA Michael Pragai once or twice at American Embassy receptions. India had no diplomatic relations with Israel at this time. Nonetheless, in the desperate situation I now was, I telephoned him and requested his assistance. He responded magnanimously and within three hours brought the mentioned WHO surgeon to DH. When the latter saw the unsightly abscess on our tiny baby's chest he gravely muttered it might be too late already. He stated that since the baby was just five days old, not even a mild anaesthetic could be used during the lancing. I accompanied him and the baby to the operation room but stayed outside. When the lancing commenced the baby shrieked so loudly and pathetically that I felt her lungs and my heart would be torn apart. The lancing and subsequent dressing lasted about 30 minutes. When the baby was brought back to Isobel's room she was so exhausted with her shrieking that she lay motionless for almost nine hours. Only her barely noticeable breathing indicated she was still alive.

Before leaving the Israeli surgeon informed me that if the lancing had been delayed by even an hour it would have been impossible to save the baby as the infection had gone so deep that it had reached quite close to her lungs. He added that the next three days were critical to her survival.

That afternoon Mary Kyaung, the British wife of the Burmese Naval Commander who was our Budd Road neighbour, visited DH and learnt from Tilly and me all that Isobel and the baby had gone through. When Mary was leaving she requested me to accompany her as she had something important to tell me. When we got to her car she stated that all Isobel's and her baby's travails were due to my cutting the tree branches in my compound. She said her many years in Burma had convinced her of the Burmese belief about spirits of their ancestors living in trees and if these are cut or even trimmed they avenge themselves in various ways on those who have done this. She urged me to make an 'offering of four cakes and two bottles of gin' to these tree spirits earliest possible. She added that my gardener could do this on my behalf. I was shocked that Mary, a devout Roman Catholic and daily Mass-goer, had given me this 'pagan advice'! But she had spoken so emphatically that I decided to do what she had urged rather than risk further ills to Isobel and the baby. I gave my Burmese gardener four cakes and two bottles of gin and told him to do the needful. He did so promptly and confessed that he had not done what I had requested him earlier because he had foreseen the ill effects of cutting the branches of these trees.

Amazingly, soon after this offering was made Isobel and the baby's condition improved. They suffered no further infections and were discharged from hospital on 7 November. Tilly's arthritis, which had become quite acute in late October, also eased at this time. I then realized that all my abnormal travails in getting to Holy Family Hospital on 23 October morning must have been caused by these 'Tree Spirits'.

It is to Burma that I owe my 'ringside' experience of tree spirits, who avenge themselves on those who disturb their abodes in old, stately trees.

In mid-November the exhilarating news was received that Prime Minister Lal Bahadur Shastri would visit Burma 20-23 December. He had recently acquired a heroic image having effectively countered Pakistan's military moves in Kutch and Kashmir by authorizing an Indian attack across the international border near Lahore. *The New York Times* had lauded him as 'The little sparrow with a spine of steel'.

He came accompanied by his wife, sons Ashok and Suman, Foreign Minister Sardar Swaran Singh and senior MEA and Home Ministry officials. His modesty despite his fame, simplicity, affability, clarity of thought and expression, heart-warming smile and piquant humour made a big impact on Burma's people and VIPs, including the not-so-easy-to-please General Ne Win. The fact that he had visited Burma so soon after the 23 September India–Pakistan ceasefire was also much appreciated.

A good example of Prime Minister Shastri's humour was the toast he raised at his return banquet for General and Mrs Ne Win. He raised his water-filled glass and said 'Your Excellency, India is the only country in the world where water flows like champagne!' This triggered loud peals of laughter and was recounted many times thereafter!

The Joint Communique issued at the end of this visit was short and bland. Its substantive part only stated that 'the Chairman and Prime Minister held talks on Indo-Burmese relations and exchanged views on international matters of common interest' and 'This visit has further strengthened the friendly relations existing between the two countries'. The vexed Indian jewellery issue was not raised. The recent India–Pakistan war and Burma's heightened strategic importance to India had made this issue of only marginal importance now.

Prime Minister Shastri's sudden demise at Tashkent just three weeks later, gave his impactful visit to Rangoon a special tinge of sadness for those who had had the privilege of meeting and hearing him.

In early March 1966, Mr Narendra Singh Sarila, Eric Gonsalves' successor arrived and took over as Counsellor (Pol). Soon thereafter MEA raised the foreign allowance for Rangoon. These developments eased my official work and financial stringency.

In early July, my IFS batchmate Pushkar Johari, then US (PA) informed me that I was being posted to EI, Stockholm. But in mid-September, I was pleasantly surprised to receive official intimation that I had been posted as Consul in CGI, New York and should report there in early January 1967.

5

An Up-in-the-Sky Apartment & a Sleek Jaguar for 'Our James Bond' in New York

(January 1967 – July 1969)

I travelled to New York via Rome. Though I had lived in Tokyo for three years, New York with its innumerable skyscrapers and the great diversity of its people amazed me.

I took charge as Consul (Passports/ Visas) and met the staff of this section on the morning of 7 January (1967). Among them was a local recruit, quiet and self-effacing with a palpable spiritual aura about him. His name was Chinmaya Ghosh. I had no inkling then that within the next 10 years he would become renowned at the UN and around the world as Shri Chinmoy.

That afternoon I called on Consul General Shantiswarup Gupta, a scholarly but slightly odd senior IFS officer. About 10 minutes after the initial pleasantries, he got up from his chair, walked to his safe at the far corner of his office, carefully worked its combination lock, opened the safe, took out one file out of it and gave it to me. This file had only one 'Top Secret' CCB telegram in it which stated that Dharma Teja, who had founded the Jayanti Shipping Company with a US$40 million loan from India's Shipping Development Fund, had defrauded this company and disappeared. His last known address was The Sherry-Netherland Hotel on 5th Avenue/60th street in New York City, and CGI NY should make best efforts to locate him and have him arrested/deported to India. Consul General Gupta told me that I should give this task top priority and regularly report to him progress made therein.

The following morning I walked to The Sherry-Netherland Hotel, which was just four blocks away from CGI, and met its general manager. He admitted that Mr and Mrs Teja had stayed there recently but 'had left without leaving a forwarding address'. I requested that we be notified as and when they next checked in, which he promised to do.

Soon thereafter I prepared a detailed note about Mr Teja and his shipping company. I then took copies of this note to the New York Justice Department and Immigration offices. Two of my fellow consuls assisted me in taking them to all consulates in New York and personally handing them over to their Consuls concerned. At the US Immigration Office, I met Commissioner Clayton Hollinger, who was friendly and helpful. So, the following week, I invited him to lunch at the Bombay Palace restaurant, which he greatly enjoyed and appreciated.

There were two less important but urgent matters I had to handle at this time. The first was to find a good and well-located residential apartment for myself and the other was to decide on my new car. On the former matter I was fortunate. MEA had recently raised rental ceilings for a Consul at New York to US$440. This enabled me to find one at York Avenue/82nd Street, within five days of apartment hunting. It was on the 32nd floor of a newly-constructed building with a panoramic view of New York across the East River. Its rent was US$440! Initially, its Management Agent Douglas Elliman declined to lease it to me, stating that they do not rent apartments to diplomats and Consuls because of their immunities and mid-lease transfers. However, when the New York City Consular Corps Committee intervened on my behalf, he did so. The lease was signed soon thereafter, and the requisite furniture hired.

For my car I had initially considered the French Citreon and British Jaguar and written to their manufacturers. The latter made the better offer. It was US$3,800 with a 10 per cent diplomatic discount ex-UK port. Since MEA had agreed to pay the UK–New York freight ($430) (as this was less than the cost of transporting my car from Rangoon to New York) the net cost of this car to me was only US$2,990! So I ordered it in early March. It was delivered on 10 April, a slightly delayed gift for my 31st birthday on 7 April.

Isobel arrived in New York on 14 April, with baby Premila and Mary, our domestic maid. She was wonderstruck by the magnificent view from every window of this two-bedroom apartment. Though tiny in comparison to our sprawling Budd Road bungalow in Rangoon, it was centrally air conditioned, had a kitchen with an electric cooking range and a dishwasher and bathrooms with tubs and showers. At nights, the lights on seven of New York's bridges, visible from its sitting/dining rooms, glistened like pearl necklaces.

On 27 May afternoon, Immigration Commissioner Hollinger telephoned me to convey that an Indian couple named Jayanti Dharma Teja and Ranjit Kaur Teja had been arrested for overstaying their visas and would be produced in the US District Court of New York (South) at Foley Square, the following morning. When I conveyed this news to Consul General Gupta (whom I shall hereafter refer to as CG Gupta) he was overjoyed and immediately cabled it to Secretary (West).

The next morning, I went to the indicated court. When Mr Teja saw and recognized me he blurted out, 'This is a shame for India. I have enjoyed the confidence of Prime Minister Nehru. Ambassador B.K. Nehru is a personal friend. Yet you have had me arrested and detained. I have spent last night in a prison cell in my dress suit.' I blandly replied, 'Mr Teja, I am here as a consular officer to assist you as I do in all such other cases.' He angrily responded, 'That is nonsense'! However, Mrs Teja courteously requested me to convey to their 'good friend' Ambassador Nehru that she and her husband had been arrested and detained by the immigration authorities, and would much appreciate his immediate intervention in having them released. I promised to do this and did so that evening, through CG Gupta. He later told me that the Ambassador's comment was, 'The Tejas should stew in the mess they have created for themselves and be extradited to India earliest possible.'

In the hearing before the District Judge John McGohey, Commissioner Hollinger and our lawyer Louis Steinberg presented detailed documentation on Mr & Mrs Teja's criminal acts, (which I had earlier handed over to them) and pressed for their continued detention pending extradition to India. The judge stated he would need four weeks to study these papers and fixed 28 June for the next hearing. The Tejas' lawyer Edward Ennis appealed for bail on their behalf which Commissioner Hollinger and lawyer Steinberg strongly opposed. At this point the good-looking and elegant Mrs Teja stood up and told Judge McGohey that she and her husband were victims of political vendetta in India because they had been close friends of Prime Minister Nehru and had been assisted by him. She asked whether the allegation of criminality against them was credible to him. The judge, visibly moved, granted them bail on a surety of US$10,000 each.

On, 28 June lawyer Ennis requested an adjournment as his clients were unable to be present for unavoidable reasons. The judge granted this and fixed the next hearing for 13 September. On that morning, lawyer Ennis produced a telegram which he stated he had received that morning from Mr Teja. It stated that having lost hope of securing justice in US courts, he and his wife had decided to 'depart that country'. To which country they had departed was not indicated. The judge declared their bail bonds forfeited and ruled in favour of their extradition to India. The latter was a favourable development for us but his secret departure from the US to an unknown country was a major setback.

On 25 September, when I returned to office after an official lunch, my Jamaican secretary Yvonne informed me that the Costa Rican consul, Alfredo Lizano had made three telephone calls during my absence and stated he had important information to convey to me urgently. So I telephoned him. He said he would like to meet me immediately. I agreed to meet him. He arrived at CGI within 20 minutes. On entering my office, he excitedly blurted out, 'The Teha's (the Latins pronounce J as H) are now in San Jose, Costa Rica.' When I asked him how he knew about this he told me the following: His Consul General Carlos Jaoquin Zuniga received a telegram from their Ministry of Foreign Affairs some days ago instructing him to issue entry visas to Mr and Mrs Teja. He pointed out that CGI had sent them a formal note stating there were criminal charges against this couple and no visas should be issued to them. Nonetheless he was instructed to issue these visas and hence did so. Consul Lizano, who was closely connected to a leading political family of Costa Rica, probed into the matter and learnt that it was their former president Jose Figueres Ferrer, who had induced their Foreign Minister to instruct his Consul General in New York to issue these visas. He also informed me that Mr Teja is said to have paid Mr

Figueres US$30,000 for his intervention and to enable him to finance his campaign for the next presidential election. Since Consul Lizano, (whom I shall hereafter refer to by his first name Alfredo) belonged to the rival political family he was determined to expose this scandal by assisting us in apprehending Teja and having him extradited from Costa Rica. I asked him how he proposed to do this. He responded that he and I should fly to Mexico City earliest possible, meet the Costa Rican Ambassador there (who was a former President and mentor of the present president), get a letter of introduction from him to the latter and proceed to San Jose, the Costa Rican capital, and request a meeting with the President. All this was such stunning information and an incredible plan of action that I decided to take Alfredo to CG Gupta and get him to repeat all that he had told me. The latter also felt this was an amazing narrative and plan of action but considering the high political importance of the Teja case, realized we could not afford to dismiss them as absurd. He instructed me to convey all this to Secretary (West), who was handling this matter at MEA. As I had not corresponded with any MEA officer at such a high level before, I pleaded with him to do this. He firmly refused. So I painstakingly drafted a CCB telegram to Secretary (West), and tried my best to make its incredible contents appear credible and sent it at about 11 p.m. that night. His response, addressed to CG Gupta, arrived at 4 p.m. the next day. It instructed him to arrange my and Alfredo's travel to Mexico and San Jose earliest possible. He and I were stunned!

It took five days to secure my Mexican and Costa Rican visas and for CGI to arrange Alfredo's and my air tickets to Mexico City and San Jose and hotel accommodation there.

We left New York on September 30 morning and arrived in Mexico City at 2 p.m. Soon after checking into our hotel we went to the Costa Rican Embassy. We were greatly disappointed to learn that the Ambassador had had a heart attack and was in hospital recuperating.

Since Alfredo was related to him he decided to visit him in hospital. So we went there. At the hospital, Alfredo managed to outsmart all those who tried to prevent us from getting to the Ambassador's room. The latter recognized him, greeted him warmly and asked who I was. Alfredo introduced me, briefly stated our purpose and requested a letter from him to Costa Rican President José Trejos Fernández to receive us. The Ambassador responded he could not do this from his hospital bed but would give us his visiting card. On the back of it he wrote 'Please receive them' and signed below it.

From the hospital, Alfredo returned to our hotel and I went to the Embassy of India to send a CCB telegram to Secretary (West) and CG Gupta about that day's happenings. Ambassador Ratnam initially stated that the frantic efforts to get the Tejas back to India was a 'hare-brained scheme' and 'wild goose chase', but later reluctantly permitted me to send my telegram from his embassy.

The next morning (1 October), we flew to San Jose, arrived there by 5 p.m. and checked into the small but elegant Hotel Presidente. When its receptionist saw me she commented, 'We have not had Indians in this hotel for many years. But recently an Indian couple stayed here and now you have arrived!' I asked for the names of this couple. She replied 'Dharma and Ranjit Teha'. This was vital confirmation that they now were in this city.

Early the next morning Alfredo told me that we would go to the Presidential Mansion. We walked there as it was quite close to our hotel. When we arrived at this mansion, he headed for its back service entrance and entered its kitchen. The President's wife was there with two of her staff, preparing her husband's breakfast. She was surprised to see us but nonetheless greeted Alfredo (her nephew) warmly. He introduced me to her and indicated we wished to meet the President. She initially stated, quite firmly, this was not the appropriate way to meet him on an official matter. Alfredo then showed her the visiting card of the Costa Rican Ambassador to Mexico and what he had written on it. She took it to her husband and came back a few minutes later to take us to him. He was seated in their private sitting room, draped in a dressing gown, reading that morning's newspapers. Alfredo introduced me to him, indicated the purpose of our visit and told me to show the President the Indian and American legal documents about Teja's criminality I was carrying. While he was scrutinizing them, Alfredo kept telling him the nefarious role which his predecessor José Figueres Ferrer had played in this case. The President said nothing but a few minutes later picked up the telephone next to him and summoned the Police Chief, who arrived in about 15 minutes. Meanwhile, the President continued reading the newspapers and his gracious wife served us breakfast and chatted with Alfredo. When the police chief arrived, the President handed over the mentioned legal documents and told him that 'the entry of the Teha couple into Costa Rica was unfortunate' and they should be deported immediately. The police chief said he would have this done by getting the foreign office to cancel their visas and instructing the airline that had brought them into Costa Rica to take them back to where they had boarded it. The President concurred with this course of action. At this point it appeared that the amazing plan of action which Alfredo had devised had worked perfectly—our objective of locating, apprehending and deporting the Teja couple first to the US and then to India would be achieved. Alfredo and I thanked President Trejos respectfully and profusely for the prompt and positive action he had taken, and Mrs Trejos for her gracious hospitality to us. We left the presidential Mansion by the front entrance this time and were escorted out by the police chief, who also was well known to Alfredo.

He suggested that we now visit his mother and siblings, but I decided to go instead to the Ministry of External Relations to report my presence in Costa Rica as also that of the criminally-tainted Teja couple. On arrival there, I requested a call on its 'Secretario General' (equivalent to Foreign Secretary), who was named Alvaro Antillon Salazar. Though I had come with no prior intimation and India had not yet established diplomatic relations with Costa Rica, he received me immediately and stated that he had done so because of his 'great admiration for Mahatma Gandhi'. I gave him details of the Teja case, expressed our great disappointment that their Consulate General in New York had issued visas to the Tejas despite our formal request not to do so. Visibly embarrassed, he said this had been done on instructions from 'a high political level'. I did not reveal to him my meeting with the President earlier that morning and his instructions to the police chief to have them deported, but gave him a set of the Indian and US legal documents about the Tejas and requested that they be apprehended and deported earliest possible. In leaving I suggested that in view of his admiration for the Mahatma he consider taking the initiative to set up a Mahatma Gandhi Society in San Jose. He promised to do so and we parted on a friendly note.

At 5 p.m. that day Alfredo telephoned the Police Chief and enquired whether action on the President's instructions had been taken. The latter gave the disappointing news that when his officers arrived at their front door the Tejas slipped out of the back door and sped away in their red sports car. The police chief expressed confidence that they would soon be found since Costa Rica was a small country and red sports cars were few.

The following morning's San Jose newspapers carried news reports about the police looking for an Indian couple who had entered Costa Rica surreptitiously. *La Nacion* and *La Republica* raised questions about how they had managed to do this and linked it to lax national security. This constrained the Ministry of External Relations to issue a press release signed by its minister Fernando Lara indicating that their visas had been issued as requested by former President José Ferrer Figueres and that he had strongly recommended this as Dharma Teja was an eminent scientist and shipping magnate, whose presence in Costa Rica would benefit it greatly. The press release also indicated that on reconsideration of this matter the visas issued to him and his wife had been cancelled and they had been notified to leave the country within 30 days. This press release appeared in the San Jose papers on October 6 morning.

The fact that former President José Figueres (who will hereafter be referred to as Senor Figueres) had intervened on Teja's behalf was now openly and officially revealed. Efforts by journalists to contact him were of no avail as he was then in Taiwan.

I left San Jose for New York on 6 October afternoon, greatly disappointed that despite having secured a Presidential order for deportation of the Tejas from Costa Rica within 24 hours of Alfredo's and my arrival there, they had managed to escape a few minutes before the police arrived at their home to arrest and deport them.

When Ambassador B.K. Nehru visited New York in mid-October, he addressed me as 'our James Bond' and complimented me on my 'good work' in locating Mr and Mrs Teja in Costa Rica and inducing the Costa Rican Government to cancel their visas and order them to leave that country within 30 days.

Senor Figueres returned to Costa Rica on 25 October. The following day he wrote letters to *La Nacion* and *La Republica* newspapers expressing anguish that 'petty politics has befuddled a great human tragedy'. He averred that 'mere allegations were presented as criminal acts' so as to have the Tejas expatriated to India. This endangered their liberty as also their lives. Their going into hiding was deplorable, but sometimes 'a small wrong doing averts a bigger one'. He urged the Tejas to come out of hiding and boldly present the actual facts of their case, 'as Costa Ricans were open minded and freedom loving'.

On 1 November the Tejas appeared at a well-attended press

conference arranged by their lawyer Rogelio Navas. Mr Teja presented his academic and scientific credentials, including his CERN (European Organization for Nuclear Research) identity card. He averred that he had enjoyed the confidence and support of Prime Minister Nehru because of which those envious of him wanted to destroy him. He appealed to the Costa Rican people for their sympathy and support and indicated that he would soon be applying for political asylum for himself and his wife. The media gave extensive coverage to this interview. It generated much public sympathy for them. Alfredo, back at his post at the Costa Rican Consulate General in New York, kept sending me clippings of all news reports about the Tejas. This enabled me to regularly update Consul General Gupta, Ambassador Nehru in Washington and Secretary (West) in MEA about every development in this case.

On 10 November, the Tejas submitted their formal appeal for political asylum in Costa Rica to Foreign Minister Fernando Lara. So, as instructed by Secretary (West), P.K. Banerjee, Minister (Pol) in EI Washington, designated as Special Envoy of GOI, accompanied by me and R.L. Mehta and Gurdas Mal of the Central Bureau of Investigation (who arrived in New York the previous day), flew to San Jose on 17 November, with all the requisite Indian and US court documents, to present our formal request for denial of political asylum to them. Mr Banerjee had been my mentor at EI Tokyo and I was delighted to work with him again.

Mr Banerjee and I were received by President Trejos the following morning. In response to our detailed presentation about the Tejas, the President commented that he was well aware of the facts of this case; the difficulty in resolving it was due to the support the Tejas had garnered from one of his predecessors and the Costa Rican news media and people.

Our formal request for denial of political asylum to Mr and Mrs

Teja was made to Foreign Minister Lara on 19 November along with our proposal for establishment of diplomatic relations between India and Costa Rica. That afternoon Mr Banerjee addressed a press conference. It received good media coverage, but two days later Mr Teja also held a press conference contradicting all that Mr Banerjee had stated. He therefore advised that I make a press release, under my name, presenting the actual facts. Fortunately, this was carried in full by the leading newspapers on 30 November.

Mr Banerjee, the two CBI officers and I left San Jose for Washington/New York via Miami that afternoon. The previous day we had appointed two leading Costa Rican lawyers Eduardo Ortiz and Guido Loria to represent GOI in all the legal proceedings connected with the Teja case. They were recommended to us by Alfredo and were given a detailed briefing about the Teja case and a complete set of authenticated legal documents about it by R. L. Mehta and Gurdas Mal of CBI.

The first good news we received thereafter was on 19 January 1968. The Tejas' request for political asylum was denied with an Executive Order signed by President Trejos and Foreign Minister Lara and they were given 30 days to depart Costa Rica. In view of this, Mr Banerjee and I were instructed to go immediately to San Jose to present our formal request for their extradition to India. This was done on 23 January morning. Soon thereafter the Costa Rican Government revoked its 15 January order requiring the Tejas to depart Costa Rica within 30 days and ordered them not to do so in view of the GOI request for their extradition to India.

By early March the initial phase of the extradition case had been completed and its substantive phase was soon to commence. Lawyer Ortiz made an urgent request for some additional documents and four Indian and US law books. So I was instructed to take them to San Jose immediately. I was unhappy about this as Isobel, now in her ninth month of pregnancy, was due to deliver her baby on 20 March, but I flew to San Jose on 15 March!

On 16 March, while I was having dinner at the popular Swiss Chalet restaurant the other diners suddenly began gazing excitedly towards its entrance. When I looked that way I saw the Tejas entering this restaurant and the Manager receiving them most respectfully. They stood at the entrance for a moment and waved at everyone as celebrities do. Many diners waved back at them. As they passed my table they saw and recognized me. Mr Teja looked away immediately but Mrs Teja, more suave, smiled and asked, 'Are you based in Costa Rica now?' I replied with a reciprocal smile, 'No, I have only come to assist you both in returning to India!' She self-confidently replied, 'How kind of you.'

When I met Lawyer Ortiz the next morning he told me that he had learnt from a reliable source that Mrs Teja was now pregnant as Mr Teja's lawyer had advised him that she having a child in Costa Rica would enhance their chances of not being extradited. (This information turned out to be true. Mrs Teja delivered a baby boy in September that year. He was named Ignacio Jayanti. Eighteen years later he moved to the US for higher studies where he met, and married Samhita Patwardhan, daughter of Arun Patwardhan, my predecessor as Consul General in New York. I met Samhita Teja in October 2012 when I was in New York to deliver the keynote address at that year's International Day of Non-Violence at the UN. She had two lovely children.)

I returned to New York from San Jose at about 10 p.m. on 19 March. Soon after I got home Isobel told me her pre-natal pains had started about an hour earlier. So I immediately telephoned her gynaecologist Dr Robert Hoenig, who advised me to move her immediately to Lennox Hill Hospital. We arrived there at 11.30 p.m. Dr Hoenig, who lived in New Jersey, arrived at 1 a.m. Meanwhile, Isobel was assisted with her prenatal pains by an Afro-American nurse named Bertha. On arrival, Dr Hoenig examined Isobel and informed us that as her first delivery was by caesarean section it would be safer to have this one the same way. We both concurred. The surgery took longer than expected. At 4.10 a.m., Nurse Bertha came out with a seven pound six ounce baby boy, told me he was my son, and asked for his name. I replied that we had not yet decided on it but had Anand, which means 'joy', in mind. She promptly stated 'Wonderful, We will label him as Andy!' That was the label she made and stuck on his wrist. It stayed there for the next three weeks until he was christened as Anand Pascal on 14 April (1968). However, he has been known to everyone as Andy since the day he was born!

On 4 April, the shocking news of Martin Luther King's assassination was received. Isobel and I admired him greatly. We had had the shock and sadness of President John F. Kennedy's assassination while in Burma five years earlier, but that had not impacted much on us as we had seen no TV coverage of it. This assassination was covered ceaselessly on every television channel. Its impact was far deeper and more indelible.

Just eight weeks later (on 6 June) occurred another equally traumatic tragedy of Senator Robert Kennedy's assassination in Los Angeles. Two days later his body was brought to New York and 'laid in repose' at St Patrick's Cathedral for two days. We attended the Requiem Mass for him there on 7 June and were deeply moved by it. Fortunately, some rows had been reserved for the diplomatic and consular corps and we managed to find two seats.

This was a particularly violent period in the United States. In many of its universities student unrest had been brewing since the beginning of that year over conscription for the Vietnam War. In April it erupted violently at the reputed Columbia University. Martin Luther King's assassination triggered it but the initial anger was over the discovery by an activist of the 'Students for a Democratic Society' named Bob Feldman that Columbia University had a secret institutional affiliation with the Institute for Defense Analyses (IDA), a weapons research think tank linked to the US Department of Defense. A subsidiary issue was its gymnasium project which involved removal of many low income black residential buildings from its neighbourhood.

I had a ringside seat to this uprising as Student Welfare was one of my responsibilities as Consul (CPV) and my younger brother John, who was staying with me, was president of its Indian Students Union. From him I received daily reports about happenings there. This student uprising achieved two of its prime objectives—Columbia's affiliation with IDA was ended and its plan for the controversial gym was scrapped.

In the third week of August, the brutal crushing of the '*Prague Spring*' uprising with thousands of Soviet troops and tanks was extensively covered on US TV. This and the strong denunciation of the Soviet action at the UNSC and UNGA made this tragedy very real and close to us.

In January 1969, P.K. Banerjee having been appointed as PR, PMI, Geneva left Washington. V.K. Ahuja, Consul General of India at New York, was appointed Ambassador of India to Costa Rica. I accompanied him to San Jose when he presented his credentials there on 29 May 1969. That was my 14th and last visit to that country.

In mid-June, I was surprised to be appointed CDA of the new EI which was being opened in Lima, Peru as a follow-up of Prime Minister Indira Gandhi's visit to Latin America the previous year. I was to arrive in Lima by early September.

During all of July there were numerous farewell parties for us. While we were at one of them, at the elegant Bombay Palace restaurant, we had the great thrill of watching on television screen the first US moon-landing on 20 July 1969, at 20:18 hours, and six hours later watching astronauts Neil Armstrong and Buzz Aldrin walking on the lunar surface, on our home TV.

We left New York for Bangalore on 20 August 1969 and arrived home in time for lunch on 22 August. All four of us, but particularly Andy, the first Nazareth grandson, received a very warm and joyous welcome from my parents and the following day also from Isobel's!

6

In the Land of the Incas and Machu Picchu

(September 1969–December 1973)

I travelled from New Delhi to Lima, the Peruvian capital, by Air France via Paris. En route it touched down at Pointe-á-Pitre in Guadeloupe.

I was received at the airport by Juan McBride, an English-speaking liaison officer, who had been assisting Ambassador of India to Peru K.L. Mehta (who was based in Santiago, Chile), on his quarterly visits to Lima. He drove me to the elegant Hotel Bolivar where Ambassador Mehta, who had arrived the previous day, was staying.

I called on Ambassador Mehta in his suite the next morning and we had breakfast together. He informed me that he would be calling on the Peruvian President General Juan Velasco Alvarado at 11 a.m. that morning, on Foreign Minister Mercado Jarrin at 4 p.m. that afternoon and the Finance and Commerce Ministers at the same times the following day and that I should accompany him to all these meetings.

I was greatly honoured and privileged to be introduced to all these VVIPs as India's new Charge D' Affaires in Peru. This gave me a very high level official start on my first two days there.

President Velasco had been in office only since 3 October 1968—the day on which he staged a bloodless military coup and deposed President Fernando Belaúnde Terry. The prolonged bickering between the President and the APRA-UNO Opposition over the license issued to International Petroleum Company (IPC) to drill in northern Peru had created the conducive scenario for his coup. When, soon thereafter the Velasco government cancelled this licence and took over IPC's assets in Peru, it received wide popular support.

On the first weekend after Ambassador Mehta's return to Santiago, I had an unexpected adventure. On Friday I received a telephone call from Jaime Stieglich, an officer in the Asia Section of the Foreign Office, who stated that his senior colleague Jaime Caceres, Deputy Permanent Representative in their UN Mission in New York, had instructed him to 'befriend' me. (Ambassador N. Krishnan, our PR in New York, had introduced Jaime Caceres to me before my departure from there.) He told me he and his colleague Fernando Belaúnde would like to take me for a drive into the cordilleras (a chain of mountains). I was delighted and readily agreed. They picked me up from Hotel Bolivar at 8 a.m. that Saturday morning and drove out of Lima for about 30 miles along Peru's arid coast and then eastwards into the Andes. In the latter section we initially passed luxurious residences with swimming pools and well-maintained gardens. There was also a golf course in this area. Soon thereafter the road ascended, gently at first but steeper at every bend thereafter. When we stopped 90 minutes later for coffee and snacks we were at 7,000 ft. From here onwards Jaime and Fernando (who I now learnt was former President Belaúnde's nephew) changed places in the driver's seat every 30 minutes and also made a 10-minute stop each time they did this so that we could get adapted to the higher altitude. Nonetheless, at the next stop I began to have breathing difficulty. Jaime, who had earlier given me a thick llama wool poncho and cap, now gave me a hand-held oxygen cylinder and this eased my breathing difficulty. By 1 p.m. we had reached El Ticlio, at altitude of 4,818 metres yet only 140 miles from Lima. We had a hot Peruvian 'antichucos' lunch here and strolled to the El Ticlio rail station, highest in the world (at that time). The view from here was stunning but mainly for its bleakness as most of the mountain slopes were treeless crags. Jaime informed me that if we drove further eastwards we would be at Iquitos, on the verdant Amazon river bank, by sunset. Peru is an amazing country. One can have breakfast on the beach, lunch at 15,000 ft and dinner in dense tropical jungle, on the same day!

At 3 p.m. we commenced our return journey, which was easier but not much quicker because of the narrow, winding roads. Back at Hotel Bolivar by 8 p.m. we had a relaxed dinner together. For me, it was and still is the most amazing and memorable 12-hour road journey I have had in my life.

Before I left New Delhi, Yashwant Sinha, Deputy Secretary in Ministry of Commerce, had assured me that he would soon be making a US$2,000 remittance to Banco de Londres y America del Sur (BLAS) via SBI New York in favour of EI Lima (which was an MoC post). But when I went to this bank on the day after my El Ticlio trip and enquired about this remittance its manager informed me it had not arrived. So I sent a telegram to Yashwant Sinha from Bolivar Hotel and was stunned by its cost: $24, at $1 per word. So the hotel manager suggested I use telex rather than telegram as the former is charged on per minute rather than per word, and a telex machine could be easily installed in my room. So I instructed him to do this, and it was done the following day. I then sent telex messages to Yashwant Sinha in MoC and Deputy Secretary (Latin America) in MEA about this, indicating why I had done so and requesting that they send their future messages to me by telex. The former did so and informed me that the $2,000 remittance was with SBI New York and would be forwarded to Lima as soon as the EI bank account had been opened at BLAS. MEA's response, by telegram and not telex, stunned me. It pointed out that I had no powers to have a telex machine installed and should explain why I had done so without the ministry's prior approval. Fortunately, Ambassador Mehta came to my rescue from Santiago and strongly supported the action I had taken on grounds of economy.

Three weeks later MoC, as advised by MEA, issued an ex-post-facto sanction for the installation of the telex machine. More notably, a month thereafter, MEA sent out a circular to all missions/posts abroad that it had recently come to its notice that telex messages were more economical than telegrams and hence it was amenable to sanction installation of telex machines in missions/posts abroad which prefer to use telexes rather than telegrams. I then discovered to my great surprise that other than the EIs at Washington and Moscow, HCI London and PMI New York, the only other EI that had it was a one man EI located in a hotel room in Lima! In the next 12 months nearly all Indian Missions/Posts had telex machines. I had unwittingly triggered MEA's 'Telex Revolution'. By mid-October I had also found suitable office and residential accommodation and secured MoC sanction for both.

A word here about each of them. Most other embassy offices and residences in Lima were housed in villas in the elegant San Isidro or Miraflores areas, where rents were high. The one I leased for the office was a compact 20' x 30' room on the fifth floor of a newly-constructed 12-storey steel and glass building, which was just across the site where the new Sheraton Hotel and the new expressway from the city centre to the suburbs, were being built. It was air-conditioned, had an open terrace at the third floor level with two flag posts on it. In signing the lease deed for this office I told the building management I would be flying the Indian flag on it every day. They agreed to this. Because of this and the strategic location of this building the Indian flag became the most visible foreign flag in Lima.

The embassy residence was a two-floor L-shaped modern villa, in Barranco. It was located on the edge of a cliff with only a small, well-maintained public park between it and a sheer 200-foot drop to a narrow beach. It had a spectacular view of the Pacific Ocean upto the horizon. The residences of the Bolivian Ambassador and Louis Berckemeyer, brother of the Peruvian Ambassador to the US, were located close to it.

Isobel, Premila, Andy and Mary, our domestic maid, arrived in Lima on 31 October (1969). The following Sunday we all went to the closest Catholic Church for Mass. When Isobel, dressed as usual in a saree, went up to receive communion the Priest asked her, in Spanish, if she was a Roman Catholic. I stepped forward and assured him, in Spanish, that we were Catholics and that I was CDA of the newly-opened EI in Lima. He gave us both a welcome smile and the 'sacred host'. The following day a local newspaper carried a news report that a 'Roman Catholic Hindu' heads the newly-opened Indian Embassy in Lima. (In Latin America all Indians are referred to as 'Hindus').

The major challenge I now had to handle was India's participation in the Lima International Trade Fair (LITF) in late November (1969). This required construction of a well-designed 'India Pavilion' and timely clearance of the various exhibits sent from India. Large expenditures were involved on both counts. The EI Liaison officer Juan McBride brought in one estimate for the pavilion construction. In view of GOI stipulation about securing three quotations I told him to secure two more which he did within three days. Both these were higher than the first! As the time frame for construction of the Pavilion was short

I accepted the lowest of the three received. This firm made a good design with typical Indian features and also constructed it in time for the trade fair opening. On that day, the President and Ministers of Finance, Industry and Trade visited our pavilion, praised its design and '*encantadora ambiento*' (enchanting ambience) and stayed longer at it than at the much bigger Brazilian and American pavilions, partly because the President got into a conversation with Isobel and chatted with her, for almost five minutes.

After LITF ended and the Indian exhibits were repacked and shipped to India I visited Juan McBride's office and was amazed to find the Indian flag on a flag pole standing next to his desk there. On his desk was a brass plate with his name and Honorary Consul of India inscribed on it. I told him the flag/Honorary Consul of India name plate were inappropriate and should be removed forthwith. He declined to do so and said Ambassador Mehta had not objected to them when he visited his office. The following week, I sent M.K. Chibber, our Vice Consul, to check whether McBride had done what I had told him to do. He informed me that he had not done so. So we made a press release that Mr Juan McBride, who had been functioning as our Liaison Officer, had been describing himself as The Hon'ble Consul of India which he is neither authorized nor permitted to do and all those who require visas or any information about them should come directly to the Embassy of India, the address of which was indicated in the press release. When McBride saw this in the newspapers he was enraged. He telephoned me and angrily stated that he would 'expose and destroy me'. Two weeks later I learnt from Ambassador Mehta that he had written to Ministry of Commerce in New Delhi with a copy to him, that the two additional quotations for the pavilion construction at LITF were from fictitious firms, had been secured on my instructions and that the firm to whom the pavilion construction contract was awarded had paid me a substantial sum of money. Fortunately, Ambassador Mehta came to Lima the following month, and as requested by MoC, made a detailed enquiry about this matter. He spoke to me, Chibber, McBride and the contractor who had constructed the India Pavilion. The contractor told him that the money he had paid was to McBride and not to me! Ambassador Mehta reported his findings to MoC and the matter was closed.

In early April 1970, an Indian Film Export Promotion (IFEP) delegation arrived in Lima. Some Indian films like *Mother India* and *Do Bigha Zamin* were being screened occasionally in cinema halls and on TV, particularly during Holy Week, as inspirational narratives of suffering and sacrifice overcome through deep faith in the Almighty. These films were popular but probably pirated. We had no previous contact with any Peruvian film importer and therefore approached the Peruvian Chamber of Commerce and got the names of two of them. They were invited to meet the IFEP delegation. After two days of discussions a major breakthrough was achieved. A contract for import of 54 Indian films for distribution all over Latin America, was signed by one of these two firms, named Promociones Filmicas Internacionales S.R. Ltda. The leader of the IFEP delegation was delighted as this was the largest such contract it had secured until then. The first two films imported into Peru with this contract were *Mera Naam Joker* and *Haathi Mere Saathi*.

The day 31 May 1970 was a Sunday. After attending Mass I had taken my family for a drive on the Pan American highway to Pachacamac, a 1,000-year-old pre–Inca fortress 50 miles south of Lima. Having enjoyed the stunning views of the countryside and the Pacific Ocean from its ramparts and a typical Peruvian lunch in a village next to it, we returned home at about 3 p.m. and got into bed for a nap. We were fast asleep when we were suddenly awakened by our bed being tossed up and down, as if some beast had got under it and was doing this. I immediately recalled what a Peruvian friend had told me. The up and down movements are far more dangerous than the sideward ones and one should run out of the house immediately when the former occur. This is what we, our children and domestic staff did. By the time we got out of the house and into the park that faced it, a large cloud of dust was already arising from the sandstone cliff on which it was located. Some portions of it had already fallen off onto the beach below. All our neighbours also ran into this park. We all stayed here until 10 p.m. that night with some of the neighbours kindly providing us and the others coffee and snacks. As there were no further tremors we went back into our home but not to our bedrooms. We had bedsheets spread on the carpets in the ground floor sitting room and left the front door unbolted so that we could run out again should another tremor occur that night. Fortunately, there was none.

The next morning we were relieved to learn from the newspapers that there was no major damage or loss of lives in Lima and that the epicentre of this earthquake (7.9 on the Richter scale) was 35 km off Peru's coast near Chimbote, which is 430 km north of Lima.

It was only two days later that Lima residents learnt of the enormous damage this earthquake had caused in Peru's northern and particularly its Callejón de Huaylas area, where the entire town of Yungay and its 30,000 residents had been buried under a 50-foot high avalanche of snow, water, rocks and earth from Mount Huascaran. Its total human toll was 66,794 deaths and about 30,000 injured. It was the world's deadliest avalanche.

Humanitarian assistance—tents, blankets, food, medicines—began pouring in from various countries. I saw little chance of securing such assistance from far away India in a short span of time. I therefore suggested to the Indian film importer that we screen *Mera Naam Joker* as a fundraiser for the earthquake victims. He readily agreed. Isobel then contacted the Chairman of the National Disaster Relief Organization (who was Peru's First Lady Mrs Consuelo de Velasco) and offered to organize fundraiser film screenings of the mentioned Indian film in aid of the earthquake victims. Her offer was promptly accepted. Three screenings of this film were made, at the best cine theatre in town. The first screening was attended by Mrs Velasco, wives of the Foreign, Finance, Commerce and Culture ministers and members of the Peru-India Friendship Society, the President of which was the renowned and wealthy Anita Fernandini de Naranjo, one of whose mansions was leased to the Soviet Embassy. She brought with her many of her high society friends. The first screening thus became a major social event. The donations made by Mrs Fernandini and her wealthy friends raised a far more substantial amount than that raised from the high-priced ticket sales at the three screenings. Besides, the wide media coverage the first screening secured was much more extensive than what even the largest foreign donations received.

When Ambassador Mehta came to Lima three weeks later and called on the President to convey India's condolences on this tragic disaster, the latter in thanking him for the condolences mentioned the EI fundraiser and offered a helicopter tour of the disaster area for the Ambassador. Isobel and I were also included. This gave us a stunning aerial view of the extensive devastation the earthquake had caused. At Yungay, the only indication of where this town of 30,000 residents was located, was the cross on top of its church and the tops of four palm trees which stood in front of it, in the town's main plaza. It was an awesome and heart-rending sight.

On 5 July I received a vital telephone call. It was from my Gandhian friend Alvar Antillon Salazar in San Jose, Costa Rica. He had retired from his Secretary General, External Affairs Ministry post but still remembered my deep interest in the Teja case. He had therefore called to convey the following: Teja's friend and benefactor José Figueres had won the April 1970 election and was now President of Costa Rica. Teja had won the extradition case—in which he had been defended in the final round by Antonio Picado, former Chief Justice of the Supreme Court!—had recently been issued a Costa Rican diplomatic passport in the name of Jayanti Dharma Konduru, and would soon be travelling to London via Paris with that passport. He (Alvar Antillon) had secured his itinerary from a relative of his who worked in the travel agency which had made Mr Teja's travel arrangements. He read it out to me, and at my request kindly telexed it. The information he had painstakingly collected and conveyed to me by telephone/telex at his own cost was of vital importance to us. I thanked him profusely and immediately thereafter conveyed it to Foreign Secretary/CG New York by CCB telegram.

The following day CBI transmitted this information to Interpol, which issued a red alert to their stations in Paris and London. In consultation with MEA and Ministry of Shipping, the CBI decided not to have Mr Teja arrested in Paris but in London, as India did not have an extradition treaty with France. When Mr Teja landed at Heathrow Airport on 24 July 1970 he was arrested. He flaunted his Costa Rican diplomatic passport, but in vain. The next day the Costa Rican Embassy in London protested his arrest but in vain as the Foreign Office pointed out that only diplomatic passport holders accredited to diplomatic missions in the UK are entitled to diplomatic immunities. A few weeks thereafter, GOI initiated extradition proceedings against Mr Teja in the UK. He was defended by the renowned Lord Dingle Foot, who argued, incredibly, that Mr Teja was being politically victimized because he had handled 'secret negotiations with Soviet leaders on India's behalf during the October 1962 Chinese invasion of India and had arranged a secret meeting between Prime Minister Nehru and President Charles de Gaulle'. Despite, or perhaps because of these outlandish claims India won the extradition case. Meanwhile Mr Teja, spent nine months in London's Brixton and Pentonville prisons and was finally brought back to India, with Indian police escort and taken to New Delhi's Tihar Jail.

(At New Delhi, Mr Teja's trial went on for many months at the court of Delhi Sessions Judge Muni Lal Jain. The clinching evidence against him was given by Fumiho Karaki, vice-president of Mitsubishi Heavy Industries (MHI), who revealed that MHI had paid Mr Teja US$220,500 for the purchase of three vessels; and a 2 per cent addition was made to the price of eight bulk carriers as a special commission to him. Besides, US$1.2 million had been paid into his London bank account on the basis of a Jayanti Shipping Corporation resolution which was later discovered to have been forged. Judge M.L. Jain's 360-page judgement found Mr Teja guilty on seven counts and sentenced him to a three-year jail term on 19 October 1972. He was then shifted from Tihar Jail to a Hyderabad jail where he is reported to have written numerous love poems, some of which were later published under the title *Penelope*.)

In 1973, Jayanti Shipping Company was merged with Shipping Corporation of India (SCI), with a Presidential ordinance. Serious though Mr Teja's crimes of defalcation and fraud were, there is no denying the fact that SCI, and India, benefitted greatly from the 16 modern bulk carriers which he purchased at favourable prices and on easy terms from Mitsubishi Heavy Industries of Japan.

I must now return to my Peru narrative.

In September 1970 I went on my first official tour out of Lima. It was to Cuzco, Peru's ancient Inca capital. Isobel accompanied me. As the flight from Lima takes only one hour and Cuzco's altitude is 3,400 metres we were advised to take complete rest on the first day so that our bodies get attuned to this altitude. This is what we did. The following day I called on the Mayor who kindly arranged a sightseeing tour for us of this historic city. We were deeply moved by 'Huacaypata' (sacred place of tears), Cuzco's main plaza. It has this name because it was here that Francisco Pizarro formally announced Spain's conquest of Peru in November 1532. Forty years later, on 24 September,1572, Túpac Amaru, the last Monarch who had ruled the remnant Inca Empire from Vilcabamba and had led an uprising against Spanish rule, was brutally executed here by being torn apart by four horsemen, to whose horses his hands and legs were tethered.

From Cuzco, we went to the famed Machu Picchu, 90 km away. It involved a two-hour train journey to a small town named Aguas Calientes and then a 30-minute bus ride, along a narrow, winding road to the top of an ant hill-shaped mountain on which this amazing archaeological site is located. En route one sees nothing but thick, tropical greenery on both sides of the road. Then all of a sudden, as the bus takes its last, sharp bend, the breath-taking sight presents itself. It is not easy to describe but is much like a 3,000-ft high anthill that has risen straight up from a riverbed and has its top sliced off to create a mini, self-sustaining township with numerous homes and terraced fields. Just beyond the fields is a sheer, 80° drop to the Urubamba river below, which from here looks like a narrow silver ribbon. Just about 50 metres away is the uncut top of Machu Picchu's twin Huayna Picchu. It is fully granite on two sides. Its near-perpendicular granite faces are widely considered the greatest challenge for mountain climbers. I had earlier seen some awesome sites like the Rohtang Pass in the Himalayas in India, Mount Fuji in Japan and Grand Canyon and Niagara Falls in the US but this was uniquely spectacular, a combination of wonders of Nature and human ingenuity.

Archaeologists generally agree that Machu Picchu was built during the reign of Inca Emperor Pachacuti (1438–1472 AD), as a secret hideout for him or his successors should any external threat emerge, as had been prophesised (and was fulfilled 50 years after his death!). Neither the Spanish conquistadores nor the world knew anything about it until American explorer Hiram Bingham discovered it in 1911.

In his later years Bingham became US senator for Connecticut. Among his publications are *Inca Land* (1922), *Machu Picchu, a Citadel of the Incas* (1930), and *Lost City of the Incas* (1948).

In mid-March 1971, I visited Cerro de Pasco Copper & Silver mines at La Oroya and thereafter the picturesque town of Huancayo, about four hours away by road. Both were stunning experiences, the first as an engineering marvel and environmental disaster and the other for its scenic beauty and invigorating air.

La Oroya, located at an altitude of 4,330 metres (14,210 ft) is the highest mining town in the world. Yet it is connected to Lima, 200 km away, by road and rail!

Silver was first discovered in this area in 1630 and mining began soon thereafter at Machcan, Atacocha, and Milpo. By 1750 these mines had become Spain's prime sources of silver.

The Lima to La Oroya railway line was completed in 1893. At El Ticlio, it reaches an altitude of 4,781 metres. Until China built its Qinghai-Tibet Railway it was the highest standard gauge railway in the world.

Cerro de Pasco Corporation (CPC) was established in 1902 by an American syndicate composed of J. P. Morgan, Henry C. Frick, Darius Mills and William Vanderbilt. In the next 10 years it bought all the small mines in this area. In 1922, it built the copper and silver smelters. By 1930, it had 13,000 workers, nearly all of whom were indigenous Peruvians.

In 1970, an NRI named Vijay Balaram arrived here as one of its senior managers. It was he who urged me to visit CPC and acquaint myself with its mining and refining operations and meet its top management.

In my discussions with the CPC top management the main point the latter made was that India was buying Peruvian copper but only at the London Metal exchange. Its benefit accrues primarily to British traders and not to Peru or India. They requested that I induce GOI to purchase Peruvian copper directly from Peru. I had intended to do this on my return to Lima, but on 25 March (1971), came the startling news of Pakistan's annulment of its 1970 national election results, Sheikh Mujibur Rahman's imprisonment and its army's brutal crackdown on its Eastern Wing. Though EI Lima had only a three-member staff and Dacca was very far away, I decided that we should do our best to bring these horrendous developments to the notice of the Peruvian Government and news media. Impactful news items from MEA's daily newsfeed and editorials and articles from the international press (e.g. NYT's 'Ballots in India, bullets in Pakistan') were culled by me, translated into Spanish by Angela (our Peruvian receptionist/translator), and made into a news bulletin, which was then cyclostyled by Krishnamurthy, my Private Secretary, and hand delivered by Chibber our Vice Consul, at the Foreign Office and leading newspaper offices. By early August, its frequency was increased to twice a week and its distribution list enlarged to include Peruvian friends and members of the Indian community. A courier service was now engaged for their distribution. None of this would have been possible if Angela had not graciously agreed to handle the strenuous and time-bound translation work involved in this. I am still deeply grateful to her.

On 16 December 1971, when news of the Pakistan army's surrender to Indian army commanders at Dacca was received and Chibber, Krishnamurthy and I rejoiced exultantly over the radical change this would bring about in South Asia's geopolitical landscape to India's advantage, Angela did likewise, almost as if she was an Indian—or Bangladeshi! (Thanks to Facebook I re-established contact with Angela in 2016, after 43 years.)

Just eight days later, on Christmas Eve, shocking news was received of a Peruvian passenger plane of LANSA Airline that had departed Lima for Pucallpa had crashed in the Amazon jungle killing all its 93 passengers and crew. Ten days later, the world was startled to learn that a 17-year-old girl had survived the crash and managed to walk/swim to a village about three miles downhill from the crash site, where she arrived on 3 January 1972. She had dropped two miles through the air but had suffered only a broken collarbone and a gash on her left leg. She had managed to stay alive for 10 days in this dense jungle replete with wild animals, poisonous snakes/spiders and man-eating fish. Her name was Juliane Koepcke. She revealed that the plane had crashed after it was struck by lightning.

Juliane did not have any tools for survival, not even a penknife. She was in a thin cotton dress and had only one sandal, the other having dropped off during her fall. What saved her was her knowledge of the jungle which she had learnt from her father, an eminent German zoologist named Hans-Wilhelm who worked at the Javier Prado Museum of Natural History in Lima. He often made trips into the jungle and sometimes took his daughter along. He had told her 'if you lose your way in the jungle, follow a flow of water and you will find your way out.' He had also told her 'piranhas are dangerous only in shallow water' and that 'water from the creeks is safe.' Besides, he had taught her to recognize bird calls and informed her that hoatzins (reptile birds) always live near lakes and rivers.

Her story gripped the world as 'powerfully life-affirming in its cocktail of luck, bravery and the invincibility of the human spirit'. Her first interview appeared in Stern magazine of Germany and then in many other magazines worldwide. But thereafter, she stayed away from all journalists and almost disappeared for four decades. Finally, in March 2012, her memoir, titled *When I Fell from the Sky: The True Story of One Woman's Miraculous Survival,* was published in Germany. When it was released she stated, 'I have now made peace with my own past!'

I must now return to the matter of direct import of Peruvian copper by India. There was initially fairly strong resistance from MoC/MMTC to this proposal on grounds of political instability in Peru. Fortunately, in November 1971 Commerce Minister L.N. Mishra accompanied by his IAS special assistant N.K. Singh (whom I had met and assisted in Tokyo in 1961) came to Lima for the G77 Ministerial Meeting prior to UNCTAD III at Santiago some months thereafter. I spoke to them about this matter. N.K. Singh promised to have it approved. This approval, for direct import of 54,000 tons of Peruvian copper by MMTC over a three-year period, was received in mid-December 1971.

The Peruvian government was so pleased that it decided to send its Minister of Mines, General Jorge Fernandez Maldonado (who four years later became Prime Minister) to sign the agreement at New Delhi in early March 1972. I was instructed to arrive there a week earlier to brief all concerned about Peru's political/economic scenario. So I boarded an Alitalia flight from Lima to Rome and was booked on Air India to fly from there to Delhi. The Alitalia flight made a brief halt at Caracas, where among the passengers who boarded it was a VVIP – Mother Teresa! She walked past me and seated herself in a window seat three rows ahead of me. The two seats next to her were vacant. So, as soon as the plane took off I went up to her and requested the privilege of sitting next to her. She readily agreed. When I had seated myself next to her she asked for my name and what I was doing in Caracas. I told her my name and that I was not in Caracas but in Lima where I had opened the Embassy of India in September 1969 and was now on my way to New Delhi in connection with a Peruvian Minister's visit there the following week. She smiled and commented 'I am glad Government of India is now sending young Christian diplomats to open its Embassies in Latin America!' This was the beginning of the most interesting and inspiring conversation I have had in my whole life.

The gist of our conversation was as follows:

The purpose of her visit to Venezuela was to open a new Missionaries of Charity Home (MCH) at Caracas.

Would she open an MCH in Lima? Yes, provided Peru's government and its Cardinal requested her to do so and provided suitable premises for it.

Where was the MCH home prior to the one in Caracas opened? In Cape Town South Africa; she had selected the fairest and darkest of her nuns and sent these two there with instructions that they should always go out together, hand in hand, 'to make the point publicly that black and white people can live and work together and love each other'.

How are all her many Homes financed? She smiled and pointed her finger upwards and said 'That is HIS responsibility; HE has never failed me.'

I had read about it and therefore asked her about her visit to Bangladesh soon after its liberation. She replied that its objective was to meet the numerous women in Dacca and nearby towns who had been raped and become pregnant. She requested all of them not to abort their babies but give them to her 'because even children conceived in sin are children of God'. She said almost 200 of them had agreed to do so and she had arranged to have them collected by her MCH in Dacca. About 75 of them had been collected already and others would be collected in the coming months for upbringing, education, vocational training and then marriage.

Estimates of pregnancies resulting from rape by Pakistani soldiers range from 70,000, according to Bangladesh government figures, to 125,000, which is the WHO figure. A victim relief programme set up by the Bangladesh government with WHO assistance recorded 30,000 'war baby' births during the first three months of 1972, and approximately 100,000 abortions all over Bangladesh in the next six months. The babies Mother Teresa's sisters collected (about 300 ultimately) were, therefore, miniscule in number but their efforts in doing so and preventing them from being aborted were noble and laudable nonetheless.

The conversation lasted 10 hours until the plane landed in Rome.

Here we both disembarked; she for a three-day stay there before she flew to Calcutta and I to board my onward Air India flight to New Delhi three hours later.

In wishing Mother Teresa a respectful farewell at Rome's Fiumicino airport I assured her that I would do my best to have a Missionaries of Charity Home opened in Lima before the completion of my term there. She smiled and responded 'If God wills it, we will have a Home there.'

The Peruvian Minister's visit to New Delhi and signing of the agreement for direct import of 54,000 tons of Peruvian copper by India over a three-year period, went off very well. The Peruvian Minister thanked GOI very much for this and indicated Peru's interest in importing Indian mining machinery and securing India's assistance in upgrading the railway network to their mines.

On the eve of my return to Lima N.K. Singh told me that he had advised the Commerce Minister to write to the External Affairs Minister (EAM) for my retention at Lima until the end of 1973 in order to ensure the mentioned agreement was implemented without any hitch. He also told me we would be meeting again soon in Santiago at the UNCTAD III Conference. I was quite sceptical about both. My successor in Lima had already been named. Besides, a batchmate of mine was DCM at EI Santiago. I was therefore stunned when soon after my return to Lima I was intimated that my tenure at EI Lima had been extended up to end December 1973 and that I should be in Santiago by 6 April 'to set up and handle the administrative arrangements for the Indian delegation's participation in UNCTAD III in Santiago, 13 April–21 May 1972'.

On my arrival in Santiago, Ambassador G.J. Malik (who had succeeded Ambassador K.L. Mehta in June 1971) informed me that the requisite number of rooms had been booked in the Carrera Sheraton Hotel and my immediate task was to interview and appoint four English knowing typists/one Liaison officer for the Indian delegation. Fourteen applications for these posts had already been received by EI Santiago. They were now called for an interview. One of them, Maria de La Luz Molina, who had a law degree and was well informed about local regulations, location of conference halls, government offices, historical sites in and around Santiago, was appointed as the Liaison officer. Four others who were proficient in English were appointed as Secretaries.

During the course of this conference, the above mentioned Liaison officer introduced me to Pablo Neruda's poetry and Chile's outstanding 'Casillero del Diablo' (The Devil's Mailbox) wine! I still have the book of Neruda's poems she gifted to me.

The Carrera Sheraton Hotel was located in Santiago's historic Plaza de La Constitution. The Presidential Palace and the Catholic Cathedral are located on the opposite sides of it. The view of this Plaza from this hotel's third floor, on which the Indian delegation was accommodated, was excellent.

Most members of the Indian delegation arrived on 10 April. Among them were Commerce Secretary H. Lal, Mr R.D. Pradhan, PR to UNCTAD/GATT at Geneva (who later became Secretary to Prime Minister Rajiv Gandhi), Mr Surendra Singh, JS in Ministry of Industrial Development (who retired as Cabinet Secretary), and Mr Vinod Dixit, JS in Commerce Ministry (whose wife Sheila some years later became Chief Minister of Delhi – thrice!).

Commerce Minister L.N. Mishra, accompanied by his Economic Adviser Manmohan Singh (who later became Prime Minister), special assistant N.K. Singh, two MPs (one of whom, Shri Sitaram

Kesri, became Congress Party President some years later), and two industrialists Mr Harish Mahindra and Mr Swraj Paul, arrived on April 12. Our Ambassador to USA Mr L.K. Jha arrived two weeks later.

President Salvador Allende's inaugural address was inspiring and impactful. He spoke of the daunting challenges developing countries faced from the developed countries and their deeply entrenched allies within them.

Among the VVIPs at the inaugural session were H.E. Luis Echeverria Alvarez, President of Mexico; Mr Valéry Giscard d'Estaing, France's Minister of Finance; General Miguel Angel de La Flor Valle, Foreign Minister of Peru; Mr Robert McNamara, World Bank President; Mr Pierre-Paul Schweitzer, IMF Managing Director and Mr Raul Prebisch, Director-General of the United Nations Latin American Institute for Economic and Social Planning (ILPES).

Handling the administrative and other requirements of the many VVIPs in the Indian delegation was a big enough challenge but to handle those of the two Indian MPs was far bigger. Their demands ranged from for *idli vadas* and *poori bhaji* for breakfast (these had to be procured from Ambassador Malik's residence) to visits to Hindu temples (none in Santiago those days!) and Gandhi statues (of which there was more than one!). I was therefore relieved when they indicated they wished to go to Buenos Aires for three days. I informed EI there about this visit, had their air tickets purchased and deputed Liaison Officer Maria de La Luz to escort them off at the airport. About an hour after their Chilean Airways plane left Santiago, news was received that, because of a severe storm over the Andes it had been diverted to Lima. So I telephoned Vice Consul Chibber there to receive them at the airport, book hotel rooms for them for two nights, arrange their sightseeing of Lima and request my wife to host a dinner for them with senior Indian community members. All this was done by him.

When the two MPs, returned to Santiago they spoke effusively to Commerce Minister Mishra about my efficiency and dynamism in making all these arrangements for their reception, accommodation, sightseeing and meeting Indian community leaders in Lima at such short notice, and urged him to convey this to EAM, which he kindly did after his return to India. (Shri Sitaram Kesri never forgot his visits to Santiago and Lima in 1972 and stayed in touch with me until he passed away in 2000.)

Besides the mentioned happenings during UNCTAD III, the other notable happening was Chile's economic destabilization, triggered by the US at this time. Initially launched soon after Salvador Allende's Popular Unity alliance won the 4 September 1970 election, it was intensified during this six-week long conference. With hundreds of foreign delegates attending it and changing thousands of US dollars into Chilean pesos every day, Chilean pesos mysteriously inundated Santiago. Its value kept dropping initially every week and later every day. This city became a diners and shoppers paradise. A three-course dinner, with wine, for four persons, at an elite restaurant would cost the equivalent of US$10! Chilean copper and silver art objects, imported perfumes, watches etc could all be bought at a third of their actual dollar values. By the time UNCTAD III ended Santiago was bereft not only of all luxury goods but even necessities like razor blades and medicines had become scarce.

Thomas Bodenheimer and Richard Gould, in their book *Roll Back: Right Wing Power in US Foreign Policy* have written about this CIA-crafted economic destabilization.

The Allende government did its best to stem this economic debacle. It stepped up the production/supply of goods and controlled their prices/distribution but with little success. This led to an erosion in political support for it, first from its supporters and some months later from the Christian Democratic Party (CDP) ally. In August 1973

CDP joined the opposition parties in the Congressional declaration of a 'constitutional breakdown'. This provided Gen. Augusto Pinochet, the golden opportunity to stage his long-planned coup, which he led on 11 September 1973. The Army, Airforce, and National Police supported him but not the Navy.

President Allende stayed on in the Casa Moneda during the army and air force attack on it and took active part in defending it. In a broadcast he made from here he declared that he would not resign but defend his constitutional office until his last breath. When all hope of doing this was lost he shot himself.

Later that day, when his clothing was gone through, a slip of paper was found in his coat pocket. It had a handwritten telephone number on it which turned out to be that of Ambassador G.J. Malik! He was a close friend of President Allende, who telephoned him on that fateful day and stated, 'I am calling you on the most difficult day of my life. We shall fight all day.' (Ambassador Malik has revealed this in his article titled 'The last days of Salvador Allende' in *The Ambassador's Club: The Indian Diplomat at Large'* edited by Ambassador K.V. Rajan and published by HarperCollins 2012.)

On my return from Santiago I followed up on my promise to Mother Teresa. I called on Cardinal Juan Landázuri Ricketts as also on the dashing Mayor of Lima, 'Chachi' Dibos (who used to drive around town in a red MG sports car). Both welcomed the proposal to have a Missionaries of Charity Home in Lima and promised to provide all the necessary requirements. As requested by me they also wrote formal letters of invitation to Mother Teresa, which I forwarded to her in early July 1972. She responded in mid-September, confirmed she would open her Home in Lima and indicated she could do this only in March 1973.

By mid January 1973, the Cardinal and Mayor had jointly identified three premises for Mother Teresa's choice. After her arrival in Lima on 25 March she chose the one on Avenida 28 de Julio, close to La Victoria slum. It was immediately repainted and furnished with the few items she requested. A large board with 'Hogar de La Misioneras de Caridad' inscribed on it was then fixed on the front gate. On the fifth morning after her arrival in Lima with two of her sisters, Holy Mass was offered in this 'Hogar' by a priest deputed by the Cardinal. I, Isobel, Premila, Andy and our maid Mary attended it. When the Mass was about to begin, Mother Teresa beckoned Andy to be the 'altar boy'. Taken aback, he told her he had never done this before. She smiled and told him she would tell him what needs to be done.

For all of us this Mass in a tiny chapel in an impoverished part of Lima, was a deeply moving and spiritually elevating experience. For Andy it was to have vital importance 12 years later, when he was critically ill at Sloane Kettering Hospital in New York.

As her visit to Peru had aroused much public interest I organized a 'Meet the Press' event for her. She initially declined to attend it but on my gentle urging agreed to do so. Among the questions she was asked was the following: 'Mother Teresa, we are very happy and honoured you have come to Lima and opened a Home here but would like to ask why you have done this when there is much more poverty in India than Peru?' Her reply was simple and impactful. 'It is in India's widespread poverty that I discovered the greatest hunger is for love not for food. That is the message I always carry with me and have now brought to Peru. As soon as two Peruvian nuns are found to manage this 'Hogar' the two Indian nuns now doing this would be sent to some other country to implant this message there.' The following morning's newspapers reported this with the title 'The greatest hunger in the world is for love, says Mother Teresa!'

The first direct shipment of Peruvian copper to India under the agreement signed with India in March 1972 commenced in January 1973 and continued smoothly once every quarter.

As I was completing my extended term at EI Lima in September 1973 and could not take my Jaguar car with me to India (as it was then classified as a luxury car), I sold it in Peru with MEA's approval in May 1973, and imported a new Chevrolet Camaro from Miami soon thereafter. It was delivered to me in the last week of June.

In early September among the new Ambassadorial appointments announced were those of A.R. Sethi, as India's first Ambassador to Peru, and Avadhuth Kakodkar (my 1959 IFS batchmate) as India's first Ambassador to Venezuela. Ambassador Sethi arrived in Lima in early December 1973. I was instructed to stay on in Lima until he presented his credentials, which he did on 14 December.

On 7 December, Isobel had pleasant surprise. A protocol officer from the Presidential Mansion arrived with a package addressed to her. It was from Peru's First Lady and contained a finely crafted pair of gold earrings and a handwritten letter of thanks for Isobel's efforts in aid of Peru's 1980 earthquake victims and 'Bon Voyage' to her.

My surprise came the following day. The Chief of Protocol (COP) telephoned and stated the Peruvian government had decided to honour me with the 'El Sol del Peru'. I was stunned. After thanking him and his government profusely for this honour, I informed him that GOI does not permit its diplomats to accept foreign decorations. He expressed great surprise and pointed out that whereas proposals for these decorations are normally initiated by the Foreign Office this one had emanated from the Presidential Mansion. It would therefore be quite discourteous to decline it. He urged that I consult Ambassador Malik in Santiago and convey to him what he had told me. I promptly did this. The Ambassador told me to send a telegram to Secretary (West), with cc to him, conveying what COP had told me. He then strongly recommended that I be permitted to accept this decoration. Secretary (West) responded favourably and to my pleasant surprise indicated that Ambassador A.B. Bhadkamkar in Cairo had recently reported to him the high praise which the previous Egyptian Ambassador to Peru, now COP in Cairo, had had for my work in Lima. In being permitted to accept this decoration I was instructed not to display it in public.

This decoration, a sun-shaped gold medal, was pinned on my 'bandh gala' by Peruvian Foreign Minister Miguel Angel de La Flor, at a lunch in the Foreign Office on December 14.

We left Lima for New York en route to India on December 15. I had spent 42 months in Lima. It was my longest tenure at any post in my 35-year IFS career.

7

Bangladesh and Europe on the Same Platter

(February 1974–December 1975)

I assumed charge as Director (EBD) in the Economic Division of MEA on 1 February 1974. My predecessor in this post was Hardev Bhalla, my Japanese language colleague in Tokyo some years earlier. It was designated as EBD because it dealt with economic relations with Bangladesh and Europe. It was an unusual combination. One colleague quipped it was 'The fish pot of Bangladesh with the flesh pot of Europe!'

Soon after taking charge, I called on my boss Secretary (Economic Relations) B.K. Sanyal. He was kind, efficient, and well-connected with his counterparts in other ministries. He told me that of all countries on my 'platter' I should give priority to Bangladesh in view of its great importance to India. He added that Prime Minister Indira Gandhi monitors economic relations with that neighbour minutely and that its Prime Minister Sheikh Mujibur Rahman was soon to visit India.

My prime task was to ensure regular movement of food grains and coal to Bangladesh by liaising closely with the Railway Board.

My colleagues at this post were the most outstanding I have had in my 35-year IFS career. Kris Sreenivasan, retired as Foreign Secretary and thereafter as Commonwealth Deputy Secretary-General. Lalit Mansingh retired as Foreign Secretary and then was appointed as Ambassador of India to USA; Kamalesh Sharma retired as PR at PMI in New York, then was appointed as High Commissioner of India to UK and thereafter elected as Commonwealth Secretary-General.

The Bangladesh PM's visit took place on 16 May 1974. Its focus was on economic issues as political issues had been dealt with during our PM's visit to Dacca in February 1972 when the India-Bangladesh Treaty of Friendship, Cooperation and Peace was signed. This summit meeting was marked by much warmth, informality and humour on both sides. When our PM mentioned that regular movement of food grains/coal to Bangladesh was being hampered by non-return of railway wagons by Bangladesh, its PM promptly responded that his people had been so impacted by her gracious generosity that they assumed everything coming from India, including railway wagons, was a gift! Everyone, including our PM had a hearty laugh! The former nonetheless promised to ensure that all India's railway wagons would soon be returned.

About a month prior to the above mentioned VVIP visit/meeting I was unexpectedly instructed to go to Colombo for the ECAFE (UN Economic Commission for Asia and the Far East) conference there 27 March–7 April, as Kris Sreenivasan, (who handled Africa/ International Organizations) could not do so because of a high-level Ethiopian delegation's visit to India at this time.

At the reception hosted by the Sri Lankan Commerce Minister on its inaugural day, among the many I met was a young man named Anura Bandaranaike. In our conversation I mentioned that I had previously served in faraway Peru, where I had opened the Indian Embassy in September 1969. He immediately warmed up, told me he loved Latin American Music and was fascinated by all he had heard and read about 'Machu Pichu' and the Incas. He invited me to a 'lively' party with some Sri Lankan and Latin music later that evening, which I accepted. At this party, held in the spacious and elegant home of one of his friends, I discovered that he was the son of Prime Minister Sirimavo Bandaranaike and that most others at this party were children of Sri Lankan VIPs. Among them was Anura's sister Chandrika. She had recently returned from Paris with a PhD in development economics from École Pratique des Hautes Études, Paris. She was as fluent in French as in English and Sinhala. Little did I realize when I spoke to her that evening that in just 20 years she would be Sri Lanka's first female President and occupy that high post for 11 long years as Chandrika Kumaratunga!

I invited Anura to dinner at my hotel on the eve of my departure from Colombo and thereafter kept track of his steady rise in Sri Lankan politics, from Leader of the Opposition (1983–1988), to Minister of Higher Education (1993–1994), Speaker (2000–2001), Minister of Tourism (April 2004–January 2007), Minister of National Heritage (2007) and finally Foreign Minister in 2005.

As Director (EBD), I was ex-officio member of the India–Bangladesh Joint Rivers Commission (JRC). The first JRC meeting I attended was the one held at Dacca in September 1974. These meetings were held every quarter, alternatively in India and Bangladesh.

Negotiating with the Bangladeshis was not easy. The difficulty was not due entirely to them. They argued that India's construction of the Farakka Barrage diverted life-sustaining Ganga waters away from Bangladesh to Calcutta's Hooghly port merely to desilt it. This was great injustice to it. India's proposal of a Brahmaputra–Ganga canal to replace the waters diverted by the Farakka Barrage was as clever as it was unfair. Bangladesh had to provide all the land for it but its entry and exit points would both be in India! The leader of the Bangladesh side slyly remarked one day, 'We are not as smart as you Indians but we are not so dim-witted as not to see that with both the entry and exit points of this canal located in India we would have our neck in your noose!'

The real tussle over Ganga waters was in the January–May 'lean season' when water flows varied from a high of 110,000 cusecs to a low of 60,000 cusecs. Bangladesh kept demanding 70 per cent of these flows (80,000 cusecs) but we kept insisting that 55,000 cusecs was our irreducible requirement. I felt that, in view of Bangladesh's acute poverty and great dependence on Ganga waters for its rice and fish requirements, we should agree to their demand but our leader (a Ministry of Irrigation JS), adamantly opposed it. Fortunately in the 1996 India–Bangladesh Ganga Waters Sharing Treaty, India agreed to restrict its share during the lean period to 35,000-40,000 cusecs only!

Among the most important matters I handled during my Director (EBD) days was the signing of the Indo-US Joint Commission on Economic, Commercial, Scientific, Technological, Educational and Cultural Cooperation agreement. It was signed on 28 October 1974 by Secretary of State Henry Kissinger and Foreign Minister Y. B. Chavan.

I have two indelible memories of this event. When Foreign Minister Chavan picked up the silver pen from the silver stand to sign this agreement's Hindi version he found it would not write because it had run out of ink. He turned to me and whispered '*Ye kalam nahin likta hai*'. Taken aback, I did the only thing I could at that moment. I pulled out the Parker pen from my pocket and handed it to him. He signed the agreement with my pen! When this Hindi version was then handed over to Secretary Kissinger he promptly turned to Foreign Minister Chavan and commented, 'Mr Foreign Minister, I cannot sign this agreement. I cannot read a word of it!' The latter's response was immediate and brilliant. 'Mr Secretary, a few months ago you signed agreements in Beijing without being able to read a word of them. This one is quite innocuous compared to those, so please sign it!' All those around them, including US Ambassador Daniel Moynihan chuckled. Even Secretary Kissinger could not resist a smile. The photo of him signing this agreement shows this.

(I met Henry Kissinger again 45 years later. J.P. Morgan had invited me to deliver a lecture on Gandhi@150 to its International Council members at Gandhi Smriti, New Delhi, on October 21, 2019. Among the 30 VVIP members of this council who attended this lecture were the Hon'ble John Howard, former Prime Minister of Australia, and Dr Henry Kissinger. After my lecture the latter, who was in a wheel chair, got out of it, walked upto me, congratulated me on the 'excellence' of my lecture and enquired about Gandhi's position on India's partition.)

Early in January 1975 I was included in Foreign Minister Chavan's delegation for his official visit to Yugoslavia. We travelled to Belgrade via Rome. After talks with the Yugoslav foreign minister we were taken by road to the stunning medieval fortress city of Dubrovnik from where we flew to the island of Brioni for the formal call on President Tito. His mansion, located on a hill, had stunning views of some Roman ruins and the Adriatic Sea. Though quite old by now he still had an imposing presence and it was exhilarating for all of us to be introduced to him. (He died five years later in a Ljubljana hospital while undergoing a heart surgery.)

Two days later, at Belgrade, when our departure details were being finalized, I indicated that I would be leaving for the airport later than the others as my return flight, which was via Athens and not Rome, was to leave three hours later. When Secretary (West) V.C. Trivedi, heard this he asked me sharply who had authorized this. I was taken aback. I had done this on my own as Air India had indicated no additional cost was involved in this re-routing. I apologized abjectly to Secretary (West) and requested his ex-post facto approval for it. He stated that only FM could approve this. So I went to FM's suite, trembling in my shoes, made my confession and sought his forgiveness and approval. His response was as amazing as it was unexpected. He asked, 'If you can travel via Athens at no extra cost, why not me and the others? I would much like to visit Athens and its famed Acropolis.' He telephoned Secretary Trivedi and requested him to come to his suite along with P.N. Menon, our Ambassador to Yugoslavia. When they arrived he told them what he had told me. Ambassador Menon, who was concurrently accredited to Greece, indicated he would speak to the Greek Foreign Minister and get back within an hour. He returned with the good news that the Greek FM had welcomed our FM's visit and promised to make all arrangements for this visit including to the Acropolis. The FM's tickets and those of other members of his delegation were re-routed soon thereafter for the return to New Delhi via Athens.

Early the following morning we flew to Athens by an Olympic Airlines flight. We were received at the airport by the Greek Chief of Protocol, and escorted to the Acropolis, then to the National Museum and finally to the Foreign Office for the call on the Foreign Minister. This was followed by an elegant and sumptuous lunch. We left for the airport at 4 p.m. and boarded our Olympic Airways flight to Beirut at 6 p.m. and our Air India flight from there to New Delhi at 11 p.m.

Never have I undergone such a radical image transformation from an indisciplined and wayward officer into a creative and dynamic one, as on this trip to Yugoslavia in January 1975, as a member of Foreign Minister Y. B. Chavan's delegation!

In March 1975 I had an unexpected opportunity to return to Lima. Minister of Industries T.A. Pai, who was leading India's delegation to a UNIDO Conference there, requested MEA to depute a Spanish-speaking officer to accompany them. Happily, I was the one deputed.

I spent much time with Minister Pai on this long travel to Lima and back, as also during the two weeks (12–26 March) of this conference and his trip to Machu Picchu on its second weekend.

At this conference, wherever Minister Pai and I, as his interpreter, went, he noticed that I was still fondly remembered. The Peruvian External Affairs and Industries Ministers greeted me warmly as 'Pasqualito' (Dear Pascal) and told Minister Pai how much Lima still missed me and my wife 'Isobelita'. He was amazed. In his report to PM about India's participation at this conference he graciously mentioned my 'outstanding and enduring work in Peru' in its concluding para. I am still very grateful to him for this.

An unpleasant surprise awaited me on my return from Lima. When I entered my office I found a slightly senior IFS colleague, R.K. Anand, seated in it. He informed me that I had been posted to Ministry of Commerce (MoC). P.C. Bharadwaj—now my former PS—came in just then and gave me the transfer order. I was greatly upset and went to Secretary (ER) Sanyal. He was apologetic and explained that for many months MEA had been trying to retrieve the Director (WANA-West Asia & North Africa) post in MoC. Commerce Secretary Y.T. Shah had recently agreed to make this post available to MEA provided I was posted there. He (Sanyal) had therefore agreed. He assuaged my frayed feelings by telling me that spending some months in MoC would be good for my career. I was sceptical about this then but a year later it turned out to be true.

At MoC the first task assigned to me was rationalization of the issue of licenses for import of dates. There was great clamour for them annually during the three months prior to Ramzan. Many who secured them sold them at inflated prices. It was, therefore, essential to ensure that these licenses were issued only to actual and reputed traders of this item. I spent two months toiling over this matter. When my detailed report was ready for submission, I took it to Commerce Minister (CM) D.P. Chattopadhyay's office to hand it over to him, as he had indicated keen interest in it. He had taken over as Minister of Commerce only four months earlier. (His predecessor L.N. Mishra had been killed in a bomb explosion at Samastipur Railway Station on 3 January 1975.) When I reached his office, I found most senior officers of MoC there and speaking animatedly to him. So I withdrew and went to his PS N.K. Singh's office who I knew quite well from our earlier meetings in Tokyo, Lima and Santiago. When I mentioned my report to him, he wryly remarked, 'The whole nation is stunned that Allahabad High Court has convicted Prime Minister Indira Gandhi of electoral malpractice and debarred her from holding elected office and you are concerned about date imports!' I was stunned. This was my first information about this traumatic judgment, and I learnt it a little after 11 a.m. on 12 June 1975. Thirteen days later, the Emergency was declared. Even more shocking news was in the offing six weeks later.

On 15 August 1975, the dreadful news was received that Bangladesh Prime Minister Sheikh Mujibur Rahman and most of his family members had been brutally assassinated in a military coup that morning. Having seen and heard him at close quarters in New Delhi a few months earlier I felt numb with grief and horror at this tragedy.

The following afternoon Foreign Secretary T.N. Kaul called an emergency inter-ministerial meeting of all officers dealing with Bangladesh, to brief them with such information as MEA had on the previous day's tragic events at Dacca (renamed in 1982 as Dhaka) and the course of action GOI proposed to take. Though I was dealing with WANA at that time, I was called to this meeting because of my previous close involvement with Bangladesh as Director (EBD). The indelible memory I have of this meeting is of Foreign Secretary Kaul reprimanding those who, overcome with shock and emotion, were babbling incoherently. He firmly stated, 'What I need at this meeting are cool heads and not cold feet.'

In the previous month (July) I had led an MoC delegation to the Gulf Countries (Kuwait, Bahrain, Qatar, Oman and Saudi Arabia) to stem the tide of Pakistan's Basmati rice exports to them which were steadily replacing India's exports of this item. Those who accompanied me were an STC (State Trading Corporation) Director and my Under Secretary Jayaraman. It was a nine-day tour.

This was my first visit to this region and I was amazed at the extent and pace of modernization it was undergoing. It was being transformed from backward, medieval desert sheikdoms into modern states. This started soon after the 1973 oil price hike and its impact was visible even in the first two years with smart new cars and buses on new expressways and new mosques, hotels, airports being built. Most of those building them were Palestinians, Egyptians, Indians, Pakistanis and Bangladeshis!

Our tour achieved limited success. We retrieved some of our previous importers and got one or two new but small ones. We however discovered that most of those we had lost had dropped us because of denial of visas or because of delayed shipments by STC. Visas were being denied to these importers because they had been blacklisted as exporters of contraband gold and electronic goods to India! I pointed out both these facts in my report and advised MoC to urge MHA (Ministry of Home Affairs) to review its 'blacklist' and STC to ensure timely shipments of their Basmati rice exports. The latter made me 'persona non grata' with STC!

In September I had to lead another delegation, this time to Sudan. The issue for negotiation was India's imports of Sudan's cotton over the next two years—at a reduced level! Those who accompanied me this time was a Director from the Cotton Corporation of India and my Under Secretary Jayaraman.

For many years India's imports of Sudan's long staple cotton was its main foreign exchange earner. In 1960, India imported 900,000 bales. Thereafter, as India's long staple cotton production grew, its imports of Sudan's cotton steadily declined but never dropped below 120,000 bales. In 1975, India had a bumper crop and decided to import only 50,000 bales. My tricky task was to induce the Sudanese to agree to this!

When we arrived in Khartoum and called on Ambassador I.P. Singh he expressed great surprise over the import figure of only 50,000 bales! He averred the Sudanese would never accept it. As matters turned out what he had said was understated. When the Sudanese Commerce Minister heard this figure from me he was outraged, said it was an insult to Sudan and indicated he would not continue the talks unless the import figure was raised 'at least to 100,000 bales'. I conveyed this to Commerce Secretary by CCB telegram and requested Secretary (ER) to intervene with him to have our import figure raised to 100,000. By 2 p.m. (Sudan time) the following day, which was a Thursday, I was authorised to raise our import figure to 80,000 bales. This was immediately conveyed to the Minister through his Permanent Secretary but he would not relent and insisted on 100,000 bales. We were to leave Khartoum at noon on Sunday. There was insufficient time to secure approval for the additional 20,000 bales by CCB telegram. Getting through on telephone from Khartoum to New Delhi was a near impossibility. The only other available option was a telex. But what had to be stated in it—the minister's unrelenting and truculent attitude—could not be done in English. In this critical moment I had a brainwave—to send the telex in Tamil! Joint Secretary Mani Narayanswamy knew Tamil, so did Jayaraman. So I dictated a message briefly describing the impasse in the talks and requesting him to do his best to induce Commerce Secretary and Commerce Minister to authorise the additional 20,000 bales for otherwise there would be no agreement and the considerable effort and expenditure on this mission would be fruitless. Jayaraman translated this message into Tamil which the EI telex operator sent soon thereafter. I had given this desperate gambit only a 50:50 chance of success. So I was thrilled when the positive reply—in Tamil—arrived within 18 hours! The three-and-half hour time difference between New Delhi and Khartoum was a boon.

The final round of talks was held at the Ministry of Commerce at 4 p.m. on Saturday and the mutually agreed text of the agreement was signed. Having won his acrimonious battle against us, the minister was now as amiable as he was smug. At the sumptuous dinner hosted by Ambassador I.P. Singh that night joyful toasts were raised by both sides to the 'long and close Sudan-India Friendship'.

Early the next morning we left our hotel to watch the sunrise at 'moqran al-nilayn'—the point where the blue and white Niles meet. It is about 5 miles north of Khartoum city centre and a stunning sight. The White Nile, actually clay coloured, flows all the way from Lake Victoria 2,300 km to the south in Uganda; the Blue Nile flows into Khartoum from Ethiopia 1,500 km in the southeast. Having met each other here, they then flow, side by side, without merging. From that point onwards it is referred to in Arabic as '*Bahr al-Nil*', the Nile Sea.

When I returned to MoC my 'Tamil telegram' was staple corridor talk. Mani Narayanswamy confessed that initially he could not 'make head or tail of it' but when he saw 'Rumba anticipated thanks' (many anticipated thanks) at the end of it, he suddenly realised it was entirely in Tamil but in English script!

In mid-October P.C. Alexander replaced Y.T. Shah as Commerce Secretary. He was more informal and friendly. Working with him was as enjoyable as it was stimulating. However, just three weeks later, he called me to his office and conveyed that I had been selected to head the Supply Wing in High Commission of India London and this would be an out-of-turn promotion for me as the London post was a Joint

Secretary level post. He instructed me to call on Cabinet Secretary B.D. Pande, who would brief me on why I had been selected for this job and what was the challenging work it entailed. I was stunned by this unexpected development.

When I called on Cabinet Secretary Mr Pande he spoke of the vital importance of HCI London's Supply Wing, as it handled purchases of critical spares for India's armed forces worth about £30 million annually. It had been headed by Ministry of Supply officers, who were finding it increasingly difficult to manage it effectively because many senior and mid-level armed forces officers manned it. The Committee of Secretaries had therefore decided to appoint an IFS officer with adequate knowledge of commercial matters for this important job, and FS and Commerce Secretary had recommended me for it. He told me that my prime challenge was to establish firm control and strict discipline in all sections of the Supply Wing and ensure it functions smoothly and efficiently. He instructed me to call on the Defence and Defence Production Secretaries as also on the Army, Navy and Air Force Chiefs and get their assessments of Supply Wing's functioning.

When I called on these VIPs, they all expressed dissatisfaction about Supply Wing's functioning. I pointed out that it was manned mainly by army, navy and air force officers. The Defence Secretary responded, 'Sadly, most of them get carried away by London's many *tamashas* and forget their armed forces discipline and dedication to duty.' Air Chief Marshal Hrushikesh Moolgavkar complained that even for AOG (Aircraft on Ground) indents, which require most immediate action, often three or four reminders need to be sent before they are handled.

As I was required to be in London only in early February 1976, I proposed to Isobel that we spend the festive Christmas and New Year season in Bangalore and travel there and back in my Chevrolet Camaro car. She welcomed the idea. Seema, our only India-born child, was then only 10 months old. Premila and Andy were thrilled.

It was an adventurous three-week journey, 10 days outward from New Delhi to Agra, Gwalior, Indore, Aurangabad, Bijapur, Badami, Hampi, and Bangalore and 11 days return via Goa, Poona, Ahmedabad, Ajmer, Jaipur and New Delhi. We stayed in friends' homes or dak bungalows along the way. The Camaro functioned perfectly on this approximately 2,500 mile-journey despite having been run on low rather than high octane gasoline on some sections of it.

My mother accompanied us on the return journey. En route she taught Premila and Andy popular poems and Christian hymns which they still remember.

Almost 80 per cent of India's rich historic and cultural heritage which Isobel, Premila, Andy and I have been deeply impacted by was seen on this three-week-long road trip.

Since Premila and Andy's school years at Jesus & Mary Convent and St Columba's Boys School respectively were to end in late April, I retained my Kaka Nagar residence until end June 1976 so that Isobel and the children could stay in it until I returned in June to take them to their new home in London.

On a cold, foggy Sunday morning in early February 1976 I flew to London and 10 hours later arrived there on an even colder, foggier morning. A pleasant surprise awaited me. I was driven to the historic and elegant Savoy Hotel on the Strand and checked in there. When I expressed my surprise at this I was told that HCI officers of Minister's rank were entitled to stay at this hotel until a suitable residence was found for them!

While I was being checked into this hotel, I noticed a book titled *Savoy: The Charm of a Great Hotel* at the reception counter. I purchased it and spent the rest of the day going through this fascinating book. There were many photos in it of Indian Maharajas and other celebrities who had stayed in this hotel. One of the Maharajas was photographed with his heavily jewelled wife and two pet leopards stretched out in front of them while another had two large silver tankards of 'Ganga Jal' on either side of him! Photos of other renowned guests were of President Harry Truman, Charlie Chaplin, Enrico Caruso, Cary Grant, Elizabeth Taylor, Richard Burton and Claude Monet and James Whistler (who had painted River Thames views from their rooms). But the most stunning of all these photos was one of Mahatma Gandhi and his goat captioned 'The only time a goat was accommodated at the Savoy'!

The following morning, after breakfast, I walked across to the High Commission of India, located in historic India House at Aldwych, and took charge of my new post of Minister (Supply).

8

VVIP Visits, 'Sun House' and a Virginity Test Crisis in London

(February 1976–April 1979)

The High Commissioner and Deputy High Commissioner when I took over as Minister (Supply) were B.K. Nehru ICS and Natwar Singh, IFS. I had known the former from my CGI, New York days (1966–1969) when he was Ambassador of India to the US; the latter from the day I joined the IFS, as he was Under Secretary (Personnel) at that time.

At the Supply Wing I found an impressive array of armed forces officers. My deputy was a Naval Commodore; in the rungs below him were an army Colonel and Captain, a naval Commander and Captain, a Wing Commander and two Flt. Lieutenants. Its civilian component was small with only a Director in charge of the shipping section. This gave me the heady feeling of being a Major General!

At my first Officers Meeting I conveyed what Cabinet and Defence Secretary and the three Service chiefs had told me about Supply Wing's functioning, particularly its handling of AOG indents. I told them my initial focus would be on clearing all pending AOG indents in a 90-day period and instructed my deputy to ensure this by sending out officers to procure the indented items by visits to manufacturers' warehouse rather than by correspondence as was then being done.

As there were delays not only in procurement but also in shipment of the procured items nearly all of which were being sent by sea Air India was approached for a concessional freight rate. Securing this turned out comparatively easy as Manek Dalal, Minister (Civil Aviation) in HCI was former Regional Director of Air India in London. He informed me that the HAL (Hindustan Aeronautics Ltd) office in London was already availing this. He advised computerization of Supply Wing's shipping section for facilitating consolidation of packages for air shipment. We were not authorized to buy a computer, so with High Commissioner Nehru's approval, hired one. Our Flt Lt Gune, who was computer savvy, created the requisite software for this. Air India's concessional air freight and computerization of the Shipping Section brought about a radical change in our functioning and enabled us to clear all the pending AOG indents within the 90-day deadline I had set. In mid-May 1976 I received the following letter of appreciation from Air Vice Marshal C.S. Naik, Asst Chief of Air Staff at Air Headquarters: *'Your prompt action in procuring/dispatching Qty 20 each of Bush Splits (Items 26FX/ 1053 and 26FX/1056) against our indents Nos. ECQ/628 dated 25 October 76 & ECQ/653 dated 27 October 75 is greatly appreciated. This has enabled us to clear five aircraft grounded at the repair facility.'*

In mid-June, I was called to India for debriefing on the steps I had taken and intended to take to further streamline Supply Wing. I arrived in New Delhi on 30 June. In the next 10 days, I made all the many calls which MEA had scheduled for me—on Cabinet, Defence, Supply and Foreign Secretaries and Chiefs of logistics of Army, Navy and Airforce. Foreign Secretary Jagat Mehta advised that I host a dinner at Hyderabad House for those I had called on and indicated that MEA would cover its cost. This dinner, hosted by me on 12 July (1976), was attended by the Secretaries/Joint Secretaries/Financial Advisers of the Ministries of Defence, Defence (Production), Supply and External Affairs, Chiefs of Logistics of Army, Navy and Airforce and Regional Director of Air India in New Delhi. On this occasion, most had praise rather than criticism for Supply Wing!

About a month after my return to London I received a telephone call from New Delhi. It was in Hindi and the caller wished to speak to Nazareth. When I asked for the caller's name, he replied brusquely, 'Raksha Mantri Bansi Lal'. I almost fell off my chair! I was even more shocked when he told me that a man named Krishna Kochar (KK) would be contacting me about three important air force indents and I should assist him on them. I had little option but to timidly mutter '*Jee Haan Mantri-ji*'.

Immediately thereafter I went to High Commissioner (HC) and reported this matter to him. He responded with the following memorable words, 'Alan, you now have the choice of either hitching your wagon to a political star or continue being an upright IFS officer. If you choose the former you will reap short term gains but lose in the long run as all political stars fade and yours too will fade.' When I made quite clear that the latter was my choice he assured me of his full support. He advised me to meet the person the Minister had mentioned and avail of the opportunity to 'probe how the nefarious arms trade is handled'. So, when the latter telephoned me the following day and invited me to dinner three days later I accepted his invitation.

The dinner was at an exclusive club, so exclusive that its *haute cuisine* menu had no price indicated against any item on it. When I asked my host about this he blandly responded that none of this club's members cared about such 'minor details'! So I ordered items I enjoyed the most and ignored the social norm of being a good guest! When desert was served he pulled out some papers from the inner pocket of his coat and showed them to me. They were photocopies of three recent IAF indents—all marked 'TOP SECRET' and none of which Supply Wing had yet received! He stated the indented items were urgently needed and securing them from their manufacturers would be time consuming; he had close contacts with a reputed vendor, who stocked a wide range of fighter aircraft spares and can supply them promptly. When I asked for this vendor's name he gave it as Staravia and indicated that he would be glad to introduce me to its proprietor, and should I wish to meet him and see his well-stocked warehouse he would escort me there. I thanked him for the information he had provided, as also the fine dinner and indicated that I would revert to him should I need the assistance he had offered.

At my next Officers Meeting I asked about Staravia and its standing. Commodore Gopal spoke well of them, but Wing Commander Chaddha gave an evasive reply.

So the next day I invited the HAL representative to lunch. At it, he gave me amazing details about Staravia. Two years earlier it had purchased six 'retired' Hunter Aircraft at a Dutch MoD auction and 'cannibalized' them, re-polished, greased and repacked their parts and was now selling them as new, proprietary items. All these parts had proprietary RR (Rolls-Royce) markings and appeared original but actually had long outlived their life spans. He mentioned that Commodore Gopal had close contacts with Staravia and lived in a home at Windsor quite close to it. He promised to send me a scan of the news report about Staravia's purchase of six Hunter aircraft at the Dutch MoD auction. This he did the same evening.

Some days later I circulated a note that all Supply Wing files related to purchases from Staravia, 1 January 1974 onwards should be put to me for scrutiny. About 30 of these files came to my office. When I went through them I found that Commodore Gopal had more than once cleared purchases from Staravia, even though Wing Commander Kewal Chaddha had urged these items be obtained from their manufacturers. Separately, I learnt from HCI Minister (Consular) that Commodore Gopal had two cars, one his own and the other used by his wife which was 'loaned' by Staravia. He confirmed my suspicion that this officer was compromised with Staravia.

I made a detailed report on my investigation of this matter and showed it to HC. He complimented me on it and instructed that it be sent to Defence Secretary. I requested his approval to send it instead to JS (Vigilance) in MEA, Frank Dewars, as he was well known to me. He kindly agreed to this. Mr Dewars responded promptly, commended the methodical way in which the investigation had been made and the report thereon compiled. He indicated that he had shown this report to FS who had approved it being sent to Defence Secretary/JS (Vigilance) in MOD.

Commodore Gopal was to complete his term in London in December 1976. He applied for a six-month extension of stay on grounds of his son's education. I declined to recommend it. The Naval adviser intervened on his behalf with HC but he too declined to recommend it. So he left London as scheduled. In March 1977 he was prematurely retired on the basis of the incriminating evidence contained in my report.

When this news reached Supply Wing, Colonel Kurup, a close friend of Commodore Gopal, began to make disrespectful notings in his files about 'swollen headed civilian officers' who knew nothing about armed forces logistics, yet acted as if they were experts. I sent for him and told him these notings were inappropriate and if they continued disciplinary action would have to be taken against him. He defied me to do so. So when he made the next such noting I took three files with such notings to HC and sought his advice on how to deal with this officer. He went through these notings and stated, 'This officer should be repatriated to India on disciplinary grounds and MoD informed that this had been done on HC's instructions'. I was stunned as I had not expected such a strong reaction from him. I tried to induce him to change his mind but he was firm, and stated 'Military arrogance must be dealt with firmly if discipline is to be established in Supply Wing'. I therefore had no option but to issue an office order instructing Colonel Kurup to hand over charge to Brigadier Hector Thacker (Commodore Gopal's successor) and leave for India within 15 days. I sent copies of this order to Addl. Secretary (Adm) in MEA and the Joint Secretary concerned in MoD and informed them that this order had been issued on HC's instructions. Colonel Kurup immediately submitted an appeal under the Army Act alleging arbitrary and unjust action against him. This made the comparatively small matter of his objectionable notings on files into a grave one of an army officer posted abroad being arbitrarily and unjustly treated. A few days later the Chief of Army Staff telephoned Foreign Secretary and urged that this office order be withdrawn. The latter telephoned HC to request this. He responded by writing him a letter, with copies to Cabinet and Defence Secretaries, stating that he had decided on the action taken against this 'arrogant, petty fogging colonel' because of his 'blatant disregard for decorum and discipline in his official conduct'. This finally defused this dicey imbroglio and Colonel Kurup and his family left London five days later.

In early February 1977, the announcement of national elections in India in mid-March was made. Two weeks thereafter Minister of State for Home Affairs Om Mehta came to London. Addressing a large Indian Community meeting, he praised Prime Minister Indira Gandhi and all that she had done to 'safeguard India's security and democracy', and declared that holding this election so soon after the Emergency was proof of her democratic spirit. He predicted her return to power with a big majority. However, High Commissioner Nehru boldly stated that India was a democratic country, its elections were free and fair and their outcome unpredictable. As High Commissioner he represented the President of India and not its government, and whatever this election's outcome, he 'like the Vicar of Bray would continue in his parish!' Four weeks later it was he not Mr Om Mehta who was vindicated.

During the Emergency, High Commissioner Nehru was quite opposed to HCI being used to target UK-based Indians who publicly opposed it. Nonetheless the DHC, who was closely allied to Prime Minister Indira Gandhi, did so furtively. It was not surprising therefore that within 48 hours after the Morarji Desai government assumed office a CCB telegram arrived instructing the DHC to hand over charge to me (I was the next senior most IFS officer) and proceed on leave. A week later he was appointed High Commissioner of Zambia and instructed to proceed there before the end of that month. High Commissioner Nehru's reaction was amazing. Though well aware that DHC had 'hitched his wagon' to Indira Gandhi's star and had actively supported her he took up for him strongly. He sent a telegram to FS stating that he would not permit his DHC to be publicly humiliated. He urged that he be given 30 days to make his farewell calls and host a farewell reception. FS, consulted PM, and agreed to this.

Soon after DHC departed London, I and my family moved to the DHC's official residence at Frognal Way in Hampstead. Known as 'Sun House' and designed by the renowned British architect Maxwell Fry, its amazing feature is that when the sun is up—not so often in London!—it brightens every room in the house including the kitchen! In the following weeks and months we often had architecture students coming to view and make sketches of it.

The Hampstead Parish Church, which was close to Sun House and where we attended Mass on Sundays, is a historic one, particularly its cemetery. Among those buried in it are the renowned landscape painter John Constable, John, Elizabeth and Catherine Dickens (parents and wife of Charles Dickens), George Eliot, Herbert Spencer, Michael Faraday and most notably Karl Marx.

In early May, High Commissioner Nehru wrote to PM (whom he knew quite well as he had worked with him when he was Finance Minister) as follows: 'Dear Prime Minister, Please accept my hearty congratulations on your assumption of this high office. I wish you much success in it. As you undoubtedly intend to dismiss me I have decided to pre-empt this by submitting my resignation, which please accept. Warm and respectful regards, B.K. Nehru.'

The PM replied promptly: 'Dear Biju bhai, Of course I intend to dismiss you but will not permit you to pre-empt me on this. You will stay at your post until you hear from me. I am coming to London for the Commonwealth Summit in June and intend to stay at your mansion as only Fori can handle my demanding dietary requirements. Keep in mind that no liquor is to be served during my stay! Best wishes, Morarji Desai.'

HC replied: 'Dear Prime Minister, I am honoured that you have decided to stay at our "mansion" during your visit to London for the Commonwealth Summit. Fori will gladly ensure your dietary requirements are meticulously met. I will ensure all liquor is securely put away. However, as you are an early riser, I have to request your gracious understanding on my inability to be with you before 9 a.m. each day. I have also requested the Almighty not to summon me before that hour! Warm and respectful regards, B.K. Nehru.'

This is the most amusing and friendly banter between a HOM (Head of Mission) and PM I have been privileged to see in my entire IFS career.

The Commonwealth Heads of Government Meeting was held at London and Gleneagles (Scotland) 8-15 June 1977. Presidents Idi Amin of Uganda and James Mancham of the Seychelles did not attend, the former because of domestic turmoil and the latter because he was overthrown on the eve of it.

The most important issues discussed at this meeting were the situations in Southern Africa, Uganda and Cyprus and sporting contacts with South Africa. The consensus reached on these issues was embodied in the Gleneagles Declaration.

On the eve of PM's departure HC hosted a dinner in his honour at his Kensington Palace Gardens Mansion. Those present at it included former Prime Ministers Harold Macmillan, Alec Douglas-Home and Edward Heath, Labour Party leader Michael Foot, Lord Mountbatten, Mrs Douglas-Home, Mrs Heath, Mrs Nehru, Principal Secretary to PM V. Shankar, Foreign Secretary Jagat Mehta, and myself. While the post dinner group photo was about to be taken, Lord Mountbatten suddenly commented that the Indian PM was 'hidden' by him and sat down, cross-legged, on the carpet. HC, FS, Mrs Nehru and I were constrained to do likewise but by the time I could do so the group photo was taken, and I still am greatly embarrassed that I am the only nonentity standing among this august array of VVIPs. This photo is among those included in this book.

As the Silver Jubilee of Queen Elizabeth's reign was being celebrated all over Britain from June 1977 onwards I induced my parents to visit us April-July 1977. I was able to get them an invitation to the Queen's Garden Party at Buckingham Palace and take them to Westminster and Canterbury Cathedrals, Oxford and Cambridge Universities and Lake Windermere, all of which they greatly enjoyed.

In early August (1977) Mr Raj Narain, Minister of Health and Family Welfare, arrived in London to discuss bilateral cooperation in this field with his UK counterpart. HC who always went to the airport to receive cabinet ministers declined to do so in this case. He instructed me to receive him and convey his apology for his inability to come to the airport because of an urgent official matter he was attending to, and also his cordial and respectful invitation to lunch or dinner at the Embassy Residence. I went to the airport with much trepidation as I had heard this minister spoke only in Hindi and my spoken Hindi was poor. When he emerged from the Air India plane at Heathrow airport and I introduced myself, he asked '*Panditji, kidar hai*? (Where is Panditji), I was taken aback. The only 'Panditji' I knew, Jawaharlal Nehru, had passed away! Fortunately, his IAS Secretary clarified that the Minister wanted to know why the HC had not come to receive him. So I conveyed the message HC had entrusted to me. The Minister petulantly replied, '*Woh mujhe milne airport nahin aye hain. Main unke ghar nahin jaunga; tumhare ghar aunga.*' (He has not come to the airport to receive me. I shall not go to his house but shall come to yours). The latter part of his reply terrified me even though I surmised it was just hyperbole!

On the drive into London he asked me, in Hindi, what arrangements had been made for his visit. I gave him the programme of official calls, meetings, visits to leading hospitals and laboratories which UK Ministry of Health had made and the meeting with Indian community leaders which we had organized for him in the HCI auditorium. He asked how many would be present at the last mentioned meeting and why no press conference had been arranged. I replied that about 120 would be present at that meeting and the press conference had not been arranged as his ministry had not requested it. He promptly replied 'I have never addressed a meeting of less than 10,000. Why was this meeting not arranged in Hyde Park? The press conference should be arranged immediately.' I agreed to the latter and timidly told him that foreign VIPs are not permitted to address public meetings in Hyde Park!

At the press conference, held three days later, the first question he was asked was why he had chosen the UK for his first foreign visit as he has always opposed the use of English and modern medicine and surgery. His prompt, self-assured and hilarious reply was that his opposition to English was because it had been imposed on India and not because he disliked it. He added that he read 'Milton, Hilton, and many other well-known English writers.' As for surgery, he pointed out that the first head transplant had been made in India, thousands of years ago, and its recipient—Lord Ganesh—is still alive and well! This press conference, which continued for almost an hour, might well be the most hilarious one held in London until then.

High Commissioner Nehru left London in late September. I was Acting High Commissioner (AHC) for three weeks thereafter.

In mid-October Lok Sabha Speaker K.S. Hegde visited London on the invitation of his British counterpart. I accompanied him on his call on the latter, and to the lunch he hosted in Speaker Hegde's honour. The following day I hosted a lunch in Mr Hegde's honour at India House. Among those who attended it were Lord Chancellor Elwyn Jones and Lord Alfred Denning.

The new High Commissioner Mr N.G. Goray arrived in London on 19 October, 1977. He was a well-known social activist, author and columnist but unfamiliar with the demanding requirements of diplomatic hospitality. Besides, being a widower, he was single. So Isobel's responsibilities, already enhanced since my elevation as DHC, were further heightened. On some days she had to spend entire mornings at the Embassy Residence attending to everything, from menus and place settings to floral arrangements. This was noted and lauded by diplomatic colleagues as also by some local journalists. The *Observer* wrote a piece about her in its 29 January, 1978 issue under the title 'Mix with the History-Makers' (It is among the annexures of this book).

On the day after Christmas 1978, I had a joyful surprise. The renowned music director Zubin Mehta telephoned Sun House to invite Isobel and me to the Richard Straus opera *Salome* which he was conducting the next evening at Royal Opera House. He said he always invited Heads of Indian Missions to his musical events and since he had learnt that I was AHC he had telephoned to invite us to this event. I thanked him and promptly accepted this invitation. That evening when we arrived at Royal Opera House we were received by his secretary and escorted to and seated in his box, which had a ring side view of the stage. At the conclusion of this fascinating opera his secretary escorted us backstage to meet Zubin Mehta and the lead singers and sip champagne with them. This was the first time we were meeting him and were struck by his friendly informality and close rapport with the musicians and singers. In taking his leave I timidly asked whether he and the lead singers would attend a reception I wish to host in their honour. He promptly replied 'We will gladly come if *samosas* and green chillies are served.' I thought he was joking about the chillies but discovered at this reception at Sun House on 29 December 1978 that he was addicted to them and munched them like gherkins.

Those who attended this reception besides Zubin Mehta and his wife Nancy, were the four lead singers of the Salome Opera, Barbara Daniels, Hildegard Behrens, Benjamin Luxon and Robert Cassily, Evan Luard, Parliamentary Under Secretary of State for Foreign and Commonwealth Affairs, Lord Paul Gore Booth, former British High Commissioner to India; Mr Trevor Jones, Manager, Royal Opera House, Sir Kenneth Robinson, Chairman, UK Arts Council, music critics of *London Times* and *The Telegraph* and senior HCI officers. A photo taken at this reception is included in this book.

Prime Minister James Callaghan visited India in February 1978. Many bilateral issues were discussed but of greatest interest to him was the sale of Jaguar fighter aircraft to India.

Prime Minister Morarji Desai's return visit was made in July 1978. Among those who accompanied him was his son Kanti. I witnessed with amazement the respectful attention senior British Defence Ministry officials paid him, and the separate huddles they had now and again with Secretary to PM.

On the eve of his departure PM came to HCI to address Indian community leaders. While this address was being delivered HCI fire alarms suddenly began to blare. There was great consternation. PM, his Principal PS and HC were promptly evacuated, all others urged to get out of India House immediately and the Fire Brigade summoned. It arrived within five minutes and its firemen moved into the basement, from where smoke was emanating into the elevator shaft and the ground and upper floors. One of them returned from there 10 minutes later to inform us that the fire had been caused by a short circuit in an electrical junction box on the front facing wall of the basement lower level. The sparks emanating from it had ignited the files stacked close to it. When the main switch in the lower basement was switched off the sparks ceased. The burning among the files was doused with fire extinguishers and not water (so as not to damage these files). The firemen left about 15 minutes thereafter. HC and I were greatly relieved that this fire had been caused by a short circuit and not by a mala fide infiltrator just when the PM was in the HCI auditorium. It was however an eerie and remarkable coincidence.

The following week, as instructed by HC, a thorough clean-up of both levels of the basement and weeding out of outdated files therein was undertaken. It took three weeks to complete. A happy outcome of this strenuous exercise was the discovery of a red leather box with the ceremonial gold key with which His Majesty King George V had formally inaugurated India House on 8 July 1930!

In mid-October 1978, when I was AHC again, I received a telephone call from PMO instructing me to convey to 'Prime Minister Callaghan personally' that GOI had decided to purchase the Jaguar fighter aircraft despite stiff competition from its rivals. I therefore called his office and requested to speak to him to convey an important message from my Prime Minister. His secretary stated that Prime Minister Callaghan had just left his office and was on way to Cardiff, his constituency. He offered to convey my PM's message to him. I declined this offer in view of my instructions. He called me back 15 minutes later, indicated he had spoken to his PM on wireless telephone and that the latter would be glad to receive my call on this telephone, the number of which he gave me. I called that number and conveyed the mentioned message to Prime Minister Callaghan. He said he was delighted to receive it and requested me to convey his grateful thanks to PM Desai for conveying this to him 'personally and promptly'. This is the only time I have spoken to a Prime Minister on wireless telephone, in his limousine speeding along a highway.

This Jaguar Fighter Aircraft deal was a big and historic one. It involved purchase of 200 aircraft—40 as outright purchase, the rest manufactured at HAL Bangalore. Its overall cost was $2.2 billion, which at 1978 prices was a mega amount.[1]

Mrs Indira Gandhi came to London in early November 1978. She was accompanied by Pranab Mukherjee. HC deputed me to receive her at Heathrow airport. She was cold but courteous. She thanked me for coming to receive her and requested me to convey her best wishes to HC. The purpose and success of her visit is best recounted in Sunil Sethi's article about it in *India Today* of 15 December 1978, some extracts from which are given hereunder:

> At the end of a week's barnstorming tour of Britain Mrs

1. 'Deal to buy and manufacture Jaguar fighter in India sent back to the drawing boards', *India Today,* 25 January 2015, http://indiatoday.intoday.in/story/deal-to-buy-and-manufacture-jaguar-fighter-in-india-sent-back-to-the-drawing boards/1/409770.html, (accessed on 5 July 2018).

Gandhi could hardly have returned home displeased. Arriving in London with electoral blood fresh about her lips (She was out of power, but had been elected to the Lok Sabha in a by-poll from Chikmagalur). She was already conscious of her new-found prowess. There was a new note of aggression in handling her detractors in the Western world. "God, she's tough," murmured a television reporter as she looked the whirring cameras in the eye, militantly took on the rapid-fire questioning and ignored large groups of protestors holding placards with 'Go Home, Fascist' written on them.

The British political establishment, judging by her appointments certainly lent a helping hand. To what extent it was a minimum show of courtesy dictated by protocol is a debatable matter. But she met them all, the prime minister downwards.

She called on Mrs Thatcher (Margaret Thatcher, then Opposition Leader); Edward Heath (former PM) called on her. She met over a 100 members of both Houses of Parliament. Nearly 200 members of Cambridge Union Society, in a startling and unprecedented move, engineered by 21-year-old Union president Daniel Janner, came down to London to hear her.

Among her friends was romantic novelist Barbara Cartland who whisked her off to see 'dear, dear Dickie' (Lord Louis Mountbatten) in her white Rolls and Michael Foot, Leader of the House of Commons and Deputy Prime Minister, drooled over her.

The man who rallied all her friends around her is a cherubic-looking Indian millionaire—possibly the only one in London—operating smoothly from his office in Portman Square to fix it all. Swraj Paul, manufacturer of natural gas tubes, is an unabashed admirer of Mrs Gandhi's. It was his spiral weld pipe plant worth nearly half a million sterling that Mrs Gandhi went to inaugurate in South Wales.

In between her crowded daily schedule, she took time off to nip down to Fenwick's, the fashionable ladies' store to buy herself a

> new coat. She took an evening off to attend London's hit musical, *Evita* and expressed her regret she was unable to go to Foyle's, the bookshop.
>
> She was 61 years old the day she left England. All the newspapers recorded her birthday in small print. She left beaming with the pleasure of someone who has some new tales to tell back home.[2]

In early February 1979, the sensational 'Virginity' crisis erupted. An Indian school teacher, who came to the UK to be married to her NRI fiancé, was subjected to a humiliating 'virginity test' to determine whether she was a virgin. The rationale for this 'test' was that since Indian men do not marry non-virgins if the test showed she was not a virgin her affidavit that the purpose of her visit to the UK was marriage, would be proved false and mala fide. The 'test' showed that she was a virgin. She was therefore admitted to the UK. She subsequently recounted to her fiancé and his family the shock and humiliation she had experienced in being subjected to this test. This news soon spread in the UK Indian community which was outraged. HC instructed me to handle it. I drafted a stern note verbale, secured HC's approval for it and then called on and presented it to Under Secretary for Foreign and Commonwealth Affairs Mr Evan Luard. He was already aware of this unsavoury episode as many Indian newspapers had headlined it and the British High Commissioner in New Delhi had conveyed this to him. He regretted this episode and promised prompt action. Two days later Home Secretary Merlyn Rees instructed immigration officers to immediately cease these tests and Prime Minister Callaghan stated in the House of Commons 'all MPs would be disturbed by what they have read'.

2. Sunil Sethi, 'Despite the hostile reception, Indira Gandhi's visit to Britain turns out to be a tour deforce', *India Today,* 15 December 1978, https://www.indiatoday.in/magazine/special-report/story/19781215-despite-the-hostile-reception-indira-gandhis-visit-to-britain-was-a-tour-deforce-823183-2014-03-07 (accessed on 5 July 2018).

On 3 February 1979, *The Guardian* wrote 'The Indian Deputy High Commissioner, Mr Alan Nazareth, yesterday registered a strong protest with Mr Evan Luard, an Under Secretary at the Foreign Office, saying that his government was outraged and wanted the practice banned. He pointed out that it was done nowhere else in the world.' The ironic fallout of the wide publicity this news report received was that I thereafter was often referred to as 'Virginity Nazareth'!

When Ambassador M.K. Rasgotra at EI Hague, saw *The Guardian* report he telephoned to congratulate me on the effective handling of this matter, indicated he was coming to London the following week on a two-day visit and enquired whether he could stay with us. I was honoured by his request and promptly agreed. During his stay with us Isobel and I were captivated by his warm and friendly informality, captivating smile and fascinating anecdotes. The close and enduring '*guru-shishya parampara*' between him and me was gestated by this visit and has endured ever since.

Shortly thereafter Ambassador Rasgotra's appointment as Ambassador to France and mine as High Commissioner to Ghana were announced. I applied for 45 days leave and decided to use the first 10 days for visits to/sightseeing of Paris, Athens and Rome. In Paris we had the privilege of staying at India House thanks to Ambassador Rasgotra's instructions to EI there. In Athens Counsellor C.P. Ravindranathan found us a well-located and reasonably priced hotel to stay at and assisted us in our sight-seeing.

At Rome, Fr. Peter Prabhu of the Vatican diplomatic service drove us in his car to Rome's historic sites including its ancient catacombs. Cardinal Lourdusamy, former Bishop of Bangalore and then Director of 'Propaganda Fide', graciously invited us to dinner at his elegant and spacious residence, close to the famed Trevi Fountains. We flew from Rome to Bangalore on April 25 night and arrived there at 11 a.m. the following day.

9

Revolutions, Executions and Tata Buses in Ghana and Liberia

(June 1979–April 1982)

Among the many calls I made on VVIPs in New Delhi before leaving for Ghana, the one on Prime Minister Morarji Desai was the most memorable. He remembered me from his two visits to London when I was DHC there and said he was glad I was going as High Commissioner to Ghana. He then lowered his voice and stated, 'Ghana is the only country where I could not get a single cup of cow's milk. The Ghanaians must have killed and eaten all their cows!'

I left for Accra from Mumbai by Air India at 1.30 p.m. on 2 June 1979. Because of the six-hour time difference, I arrived there at 3.30 p.m. I was received at the airport by the Ghanaian Chief of Protocol (COP) and HCI Accra Chargé d'Affaires Upendra Lal. I handed over to the former a copy of my credential letter. The latter invited us to a welcome dinner at his residence the following evening.

The Embassy Residence (ER), a large, colonial style, two-floor building set in a large compound with a sizable lawn and peepal, mango, custard apple and papaya trees, was located on Switchback Road, so named because it branched off Liberation Avenue just in front of the main gate of Flagstaff House, (Ghana army headquarters) to re-join it again about a mile away.

Isobel and I were glad to notice that the entire residence was wire-meshed for protection against the dreaded, encephalitis-causing Ghanaian mosquitos. Besides, the Catholic Church and Christ The King School were just across the road from it.

Upendra Lal's welcome dinner the following day, at which EI diplomatic officers and Accra Indian Association office-bearers were present, was sumptuous and enjoyable. When we got home that night, I promptly got into bed and soon fell soundly asleep. At about 3 a.m. Isobel awakened me and stated that she had been hearing gunfire. Still very sleepy, I muttered it was quite likely a Ghanaian festival being celebrated by firing guns. About an hour later she woke me up again and stated she could now hear helicopters over our residence. Soon thereafter the telephone rang. It was an NRI named Mohan Singh, who worked at Accra airport, who conveyed that it had just been taken over by army/air force personnel, which was clear indication a military coup was taking place. He pointed out that in previous coups some bullets had struck ER walls and windows as it faced Army headquarters, hence all of us should move into a room with no windows. Soon thereafter, our four-year-old daughter Seema, whose glass-paned bedroom faced the entrance driveway, came running into our bedroom exclaiming, 'Daddy, there are Germans in our compound.' Having previously lived in London and seen war movies in which 'good boys' were always British and 'bad boys' Germans, she felt sure the soldiers she had seen were Germans! When I hastened to her bedroom and looked out, I was amazed to find that there indeed were soldiers in our compound. I therefore went downstairs and into the compound and told the young captain, deploying his soldiers behind our back walls with their guns pointed at Flagstaff House that this was the Indian High Commissioner residence and therefore 'diplomatic premises' which none of them had the right to enter. He replied crisply, 'High Commissioner, the bullets are about to fly. Please go in now. We will deal with the "diplomatic premises" matter later.' I intuitively felt 'discretion is the better part of valour' and withdrew into the Residence. Soon thereafter, the firing started into and from Flag Staff House. Isobel, Seema, Josephine (our Indian cook) and I, huddled on the floor of the master bedroom. We heard some of the bullets striking its outside wall. Fortunately it was sufficiently thick and had no glass paned windows.

By 7 a.m., the coup ended, successfully for those who had staged it. The coup makers had secured control of their two main targets Flagstaff House and Ghana Broadcasting Station, and announced to the nation that General Fred Akuffo (the President to whom my credentials were addressed!) and his government had been overthrown and an 'Armed Forces Revolutionary Council' (AFRC) chaired by Flt Lt Jerry Rawlings had taken over Ghana. The announcement also indicated that the AFRC would hold power only temporarily, make a thorough 'house cleaning' of Ghana's armed forces and society and then hold the presidential and parliamentary elections. Scheduled for mid-July, they were rescheduled for early September.

Among those killed at Flagstaff House that night was Chief of Army Staff Major General Odartey-Wellington.

Flt Lt Rawlings' emergence as Chairman of Ghana's Armed Forces Revolutionary Council (AFRC) on 4 June 1979 was an amazing reversal of his fortunes. Just 19 days earlier, on 15 May 1979, he and six other JCOs had been tried by a military tribunal and sentenced to death for a previous coup attempt mounted earlier that month. At his trial he had made an impassioned defence of himself on grounds of the widespread corruption in Ghana's armed forces and society which had impoverished its people. This had resonated well at the grassroots level in every sector. Hence, while awaiting execution, Rawlings was released from his military prison on the midnight of 4 June 1979 by a group of his armed forces colleagues and urged to lead this coup.

The AFRC was composed of 15 army, navy and air force officers of whom 12 were Junior Commissioned Officers, three were Non-Commissioned Officers with Flt Lt Rawlings as its Chairman.

The first to be 'house cleaned' by AFRC were the armed forces. After secret military trials two rounds of executions took place. On 17 June, former head of state Maj Gen Ignatius Acheampong and former Border Guard commander Maj Gen E.K. Utuka were executed along with Maj Gen R.E.A. Kotei, a former army commander, Air Vice Marshal George Yaw Boakey, former air force chief, and Admiral Joy Amerdume, former chief of the navy. All were found guilty of misusing their positions to enrich themselves while in office.

On 26 June, six more senior military officers, including two of Ghana's former heads of state Gen Fred Akuffo and Gen A.A. Afrifa, (who was head of state from 1966-69) and former foreign minister Roger Felli were executed for the same reason.

All these executions were carried out by the firing squad at the Teshie military range, a few miles outside Accra.

These were the bloodiest 10 days in Ghana's post-independence history. Most diplomats, international observers and educated Ghanaians were shocked and revulsed, but many ordinary Ghanaians rejoiced. Flt Lt Rawlings (an Anglo-Ghanaian) acquired a heroic image among the latter who hailed him as 'Junior Jesus' (J.J. were the initials of his name).

Soon after the Armed Forces' 'house cleaning', that of the wealthy

Lebanese and Indian businessmen began. Traumatized by the summary executions of Gen Akuffo and others, they greatly feared the same fate awaited them. Teams of five or six armed soldiers would suddenly appear and search their offices by day and homes at night, take away documents, electronic and other items they fancied and in some cases their owners as well for interrogation, leaving their wives and children terrified.

One morning in early July there was an urgent distress call to ER from a terrified, recently-married Indian woman whose husband had been taken away for interrogation. She pleaded for 'protection'. So Isobel offered to go and spend some time with her. As I had to go to the Foreign Office for a meeting with Chief of Protocol (COP), I dropped her at this woman's home and promised to pick up both of them on my way back.

I went to the Foreign Office to request a call on Foreign Minister Gloria Amon Nikoi (a former diplomat, whom AFRC had appointed as FM) to convey to her that the harsh treatment being meted out to Indian businessmen was unacceptable to GOI. I was received by the COP, who visibly embarrassed courteously told me the call on Foreign Minister I had requested could not be scheduled as I had not yet presented my credentials. I pointed out to him that unlike Ambassadors, when a High Commissioner on arrival presents the copy of his credentials to COP he is considered informally accredited to that country's Government and should be received by its ministers. (I had learnt this convention and difference between High Commissioners and Ambassadors during my tenure as DHC in London). I suggested he consult the British High Commissioner if he doubted this. After some hesitation he did so and was surprised when the latter confirmed this. He then escorted me to the Foreign Secretary (who I discovered to my pleasant surprise was Sam Quarm, a friend from our days together in Tokyo in the early 1960s) who accompanied me to

Foreign Minister's office. She was cordial but courteously countered my protest by pointing out the present was an abnormal situation in which AFRC took all the decisions and MFA had a negligible role. She, however, promised to convey my protest to AFRC. Mr Quarm kindly promised to keep track of this matter and keep me informed of action taken and developments thereon.

On my way back from the Foreign Office I went to the home where I had dropped Isobel and was surprised to find it locked. Its Indian neighbours excitedly told me that Isobel and the young Indian wife had both been taken away in a military truck about half an hour earlier. Shocked and bewildered I returned promptly to the Embassy intending to get our well-connected CDA Upendra Lal to make urgent enquiries about Isobel's whereabouts. When I reached there my PS informed me that Isobel was safely back at ER and had telephoned him to convey this. When I went home for lunch she recounted her amazing and amusing experience. About 20 minutes after I had dropped her at the mentioned home two soldiers arrived there and stated they had come to take the wife for cross-examination about her husband's assertions to them. Panic stricken she clung to Isobel and pleaded that she protect her. So Isobel offered to accompany her. The soldiers initially hesitated but later agreed. The two women were 'uploaded' into the back of the military truck and driven off. The Indian neighbours, who had witnessed this, soon spread the sensational news that the Indian High Commissioner's wife had been arrested with the young Indian wife and taken away in a military truck!

When this truck arrived at the interrogation centre and the Captain in charge discovered who Isobel was, he politely but firmly told her she should not have accompanied the 'suspect' and that his car would take her back to the ER. Isobel had no option but to comply, but requested the Captain that this wife be sent to ER after her interrogation. She came the next day, with her husband. Both of them expressed deep gratitude to Isobel and apologized for the embarrassment they had caused her.

Fortunately, by the end of July the harsh treatment of Indian businessmen began to ease. Whereas searches of their offices and homes continued, the dreaded night time raids/arrests ceased. I learnt from Foreign Secretary Quarm that Foreign Minister Nikoi had met Chairman Rawlings and pointed out that India was an important country and a long-standing friend of Ghana, and hence care needs to be taken not to upset it by treating its nationals harshly.

Just as the acute pressure on Indian businessmen eased we were struck by a tragic calamity. In early August, our staff car taking two ITPO (India Trade Promotion Organisation) officers (from New Delhi) and our First Secretary (Com) S. Dayal from Accra to Lome in Togo (to which I was concurrently accredited), had a tyre burst, veered off the road and fell into a deep ditch. Mr Dayal was killed and ITPO officer, Mrs Vasantha Bharucha, was seriously injured. The Akatsi Police Station near the Togo border informed us of this on telephone and arranged an ambulance to bring Mr Dayal's body, the two ITPO officers and our staff car driver to Accra. The most challenging task now was to convey the tragic news to Mrs Dayal, who was not in the best of health. I, accompanied by Isobel, went to her home, informed her of the accident and told her that her husband and Mrs Bharucha had been injured and were presently in the Accra General Hospital. She immediately asked 'Is he alive? Please tell me the truth.' I could not muster the emotional strength to reveal it. I told her to trust in God and that we both had come to escort her to the hospital where Dr Chitale (an NRI doctor working in Ghana) would tell us the nature of Mr Dayal and Mrs Bharucha's injuries. When we reached the hospital Dr Chitale broke the tragic news to her and sought to console her by stating Mr Dayal's injuries were such that he must have died instantly and not suffered. Nonetheless, Mrs

Dayal burst out weeping and wailing. It was heartbreaking for Isobel and me to witness her grief. Isobel spent the whole of that afternoon consoling her and her children. Meanwhile, Counsellor Upendra Lal made arrangements for cremation of Mr Dayal's body.

I had never witnessed a cremation before and dreaded witnessing this one. However, while it was actually taking place and the jasmine-scented smoke kept wafting upwards towards the sky, I perceived its ethereal beauty and of the symbolism of the soul rising heavenwards with the smoke. Nonetheless, I greatly hoped this would be the last time I would have to witness the cremation of a valued colleague and his wife's intense sorrow.

Three weeks later the Indian Association president, Mr Ashok Sadhwani and his wife were brutally murdered in their home. When I learnt of this tragedy I, accompanied by Counsellor Upendra Lal, visited the Sadhwani home. What we saw was a gruesome sight. His body, in blood-stained night clothes and a deep gash in his skull, lay on the bedroom floor. His wife's body, her night clothes also blood stained, lay in their bed, with a deep gash on her chest and left arm. In both cases the lethal instrument was a long grass-cutting knife which, blood stained and with bits of human flesh on it, had been flung in the far corner of this bedroom. As most of the jewellery and silver objects had been taken it was obviously a burglary. As the AFRC comprised only army, navy and air force JCOs/NCOs most police personnel had forsaken their posts and returned to their villages. Hence law and order had collapsed and burglaries had spurted.

In late September, we narrowly escaped the same fate as the Sadhwani couple. Early one morning, our Indian cook Josephine rushed to our bedroom and excitedly told us that the downstairs had been burgled and all the silverware and electronic equipment had been taken. The latter included my high-priced B&O sound system. The ominous 'visiting card' the burglars had left behind on the dining table was a long grass-cutting knife akin to the one in the Sadhwani home. Fortunately for us the stairway leading to bedrooms upstairs had a sturdy teak wood door with two metal bars across it and hence could not be forced open. The silver lining to this hair-raising episode was that soon thereafter MEA sanctioned an India-based security guard for the Accra EI Residence.

Because of the above mentioned tragic and gruesome events the June–September 1979 period was most nerve-racking and challenging in my entire IFS career.

AFRC Chairman Rawlings kept his word about the Presidential and Parliamentary elections. Despite the widespread law and order breakdown these were held in early September. This enhanced his 'Junior Jesus' aura!

The presidential election was won by Mr Hilla Limann (who had studied at London and Sorbonne Universities and served in Ghana's Mission to UN at Geneva). He was the People's National Party (PNP) candidate. PNP also won the parliamentary election by a narrow margin.

Mr Limann was sworn in as President of Ghana on 24 September 1979. He had a very difficult political and economic scenario to handle. Ghana had been under army rule for 13 long years (1966-1979) during which all political activity had been severely restricted. AFRC's execution of its senior military officers, including three former heads of state, had greatly angered Nigeria (then under military rule) which had stopped oil exports to Ghana. This had undermined its transportation system and hampered its cocoa collection and essential items distribution. Because of AFRC raids on their premises, many Lebanese traders who operated the wholesale trade had fled Ghana taking much of their capital with them. The only positive effect of the AFRC regime was reduction of corruption and people queuing up to pay their taxes!

I had to wait almost a month after President Limann was sworn in to present my credentials to him. (I had waited for four long months prior to that!). This ceremony took place on 18 October at the historic Osu Castle (previously known as Christianborg Castle it was built in 1649 as a slave collection/export fortress by the Danes). It was the 'seat' of Ghana's government from Independence in 1957 until 2013, when it moved to Flagstaff House (the former Army Headquarters just opposite IER).

On the appointed day, two old Rolls Royce cars arrived at the Embassy Residence at 10 a.m. I and the COP were seated in the first one; Isobel and the Deputy COP in the second. We were driven to the 'Castle' with an escort of six motorcycle riders. On arrival, there was traditional drumming until the Guard of Honour ended and I entered the Castle.

In the 30-minute post-presentation of credentials conversation, President Limann spoke of the severity of Ghana's economic problems and of his keen desire to secure India's assistance in various fields, particularly the transport and mining sectors. He also spoke of keen interest to visit India to see for himself the great progress that it had made despite the enormous challenges it had faced when it attained Independence.

Among the many ministers I called on after my meeting with the President, the Minister of Transport Harry Sawyer was the keenest about Indian assistance. He stated that Ghana's road transport system was in a mess primarily because it had acquired luxurious and expensive Willowbrook and Neoplan buses from the UK and Germany. They were quite unsuited for Ghana's pot-holed roads. Almost 100 of them were always 'under repair' because of broken windshields or springs, which needed to be imported from abroad and took many weeks to arrive. He had seen Indian buses operating quite well in East African countries and would much like to get some of them into Ghana. I therefore undertook to secure detailed information/quotes from Telco and Ashok Leyland about their Tata and Leyland buses and submit them to him before long.

Telco responded promptly and quoted a price of US$33,000 per bus CIF (Cost, Insurance, and Freight) Accra on an order for 400 buses. They also undertook to arrange five-year EXIM bank credit and set up repair/maintenance facilities in Ghana for these buses. When I took this offer to Minister Sawyer he was delighted and stated the Telco price was almost one-third of what Ghana had paid (US$88,000) for Willowbrook and Neoplan buses. He promptly set up a study team of senior officers of his Ministry, Ghana Army and University of Ghana, to examine the suitability of Tata buses for Ghana's needs. This study team submitted its report in 60 days and recommended the import of Tata buses.

This caused great concern to the British High Commissioner and German Ambassador, who tried their best to dissuade Minister Sawyer from going ahead on this proposal. Their Ghanaian friends circulated rumours that these Tata buses were obsolete and much used Mercedes buses which had been fitted with new bodies and repainted. Nonetheless, Minister Sawyer decided to place an initial order for 200 buses with an option for 200 more, if the first lot were found satisfactory.

As High Commissioner of India to Ghana I was concurrently accredited as Ambassador of India to Liberia, Togo and Haute Volta (now known as Burkina Faso).

I presented my credentials to President of Liberia William Tolbert Jr at Monrovia on 5 December 1979. He was a well-educated Baptist pastor and wore a gold chain with a big cross on it, even at official events.

The presentation of credentials ceremony at Monrovia was far more impressive than at Accra. Here, besides the President and Foreign Minister, all other Cabinet ministers, Chairman of the Senate, Speaker of House of Representatives and Chief Justice of the Supreme Court were also present. Foreign Minister Cecil Dennis and Finance Minister Ellen Johnson Sirleaf had studied and graduated from prestigious US universities.

In Monrovia, after presentation of credentials the Ambassador is expected to make a formal address to the distinguished gathering. In it I referred to the single star in Liberia's flag and lauded it for being 'the lone star of Freedom in Africa' for over a 100 years (Liberia, established in 1847 by liberated US slaves, was Black Africa's only independent country until Ghana's independence in 1957). This was much appreciated not only by all those present but also by the Liberian print and electronic media. The latter kept repeating this sentence in all their news bulletins for the next two days.

Presentation of credentials to President Gnassingbé Eyadéma of Togo was made in early January 1980. His bio was amazing. He served in the French army for nine years, fought in Vietnam and Algeria and after his return to Togo took part in the 1963 and 1967 coups which toppled Presidents Sylvanus Olympio and Nicolas Grunitzky. He took over as president on 14 April 1967. Much influenced by Kim Il-Sung of North Korea, he adopted his political and social mobilization strategies. The politico-socio-cultural party he set up in 1970 was named Rally of the Togolese People and regularly held mega cultural events in which about 1,000 well-trained women sang and danced in praise of him. Besides, large statues of him were installed in Lome and other Togolese cities.

For presentation of my credentials to President Aboubakar Sangoulé Lamizana of Haute Volta I decided to travel to its capital Ouagadougou by car. Isobel and our three children (the elder two had come to Accra for their Christmas vacation) accompanied me. We travelled via Lome in Togo, rather than Kumasi in Ghana as the former road was in much better condition. It was also more scenic and exciting as it traversed the Keran National Park. We made overnight stops at the charming towns of Dapaong and Kara, just north and south of this park, on the outward and return journeys.

Whereas in Togo the Indian community was mainly Sindhi traders, in Haute Volta it was mainly agricultural scientists, most of whom worked at the International Crop Research Institute for Semi-Arid Tropics (ICRISAT) and the others with American, French and Swedish aid agencies. Amazingly, all of them had graduated from India's renowned Pantnagar Agricultural University!

Both in Togo and Haute Volta the currency was the Central African Franc (CFA), which was linked to the French Franc. France thus exercised firm and effective economic control of these countries. However, the silver lining for them was the stability of the CFA unlike the Ghanaian Cedi.

When I presented my credentials to President Aboubakar Sangoulé Lamizana he praised the work of Indian agricultural scientists in his country as also India's advances in diverse sectors and expressed interest in its mini hydel plants and student scholarships in the agricultural and medical fields.

At about 1 p.m. on 12 April (1980), at EI Accra, I received a telephone call from an NRI in Monrovia that President Tolbert had been assassinated in a bloody coup. The following day I learnt that this coup had been staged by 16 NCOs, all indigenous Liberians. They were led by Master Sergeant Samuel Doe who headed the Presidential bodyguard. He and his co-conspirators had burst into the President's bedroom a little after midnight, pulled him out of bed and bayoneted him several times in the presence of his wife. Thereafter they had taken his body and thrown it into a newly-dug pit into which bodies of all others killed in this uprising were also dumped. Later that day all top State officials, including Chief Justice James Pierre, Senate President Frank E. Tolbert (brother of President Tolbert), House of Representatives Speaker Richard A. Henries, and all Cabinet ministers, except four (among whom was Finance Minister Ellen Johnson Sirleaf) were arrested/imprisoned.

The brutal killing of President Tolbert was shocking and repulsive enough. But worse was to come. On 22 April, all those arrested/imprisoned were tried by a kangaroo court and sentenced to death. They were then taken to a public beach near Barclay Training Center outside Monrovia, tied to poles and executed by firing squad. The first volley missed the chief justice and foreign minister. However, the former died of a heart attack before the second volley was fired. This public execution was watched by over 10,000 people. Some took photos and sold them to printers who made black and white/colour posters of these VIPs before and after their executions. The former were priced at US$1, the latter at US$5! This is the nadir of human brutality and depravity, but the sad and stark fact is that it was Liberia's history in the making.

None of those executed at Accra 10 months earlier were personally known to me. But among those executed at Monrovia I had met, dealt with and greatly admired Foreign Minister Cecil Dennis. His execution, and the shoddy manner in which it was carried out, were therefore deeply shocking and painful to me.

That the indigenous Liberians had harboured great hatred for the Americo-Liberian elite which had ruled Liberia since its foundation in 1847 was well known. I had first learned of this from the British Ambassador in Monrovia and subsequently from an Indian professor at Liberia University named Jyotirmoy Pal Chaudhuri. The grotesque brutality of this coup and the executions thereafter are an indication/measure of the intensity of this long-dormant hatred.

Shortly after the coup, Master Sergeant Samuel Doe promoted himself to the rank of a General and established a People's Redemption Council (PRC) with himself as chairman. PRC ruled Liberia until the 1985 presidential 'election', in which General Doe was elected President. He was sworn in on 6 February 1986. This was the first time in Liberia's then 128-year history that an indigenous Liberian had occupied this high office.

On 8 May 1980 Pope John Paul II visited Accra to inaugurate the centenary celebrations of the founding of the Catholic Church in Ghana. Thanks to the gracious efforts of the Papal Nuncio to Ghana, Giuseppe Ferraioli, Isobel, our five-year-old daughter Seema and I had the great privilege of a private audience with His Holiness. A photo taken on this occasion is among those included in this book.

In late May (1980), the first 50 of the 200 Tata buses Ghana had ordered arrived in Accra. So did 100 drums of bitumen which GOI had gifted to Ghana (as requested by me) for repair of Accra's long-neglected roads. This generated much goodwill for India. But the big and proud moment for India was on 1 July (Ghana's Republic Day) that year (1980). All the 200 Tata buses which Ghana had ordered had arrived by then. They were all lined up in 10 rows of 20 buses each and formally presented by President Limann to the Chairman of Ghana State Transport Company. I was given a seat on the 10-foot high dais on which President Limann, Vice President J.W.de-Graft Johnson and Minister of Transport Harry Sawyer were seated. In his remarks, the President lauded me for my 'valuable contribution in making the Tata bus project a reality' and as a token of his appreciation presented me with a traditional Ghanaian hand-woven tunic. Transport Minister Sawyer added the icing on this cake by announcing that the second lot of 200 Tata buses had been ordered and would be arriving before the end of that year.

The *New York Times* carried a half page report about Ghana's import of Tata buses in its October 2, 1980 issue. It carried a photo of Minister

Harry Sawyer and me.[1]

I have already mentioned Ghana's dire economic situation in the 1979-80 period. How dire it still was in December 1980 was revealed by the surprise visit which 'Paa Willie' (William Ofori Atta) Ghana's former foreign minister and its senior most politician, made to us three days before Christmas to request a pound of sugar so that his wife could make her Christmas cake! Isobel gave him three pounds of it as also a packet of plums. He was overwhelmed and thanked her profusely. Those days to present any Ghanaian with a pound of sugar or a bottle of Nescafé was considered a very valuable gift.

In April 1981 President Limann commenced his foreign visits, initially to neighbouring countries—Togo, Ivory Coast, Upper Volta, Mali and Nigeria—and subsequently to East African countries. He indicated to me, that much as he would like to visit India, he would be able to do this only in the last quarter of 1981.

Between September 1980 and April 1981 there was a steady stream of Indian visits to Ghana. The most notable of these were those of NDC (National Defence College), BHEL (Bharat Heavy Electricals Ltd), BEML (Bharat Earth Movers Ltd), EEPC (Engineering Export Promotion Council), SCI (Shipping Corporation of India), WAPCOS (Water and Power Consultancy Services (India) Ltd), ICICI, ITDC (India Tourism Development Corporation); KVIC (Khadi and Village Industries Commission) and Central Silk Board. These visits resulted not only in considerable expansion of India's contacts with Ghana's ministries and corporations but also in some major successes for it. BHEL won a Volta River Authority contract to build two sub-stations at Prestea and Kumasi; WAPCOS was engaged to study the potential for mini-hydro plants and minor irrigation on

1. Pranay B. Gupte, 'Ghana Moves to Rebuild Transport System', *The New York Times,* 2 October 1980, https://www.nytimes.com/1980/10/02/archives/ghana-moves-to-rebuild-transport-system-controversial-bus-purchase.html.

the Volta River and its tributaries; HMT (Hindustan Machine Tools) and Eicher won contracts to supply 25 HP tractors and tractor-driven road rollers for building feeder roads; KVIC and Central Silk Board were engaged to make feasibility studies for producing crude sugar (khandsari) and Tussar silk; ICICI secured a two-year management support contract from Ghana Bank for Housing and Construction; SCI was granted permission to commence a direct Bombay–Tema Shipping Link. ITDC was engaged to install a light and sound show in Accra's Freedom Square about Ghana's struggle for independence.

From early June 1981 I liaised with the Ghanaian Foreign Office and MEA for ascertaining mutually convenient dates for President Limann's visit to India. Those finally agreed, were 9-15 October 1981. This was a momentous challenge for me as I had never before handled a presidential visit. So I made strenuous efforts to ensure it would be a very successful one and raise India–Ghana relations again to the high level attained during the period under Kwame Nkrumah, the first President of Ghana.

I arrived in New Delhi a week earlier to assist in the preparations for this visit and the agreements to be signed during it. Early on the day President Limann was to arrive in India, COP and I flew in a chartered plane to Mumbai to receive the Presidential delegation (which included the Foreign, Transport and Mines Ministers) and escort it to New Delhi.

President Limann was given a ceremonial welcome at Rashtrapati Bhavan and he and his entourage accommodated at it. All of them were greatly impressed by its grandeur and elegance. For me, having gone through all the mental and emotional strains of burglaries, murders, coups, and executions in Ghana and Liberia in the previous 28 months being in the grand and elegant tranquillity of Rashtrapati Bhavan and in close proximity to India's VVIPs was an exhilarating and deeply satisfying experience. So were the many bilateral agreements that were signed and the warm and cordial interaction between our VVIPs and President Limann and his ministers.

From New Delhi President Limann and his ministers flew to Bangalore (where they visited HAL /HMT/BHEL), Pune (where they visited the TELCO plant and saw Tata Buses being manufactured/rigorously tested) and Mumbai (where they visited a diamond cutting/polishing centre and attended a reception hosted by Maharashtra Governor Air Chief Marshal O.P. Mehra at which J.R.D. Tata was present).

At Bangalore airport, I had the joy of introducing my parents to President Limann, who told them 'Your son is doing a great job in Ghana.' Needless to say my parents were thrilled to hear this.

At the Maharashtra Governor's reception I had the honour of meeting J.R.D. Tata and being thanked by him for my role in Ghana's import of Tata buses.

When I returned to Accra after this VVIP visit to India I had the happy feeling that the Ghana–India relationship had been raised to their previous zenith. Sadly this euphoria was rudely shattered just 75 days later.

On 31 December 1981, Isobel and I were at a New Year's Eve party at the Italian Ambassador's residence when news was received that there was unusual movement of military trucks along Accra's main streets particularly near Flagstaff House. So we rushed home. En route we noticed troops and armoured vehicles blocking the main roads and traffic being diverted into side streets. When our car was stopped and instructed to do likewise our chauffeur pointed to the Indian flag on our car and indicated its occupants were the Indian Ambassador and his wife. So it was allowed to proceed. When we reached home we found Premila, Andy and Seema (the former two were again in Accra for their Christmas vacation) quite exultant about being in 'the middle of a revolution'. Rawlings had obliged them on this!

In his nationwide broadcast the next morning Rawlings declared that 'this was not a coup but a revolution'. He alleged the Limann government was 'the most disgraceful government in the history of our country; criminals have become respectable; our hospitals have been turned into graveyards; our clinics into death camps' and added 'the time has come to restructure this society in a real, meaningful, democratic manner'. He announced the setting up of 'Peoples Defence Committees' in every work place, village and town so that decision making would be in the hands of the people and not 'corrupt politicians' and indicated the new government was named 'Provisional National Defence Council' (PNDC).

Rawlings' condemnation of the Limann government was as false as it was cynical. The prime reason for Ghana's mega economic difficulties in the October 1979–December 1981 period was Nigeria's suspension of oil exports to Ghana and its adverse consequences on its cocoa collection exports and consequent fall in its currency's exchange value. This had been caused primarily because of Rawlings' execution of Ghana's senior military leaders most of whom were close friends of Nigeria's military rulers.

The faint glimmer of hope I saw for safeguarding the gains India had made in Ghana in the previous 28 months was Brigadier Joseph Nunoo-Mensah's appointment as the new Chief of Army Staff. I had first met him when our NDC team visited Ghana in September 1980. He was then Director of Ghana Military Academy and having been awarded the Military Cane of Honour by Sandhurst Royal Military Academy in 1963 was highly respected. So I called on him about a month after this coup and in the course of conversation expressed the hope that the substantial improvement made in India–Ghana relations in recent months would be safeguarded. He assured me they would be but significantly added 'Ghana's external relations perhaps need some rebalancing towards its prime donor countries'. He also stated the 'much-talked about Tata buses had been found not as excellent as they were made out to be'. This gave me an inkling of the new path PNDC would be taking and that the British and Germans might have instigated this coup. The fact that Rawlings had a British parent and his favourite riding partner was the wife of a first secretary in the German Embassy strengthened my suspicion on the latter.

The only gains India made during the January–April 1982 period was an order for six Tata buses from the Liberian government and one mini-hydro plant from Haute Volta for installation on a tributary of Volta River in its Bobo-Dioulasso region.

As my parents were celebrating their golden wedding anniversary on 17 May 1982, I requested and received MEA's permission to leave Ghana four weeks before I completed my term there. I left Accra on 10 May 1982.

Before concluding this chapter, I would like to briefly recount what subsequently happened to its principal dramatis personae.

President Limann

Overthrown and imprisoned a little before midnight on 31 December 1981 Limann was finally released in March 1982. He lived a quiet private life until induced to contest the 1992 presidential election as the PNC candidate. He lost badly. He then tried to reunite the fractured PNC party but was unsuccessful in this also. He died in January 1998.

Jerry Rawlings

Rawlings ruled Ghana for 12 years as PNDC Chairman and survived seven assassination attempts during this period. In early 1992, he resigned from the Ghana Air Force, set up the National Democratic Congress (NDC), legalized political parties and organized Presidential and Parliamentary elections. He contested the 1992 presidential election as an NDC candidate and won. In 1996, he was re-elected as President. As the new Ghanaian constitution he had promulgated did not permit him a third term, he supported his Vice President John Atta Mills' candidature in the 2000 presidential election. However, Mills was beaten by John Agyekum Kufuor, of the New Patriotic Party.

Rawlings' 1 January 1982 condemnation of the Limann Government as 'the most disgraceful government in the history of our country' boomeranged on his own. None of the Limann Government Ministers/senior officials who were imprisoned by him and subsequently investigated were found to be guilty. On the contrary, when the 1983 abduction and killing of four Ghana High Court judges (one of whom, Justice Cecelia Koranteng Addo, was a woman) was investigated by the Special Investigation Board chaired by former Chief Justice Azu Crabbe, it was found that this crime had been masterminded by Capt. Kojo Tsikata, the PNDC member in charge of National Security and four Lance corporals who carried it out had done so on his orders. Rawlings had condemned the killing of these judges as 'anti-revolution', and ordered the execution by firing squad of the four NCOs. However, one of them, Matthew Adabuga, managed to escape and 21 years later, (in May 2003) testified to Ghana's National Reconciliation Commission that PNDC Chairman Rawlings had popped champagne when informed this heinous deed had been carried out. [2]

Rawlings made two semi-official visits to India, the first was a transit stopover in Bombay on his way back from Beijing in 1993 and the second in September 1999 to attend Mother Teresa's funeral at Calcutta.

Samuel Doe

Doe ruled Liberia autocratically for three years as PRC chairman,

---

2. 'Rawlings ordered killing of Judges: Adabuga', *Modern Ghana*, 23 May 2003, retrieved from https://www.modernghana.com/news/35081/rawlings-orderd-killing-of-judges-adabuga.html.

then had a new constitution providing multi-party democracy drafted/ approved by referendum in 1984. On 15 October 1985, he was elected President in a heavily rigged election. In December 1989, Charles Taylor, an Americo-Liberian launched a guerrilla war against him, which morphed into a civil war and brought in UN peacekeepers. In September 1990, when President Doe was at a meeting with General Quinoo, head of ECOMOG, some of Taylor's guerrillas suddenly arrived there and captured him. They took him to their forest camp, chopped off his ears, toes and fingers and then beheaded him. All this was videotaped and released to the news media. Many TV channels within Liberia and some in neighbouring countries telecast it. Americo–Liberians thus settled scores with indigenous Liberians for their earlier brutalities against their elite.

Ellen Johnson Sirleaf

Johnson, former Finance Minister (who was present at my credentials presentation ceremony), fled to the US soon after the April 1980 coup. She secured a job at World Bank in 1981, then moved to Citibank and was appointed Vice President of its African Regional Office in Nairobi in 1992. She resigned in 1997 to contest in Liberia's presidential election but lost. She contested again in 2005 as the Unity Party candidate against world-class soccer star George Weah, won an impressive 59.4 per cent of the votes and became the first woman Head of State of an African nation. Her swearing-in ceremony as President on 16 January 2006 was attended by many foreign dignitaries, including US First Lady Laura Bush. She appointed women as well as some Opposition leaders in her Cabinet and like Nelson Mandela, set up a Truth and Reconciliation Commission. Her enlightened approach and strenuous personal efforts succeeded in ending Liberia's 15-year-long civil war. In 2011, she was awarded the Nobel Peace prize, (jointly with Leymah Gbowee of Liberia and Tawakkul Karman of Yemen) for 'securing peace, promoting economic and social development, and strengthening the position of women in Liberia'.

Victoria Tolbert

Victoria, President Tolbert's widow (who died in the US in 1997), in her autobiography titled *Lifted Up* has revealed that it was a 'masked man with a white hand' who first bayoneted her late husband. In August 2008, Chea Cheapoo, President Doe's former justice minister, told the Truth and Reconciliation Commission that the CIA provided the map of the Executive Mansion, enabling the coupsters to break into the president's bedroom and that 'Americans were responsible for Liberia's nightmare'.

Gnassingbé Eyadéma

President Eyadéma survived numerous assassination attempts, won numerous elections unopposed and stayed on in power to become Africa's longest serving Head of State. In 2000, he was elected the Chairman of Organisation of African Unity (OAU). He died on 5 February 2005, on board a plane en route to Tunis where he was being taken for an emergency medical treatment. His funeral on 13 March was attended by the Presidents of Benin, Ghana, Ivory Coast, Niger and Nigeria. Since he had got the Togo parliament to reduce the minimum age for becoming President from 45 to 35 in 2003, his son Faure succeeded him on the day he died! He is still in that high office!

Sangoulé Lamizana

President Lamizana of Haute Volta was overthrown in a military coup in November 1980 but fortunately this coup, unlike those in Ghana and Liberia, was bloodless.

Governor Sir Archibald Nye and Lady Nye at my grand-uncle L.C. Pais' home in Mangalore on 8 October 1946. SAC Rector Fr Jacques is seated second from left

Prime Minister Jawaharlal Nehru being received at Cuddapah in May 1952 by Madras Presidency Governor Sri Prakasa, my father and District Collector P.C. James

My father Pascal Ambrose, mother Elizabeth Lucy, sisters Corinne, Joan and Margaret, brother John and me, in Bangalore on the eve of my departure for Metcalfe House (IAS/ IFS Training School), New Delhi on 9 May 1959

Metcalfe House, New Delhi

My IFS batch at the National Academy of Administration, Mussoorie on 20 November 1959 with its Director A.N. Jha ICS and Dy Director R.K Trivedi IAS

Extended family reunion on board the *S.S. Vietnam* in Bombay on 23 July 1960, to see off my mother and me to Japan

With my IAS batchmate Louis Menezes as best man and Isobel's sister Sylvia as bridesmaid at our wedding in Bangalore on 1 September 1962

Isobel having lunch with Japan's renowned painter Saburo Miyamoto and his wife at their home in Tokyo in April 1963

P.K. Banerjee, GOI Special Envoy, conferring with H.E. Senor José Trejos Fernández, President of Costa Rica, about the Dharma Teja extradition case at the Presidential Mansion in San Jose in November 1967

Peru's First Lady Senora Consuelo de Velasco thanking Isobel after the EI fundraiser for the 31 May 1970 earthquake victims in northern Peru, in Lima on 15 June 1970

External Affairs Minister Y.B. Chavan and US Secretary of State Henry Kissinger signing the agreement for setting up the Indo-US Commission on Scientific, Educational & Cultural Cooperation in New Delhi on 28 October 1974

My presentation of credentials to President Tolbert of Liberia in Monrovia on 5 December 1979. Foreign Minister Cecil Dennis, Finance Minister Ellen Johnson Sirleaf and the Chief Justice are also in this photo

Signing of India-Ghana agreements in presence of Prime Minister Indira Gandhi and President Hilla Limann in New Delhi on 11 October 1981

Prime Minister Indira Gandhi with Bolshoi Ballet dancers at her residence on 23 October 1983

Congress General Secretary Rajiv Gandhi and I as DG (ICCR) enjoy a light moment in New Delhi on 20 November 1983

Minister of Culture of Greece Mrs Melina Mercouri with a set of books on Indian culture, presented to her by me at the European Culture Centre at Delphi in Greece on 8 June 1984

A stunning photo taken at HCI Residence in London at the banquet in honour of Prime Minister Morarji Desai in June 1977, where former British Prime Ministers Harold MacMillan, Douglas Home and Edward Heath; Leader of Opposition Michael Foot (extreme right), and Lord Mountbatten (seated cross-legged on the floor) are seen

Lok Sabha Speaker K.S. Hegde, Lord Alfred Denning, Lord Chancellor Elwyn Jones and me (as AHC) in London in October 1977

Isobel and I with music maestro Zubin Mehta, his wife Nancy and Royal Opera House singers at Sun House, London in December 1978

President Zail Singh presenting the 1983 Jawaharlal Nehru Award for International Understanding to former Chancellor of Austria Bruno Kreisky in New Delhi on 11 January 1985. Also seen are Prime Minister Rajiv Gandhi and me as DG (ICCR)

With former US President Jimmy Carter at the ball organized by the Society of Foreign Consuls (SFC) in New York City in November 1988

Pope John Paul II blessing baby Seema at Accra, Ghana on 8 May 1980

Isobel receiving Mother Teresa when she came to thank her for her constant support for their Home for Aids Patients in New York on 23 May 1989

With Nobel Laureates Rigoberta Menchú Tum in Mexico City in September 1993 (left) and Archbishop Emeritus of Cape Town Desmond Tutu in Bangalore in December 2009

With His Holiness The Dalai Lama in Bangalore on 12 January 2014

My daughter Seema and Justice M.N. Venkatachaliah 'blessing' Premila on her wedding morning (23 October 1996) in New Delhi. The latter raised the toast at that evening's reception

President K.R. Narayanan speaking at the first Business Standard Seema Nazareth Award presentation at Rashtrapati Bhavan on 21 February 2000

NATION

TUESDAY, JULY 9, 1996, THE TIMES OF INDIA, MUMBAI

Trustees of the Sarvodaya International Trust Amjad Ali Khan, Raj Mohan Gandhi, Mrinalini Sarabhai, Bindeshwari Pathak, Air Chief Marshal (retd) Arjan Singh, Justice M.N. Venkatachaliah and others at a meeting in Gandhi Museum, New Delhi, recently.

THE ASIAN AGE BANGALORE 18 JUNE 2004

Ex-President of Philippines joins noble cause of Gandhian trust

BY IYER SANJIVANI

Bangalore, June 17: The Sarvodaya International Trust, which works to promote Gandhian ideals, has recently gained a Philippine connection in former Philippine president Corazon Aquino.

The trust, with its headquarters in Bangalore, invited Ms Aquino to become its eminent counsellor in March 2004 and she, to its delight, has formally sent her acceptance.

Ms Aquino, who led the historic non-violent struggle against the Marcos dictatorship in the mid-80s and subsequently became the President of Philippines, has in her letter to Mr P.A. Nazareth, the managing trustee of SIT, written, "I accept your invitation and consider it an honour to be included in your honour panel of eminent counsellors."

Started in 1995, the trust today has six regional chapters in India. Says Mr Nazareth, "I had met Ms Aquino on a visit to Philippines in February. While speaking with her, I learnt of her deep reverence for Mahatma Gandhi. So, I requested her to join our movement."

Ms Aquino's association with the Gandhian ideal of non-violence dates back to the days of the Marcos dictatorship. Her husband Benigno Aquino, who returned from his exile in the US to Manila on August 21, 1983, was assassinated.

And his final statement read, "According to Gandhi, the WILLING sacrifice of the innocent is the most powerful answer to insolent tyranny that has yet been conceived by God and man."

Says Mr Nazareth, "Eminent counsellors serve as a source of inspiration for us. We keep them informed of our activities. In turn they acknowledge our efforts, encourage and advise us."

According to him Ms Aquino carries a book of quotations of Gandhi with her. Her role with the trust could mean a future visit to India on a lecture or an important seminar. Other eminent counsellors of SIT include noted social worker Baba Amte, Nobel laureates Desmond Tutu and Dalai Lama, former Mexican president Dr Miguel de la Madrid and former UN Secretary General Dr Xavier Pérez de Cuellar.

THE ASIAN AGE 4 OCTOBER 2003 4

INDIA

AROUND INDIA

In Other News

Sarod concert

A bhajan in Odissi

Gandhiji laid stress on truth than on traditional practices: Thakur

'He rejected any religious doctrine that did not appeal to reason'

THE HINDU

Friday, October 12, 2001

Vyjayanthi Kashi and her group.

Weave of movement, idea and visuals

THE TIMES OF INDIA

MONDAY OCTOBER 2, 2006

Bangalore

A unique tribute to Gandhiji

NATIONAL NETWORK 5

Tolstoy admired Gandhiji, says author's great grandson

PRESS TRUST OF INDIA
NEW DELHI, OCT 18

IF Mahatma Gandhi drew his inspiration from Leo Tolstoy during his South African days to set up a farm named after the Russian author, Tolstoy himself turned an admirer of Bapu when he was hailed as an "apostle of non-violence".

"Tolstoy had a great regard for Gandhi and his popular works show that he also had a deep interest and love for India, its philosophy and religion, particularly during the last days of his life," says Vladimir Tolstoy, the author's great grandson.

Just as Tolstoy's books carry the imprint of his early life, his characters also reflect his personal thoughts, thinking and world views. "The main traits of his characters are his own sincerity and truthfulness, all of which are so cardinal to Gandhi's philosophy," said

Another similarity he drew between the two personalities was the renunciation of their comfort. As Gandhiji chose to lead a simple life with the barest of essentials, so did Tolstoy violating the norms and customs of his aristocratic family.

"He chose to live like the poor as he understood the privations of the underprivileged and the downtrodden," Vladimir said delivering a lecture yesterday on the influence of Count Tolstoy on Russia.

"Tolstoy's main vision was self-reliance in agriculture," Vladimir said, referring to the major lesson to be learnt from Tolstoy's life.

"Russia is wasting a lot of resources and is not looking at its rich tradition. When we think of the war in Chechnya, one wishes the powers that be had read of Tolstoy's version of 100 years of war in Chechnya".

Behind the author's philosophy of peace lay his experience during military service, said Vladimir, director of the Leo Tolstoy museum at Yasnaya Polyana, the author's birthplace and hometown.

"So shattered was he by the contrast between his home and the battlefield that he became anti-war for life," he said.

Collage of Sarvodaya International Trust activities

Release of the Japanese edition of my book, *Gandhi's Outstanding Leadership* by HIH Princess Takamado at Vivekananda Cultural Centre in Tokyo in April 2018

Hon'ble President of India Shri R. N. Kovind receiving a copy of my book, *Gandhi: The Soul Force Warrior* at the Rashtrapati Bhavan, New Delhi on 5 December 2018

On board the *Seabourn Encore* with its Captain Tim Roberts, fellow lecturer Dr Terry Jones, Mrs Ginny Jones & Isobel in April 2017

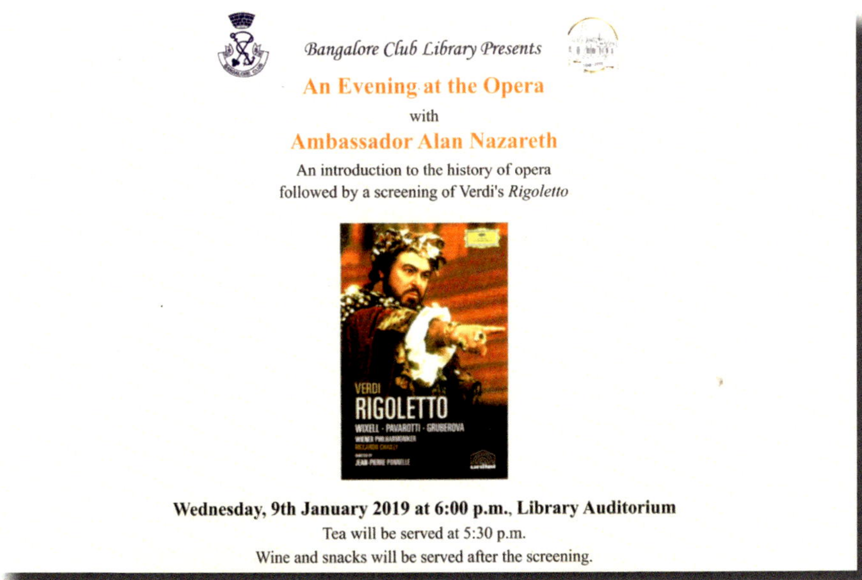

The poster of 'An Evening at the Opera with Ambassador Alan Nazareth'

10

Theatre, Poetry, Ballet and NYPO in New Delhi
(July 1982–October 1985)

Having served three years in Africa and before that four years in Latin America, I had expected to be posted as Joint Secretary (Africa) or Joint Secretary (LA). I was therefore quite disappointed when JS (Adm) Kishan Rana informed me that I had been posted as DG, Indian Council for Cultural Relations (ICCR). As two previous occupants of this post were women, the general impression among IFS colleagues was that it was a 'female post'. So I requested a call on Foreign Secretary, who was M.K. Rasgotra, who knew me from my DHC days in London.

When I voiced my grievance to him he asked, 'Alan, if it was not good for you would I have posted to you to ICCR?' He then indicated that Prime Minister Indira Gandhi wanted ICCR to be revamped so as to become a more effective cultural arm of India's diplomacy and bring the best of world culture to India and take the best of its culture to the world. He said India's cultural diplomacy hitherto had focused primarily on providing cultural nourishment to expatriate Indian communities in the Indian and Pacific Ocean islands and the Caribbean. This needs to be changed, diversified and transformed into a two-way flow. A new vision and dynamic approach were needed as 'India is the super power in the field of culture.' He assured me of his full support and advised me to call on the two 'czarinas of Indian culture', Mrs Pupul Jayakar (Advisor [Culture] to PM) and Smt Kapila Vatsyayan (Addl. Secretary, Ministry of Culture). I left Foreign Secretary's office, fully enthused about my new job and determined to do my best at it.

When I arrived at Azad Bhavan where ICCR is housed, I was pleasantly surprised to find it a large building with a sizable auditorium and lawn. It was located in Indraprastha Estate and close to the Sahitya and Sangeet Natak Akademies. However, its offices and corridors were poorly lit and office rooms overcrowded with desks, almirahs, and files. So my first instructions were to have brighter lights installed in them and obsolete files weeded.

The first cultural event I had to handle came up on the fifth day after I took over as DG (ICCR). It was a presentation at Kamani auditorium of 'Ballet Nacional de Cuba', led by its renowned founder/prima donna Alicia Alonso. The VIPs who attended it were Vice President of India Justice M. Hidayatullah (who was ICCR Chairman), Prime Minister Indira Gandhi, Lt Governor of Delhi S.L. Khurana, Cuban Ambassador Jose Perez Novoa and Foreign Secretary Rasgotra, who kindly introduced me to all of them as the new DG (ICCR). I, thus, had a high-level launch at my new job! However, the PM had a complaint against ICCR. She said renowned British poet Kathleen Raine, a good friend of hers, had come to New Delhi recently as an ICCR invitee but she learnt about this visit only after Ms Raine had left. I apologized on ICCR's behalf and promised to keep her office informed of all important cultural visits and presentations hereafter.

I had the privilege of meeting the PM again three days later when I escorted the Cuban ballet dancers and the Cuban Ambassador to her residence. She graciously spent almost an hour conversing with and posing for photos with them.

The following week I called on Mrs Pupul Jayakar and Smt Kapila Vatsyayan. This initiated my close association with them, particularly Mrs Jayakar, in handling the 'Festivals of India' in the UK and USA.

During my 42 months at ICCR, many notable cultural events were organized or handled by it. These included: an International Poetry Festival, a Buddhism and National Cultures Conference, an international Tal Vadya Utsav (drum and percussion festival), an international Gypsy Music festival, an Australian Aborigine music concert, National Dance Troupe of Turkey (with the Whirling Dervishes), Sadler Wells Royal Ballet, Paris Opera Ballet (with Rudolph Nureyev), the Bolshoi Ballet (with Natalia Bessmertnova and Alexander Bogyatrev) and the New York Philharmonic Orchestra (conducted by Zubin Mehta). It also handled the cultural presentations for the 1983 NAM Summit in New Delhi. Besides, Indian classical and folk music and dance groups, and art exhibitions were sent to innumerable countries, and the 'Festivals of India' held in the UK and USA.

Notable details of some of these cultural events are given hereunder.

The PM who attended the British Wheel Chair Theatre presentation had earlier indicated she would attend only the first half as she was hosting a dinner at her residence that night. So during the interval I escorted her backstage to meet the actors. They were thrilled that she had come to meet them but greatly disappointed that she was leaving before the second half. The lead actor pleaded with her, 'Madam, the climax of the play and its message that the handicapped are as human and talented as all others, is in the second half. Please stay for it.' Amazingly, she agreed and instructed me to convey to her daughter-in-law Sonia that she should receive the guests as she would be returning home about 30 minutes later than expected. I did this and discovered that night how deeply compassionate she was despite her regal and stern presence.

The *Barber of Seville* Opera, presented at National Centre for the Performing Arts (NCPA) Bombay, with six singers from La Scala Opera House in Milan and the Paranjoti Choir and Bombay Chamber Orchestra, was conducted by Daniel Nazareth, Music Director of the Verona Opera Company. The Italian Ambassador to India had kindly assisted in bringing the La Scala singers and Daniel Nazareth to this event. When I called on the PM to invite her to it, she stated that while she enjoyed opera she doubted many Indians appreciated it. I reminded her respectfully that in most Indian films lead actors keep singing even after they have been stabbed or shot; hence our people were well conditioned for opera. She chuckled and said, 'You might be right!' and graciously agreed to attend this event.

At the post-opera reception she asked Daniel how challenging it was conducting this opera with diverse Italian and Indian components. He coyly replied, 'Madam Prime Minister, it was much like taking an old ship out into a stormy sea and bringing it safely back to port!'

During the 1983 NAM Summit in New Delhi, the PM's social secretary Usha Bhagat telephoned me to convey that the PM wanted me to host a dinner for the renowned writer and Nobel Laureate Gabriel Garcia Marquez, whom she admired greatly having read his *One Hundred Years of Solitude*. She therefore wanted this dinner to be 'lively and stimulating' and the 'no alcohol' rule to be ignored. Mr Marquez had come to the NAM conference as a member of the Cuban delegation. So I contacted the Cuban Ambassador, invited him and his wife to this dinner and got from him the names of Indian writers/professors in New Delhi well acquainted with Mr Marquez's books. Of the names he suggested only Khushwant Singh and Prof. Susnigdha Dey of JNU were able to attend this dinner. The others who graced the dinner were Dr Karan Singh (ICCR Vice Chairman), the Mexican Ambassador Prof. Graciela de La Lama, Colombian Ambassador Ms Nelly Turbay de Munoz, my deputy Shashi Tripathi and Isobel. The ebullient Colombian Ambassador contributed the most in making this dinner, held at Ashoka Hotel, a memorable one. Mr Marquez greatly enjoyed her banter with him, appreciated his scholarly interaction with Karan Singh and Khushwant Singh and was amazed that Isobel and I spoke Spanish and were well informed about Latin American writers. He conveyed all this to the PM the next day and she conveyed her appreciation to me through Foreign Secretary Rasgotra.

The India-Greek Symposium, held in June 1984, had been suggested to the PM by Greek Minister of Culture Melina Mercouri during her official visit to Greece the previous year. She had offered to host it at the European Cultural Centre (ECC) at Delphi. On her return from there PMO instructed ICCR to organize this symposium. We initiated action on this by contacting the ECC Director at Delphi Pericles Niarchos. Thereafter both sides identified eminent scholars in diverse fields. Among those we assembled were Prof. Lokesh Chandra, Chairman, International Academy of Indian Culture/Vice President ICCR, Prof. D.P. Chattopadhyaya, Dean, Department of Philosophy, Jadavpur University, Rev. Paulos Mar Gregorios, Metropolitan of Malankara Orthodox Church, New Delhi, J.P. Joshi, Director, Archaeological Survey of India, eminent Indian artist K.K. Hebbar and Saryu Doshi, art historian and Editor, *Marg*. The Greek side was led by its Minister of Culture Mrs Melina Mercouri and included George Sioris, Ambassador of Greece to India and Pericles Niarchos, Director of European Cultural Centre at Delphi, Dr M. Sigabidou Ephor, Curator of Macedonia Antiquities of Pella Museum and G.

Amaryiannakis, Professor of Musicology, University of Crete.

The music, dance and theatrical performances of both sides were held at the ancient Delphi amphitheatre overlooking the Temple of Apollo. The Indian play presented was Ratan Thiyam's *Chakravyuha*. His Chorus Repertory Theatre's impactful performance of it was much appreciated.

In her inaugural address Minister Melina Mercouri described India and Greece as 'Mother Civilizations' and the 'algebra and geometry of world cultures'. After the valedictory event she hosted a memorable reception for this symposium's participants at the Cape Sounio Grecotel (a few miles outside of Athens), during which we watched a stunning sunset over the famed Temple of Poseidon.

The papers presented at this symposium were published in 1985, as an elegant and scholarly book titled *India and Greece—Connections and Parallels* by *Marg* Publications. It was designed and illustrated by its editor Saryu Doshi.

Among the many painters and sculptors ICCR sponsored for foreign tours during 1982-85 were J. Swaminathan and Krishen Khanna to Mexico, K.K. Hebbar and Arpana Caur to Greece, M.F. Husain to China, Balan Nambiar to Indonesia, Biman Das to Yugoslavia, and S. Nandagopal to Sri Lanka. The one among these who made the most unusual and biggest impact was M.F. Husain. His two-week visit to China in April 1985 was arranged under the India–China Cultural Exchange programme and took almost four months to finalize with China's snail-paced cultural bureaucracy. When his departure day finally arrived and I saw him off at Palam airport he presented me a line drawing of himself, with paint brushes in one hand and a painter's canvas under his arm, headed for China. Just 48 hours later, Ambassador A.P. Venkateswaran telephoned from Beijing to inform me that M.F. Husain was on a flight back to New Delhi and would arrive there that evening. He indicated that on the evening of his arrival he had hosted a reception in his honour at India House and thereafter had him taken back to his hotel in an EI vehicle. Mr Husain then went for a walk, barefoot, as usual. On his way back, while crossing from one side of the street to the other, his right toe struck the pavement (which is higher than in India) and was injured severely. He limped back to his hotel, which immediately summoned an orthopaedist and informed the Ambassador. The former diagnosed the injured toe as a fracture, encased it in plaster and advised a seven-day bed rest, whereupon Mr Husain decided to return to India the next day. Ambassador Venkateswaran's efforts to dissuade him proved of no avail. When I received him at Palam airport, he apologized for his 'galloping return', showed me a small notebook with sketches of people with straw hats riding bicycles, working in rice fields and roadside eateries and stated he had 'enough sketches for 30 canvasses'. I ignored this statement, but six weeks later was amazed when, at his request, I went to his studio to view his 'China paintings'. He had 35 of them, 15 were big, the rest medium and small size but all based on sketches in the little note book he showed me at Palam airport on the day he returned! Four weeks later ICCR organized an exhibition of these paintings at Lalit Kala Akademi. Minister of Science and Technology and former Ambassador of India to China Mr K.R. Narayanan inaugurated it and expressed amazement that 'a mere 24 hour visit to China' had yielded such a 'bumper artistic harvest'.

Presenting New York Philharmonic Orchestra (NYPO)'s four concerts, (one each in New Delhi and Calcutta and two in Bombay,) in September 1984 was the most challenging and expensive undertaking ICCR or any Indian cultural organization had ever handled. One hundred and seventeen musicians, with their musical instruments, some as small as a piccolo and two as big as a grand piano, about 30 sound and stage technicians and renowned music director Zubin Mehta and his wife Nancy were arriving in two chartered Lufthansa

707 planes and insisting that their New Delhi–Calcutta–Bombay travel also be made in these planes as they had been specially configured for their needs. Foreign planes had never before been permitted to fly on domestic sectors; so DGCA (Directorate General of Civil Aviation) refused to allow this. They reluctantly permitted this only after PMO's intervention. For the New Delhi concert at Siri Fort Auditorium, a special 'acoustic shell' had to be erected as this auditorium's acoustics were found to be inadequate. The estimated cost of NYPO's four concerts in India was Rs 14 lakh, an enormous figure those days. As this could not be met from ICCR's Rs 3.3 crore budget, commercial sponsorships had to be secured, which had never been done before. Approval for this was therefore obtained from its Governing Board. The sponsorships secured were from TISCO (Tata Iron and Steel Company), IOC (Indian Oil Corporation), ITDC, HDFC, Godrej & Boyce and Larsen & Toubro. Funds were also raised through advertisements in the elegant souvenir brochures brought out for these four concerts. The Rs 14-lakh expenditure was thus fully covered.

At the end of the New Delhi concert, after the 117 musicians were draped with sandalwood garlands by ICCR female staff, Isobel came on stage with a garland of 100 red roses and draped it on Zubin Mehta. He recognized her and gave her a big hug. The PM, seated in the VVIP box with American Ambassador Harry Barnes on one side and Mrs Jayakar on the other, turned to me, seated just behind her, and commented, 'Isobel must be the most envied woman in the country today!' This may or may not have been true but Zubin's hug must have been seen by thousands all over India as this concert was telecast nationwide thanks to the sponsorship ICCR secured from the Nikitasha Home Appliances Company for this telecast.

The Buddhism and National Cultures Conference, held at Vigyan Bhavan, New Delhi from 10 to 12 October 1984, was attended by almost 100 scholars from all over the world, some of whom e.g.

Mongolians and Brazilians could speak to each other only in Sanskrit! For rendering the Buddhist invocation at the inaugural event the only reputed Indian musicians we could find were the Dagar brothers!

The PM delivered the inaugural address in which she pointed out that it was through Buddhism that India's millennial message of non-violence and universal brotherhood had been initially spread, and the cultures of most Asian countries enriched and transformed without damaging any of them. That night Mrs Jayakar hosted an informal dinner at her residence to which she invited the PM and 10 of the most eminent scholars who had come for this conference. I was invited as DG (ICCR) and thus privileged to witness the PM respectfully questioning these scholars about Buddhism's impact in their countries in various spheres. Before leaving she complimented Mrs Jayakar and me on organizing this well-attended and intellcctually stimulating conference. Sadly, just 19 days later she was assassinated!

At about 9 a.m. of the morning after this tragic and traumatic event, Mrs Jayakar telephoned and requested me to accompany her to Teen Murti House (TMH) as some ICCR assistance in the form of flower arrangements and experienced ushers might be needed there after the late PM's body was brought there at 11 a.m. So I rushed to her residence. En route to TMH, she tearfully recounted that she had assisted in bathing and dressing the late PM's 'bullet-ridden body' and this was the 'saddest, most painful task she had ever handled'. She added she and Indira were 'like sisters since their teens in Allahabad'.

We arrived at Teen Murti House at about 10.30 a.m. Mrs Gandhi's body was brought there at 11 a.m., and was accompanied by Prime Minister Rajiv Gandhi and members of his family. Soon other VIPs arrived in an endless stream and crowds gathered outside, some of whom began to chant '*khoon ka badla khoon*' (blood for blood). We saw the young PM being enraged by this, going out promptly and sternly instructing the security officers there to have this chant stopped forthwith. I left Teen Murti House at about 1 p.m. and still retain indelible memories of that intensely sad morning.

At 2 p.m. on 31 December 1984, when I and all others at ICCR were much involved in finalizing details for the Paris Opera presentation at Siri Fort Auditorium that evening, my sister Margaret Alva telephoned. She stated that Prime Minister Rajiv Gandhi had summoned her to Rashtrapati Bhavan at 5 p.m. that evening for being sworn in as a minister. She added that as husband Niranjan was away in Mangalore she much hoped I, her elder brother, would accompany her to this important event. I was delighted by the excellent news she had conveyed, but was taken aback by her request because of the importance of that evening's ICCR event. Nonetheless, I agreed, picked her up at her residence and took her to Rashtrapati Bhavan. I requested my deputy Shashi Tripathi to receive the VIP guests and inform them why I was absent.

When we arrived at Rashtrapati Bhavan the security staff permitted Margaret to enter but not me as my name was not on their list of invitees. Fortunately Foreign Minister P.V. Narasimha Rao, who was ICCR chairman, arrived just then and intervened on my behalf. I accompanied him into the Durbar Hall, where the swearing-in ceremony was to take place.

When the ceremony commenced I waited with bated breath, after all the Cabinet ministers had been sworn in, for Margaret to be called up. She was the fifth of the Ministers of State to be called up. When she walked up to be sworn in, I felt a great surge of emotion and recalled my revered father, who had passed away in January that year. He was present when Margaret was sworn in as a Rajya Sabha MP in April 1974 and had shed copious tears of joy on that occasion. This was a far more important event and much grander venue. He would have been more deeply moved.

The swearing-in ceremony was completed by 6 p.m. and I was

able to reach Siri Fort Auditorium before the French Ambassador and other VIPs arrived there. The stunning performance of the Paris Opera Ballet stars was the crowning glory for me of that memorable last day of 1984.

While the above-mentioned happy and tragic events were taking place extensive planning and intense efforts were being made to organise 'Festivals of India' in Britain, the US and the Soviet Union. Much of this took place at Mrs Jayakar's residence.

The basic concept for these Festivals was that in order to 'break through the culture barrier' adequate mass and momentum had to be assembled and then be launched effectively as happens while 'breaking through the sound barrier'. Those who worked on creating this concept and assembling the Festival packages were Smt Kapila Vatsyayan, Addl. Secretary (MoC), V.K. Narayana Menon (Chairman, Sangeet Natak Akademi), Laxmi Prasad Sihare, Director, National Gallery of Modern Art, Mrs Mrinalini Sarabhai, Director, Darpana Academy of Performing Arts, Ahmedabad, Saryu Doshi, Director, National Gallery of Modern Art, Mumbai, architect Charles Correa, designer Rajeev Sethi and myself as DG (ICCR).

The package created for the Festival of India in the US best clarifies the mentioned concept and its praxis as also the methodology for funding it. This Festival was launched at Washington DC (on 13 June 1985) with a concert of Indian classical music and dance at Kennedy Center, an exhibition of 300 stone and bronze sculptures (dating from 500 BC to AD 1500) at the National Gallery and a two-week long colourful Indian Mela on the Mall. The US FOI went on for 18 months with Indian music and dance troupes, artisans and their crafts presented in 90 cities of 37 states. Almost 80 per cent of the expenditure on this mega projection of Indian culture was met from NRI donations and sponsorships from hotels/banks/airlines with branches in and flights to India.

I must mention here three big battles I fought, and won, at ICCR.

During my tenure at HCI London as DHC, I had learnt that GOI (Ministry of Culture) was annually providing £20,000 to a London-based impresario named Birendra Shankar for organizing a three-week long Indian Music and Dance tour of eight or ten UK cities. He was also provided rent-free 'studio space' in the basement of HCI's South Audley Street building, for rehearsals of these tour artistes. However, reputed Indian dance troupes e.g. Mallika Sarabhai's Darpana were being toured through the UK and Europe by the European Festivals Association (EFA) at no cost to GOI and being paid far higher fees than Birendra Shankar was paying to his tour artistes.

About three months after taking over as DG (ICCR) I contacted EFA (headquartered at Ghent, Belgium) through EI, Brussels. Six weeks later an EFA executive, on his way back from China, came to ICCR for discussions, which were fruitful. A contract was signed with EFA whereby ICCR would deliver a mutually agreed composite classical and folk dance troupe to EFA at Frankfurt, who would then present them at seven European festivals, including the prestigious Edinburgh one, meet all their travel/hotel/publicity expenditure and pay ICCR US$10,000. This arrangement worked excellently. Our artistes got maximum exposure and far better honoraria and ICCR recouped about 50 per cent of their Delhi–Frankfurt–Delhi air fares. The following year's contract raised the number of festivals to 11 and the honoraria to US$15,000. This was a major breakthrough for ICCR's cultural projection abroad.

In view of the above, in early 1984 I proposed to Foreign Secretary Rasgotra (as ICCR Vice Chairman) that Ministry of Culture (MoC) be informed of ICCR's EFA breakthrough and advised to terminate Birendra Shankar's annual UK cultural tour and the subsidy for it. He wrote accordingly to Addl. Secretary Kapila Vatsyayan in Ministry of Culture. When Birendra Shankar learnt of this, he first got High

Commissioner Seyid Muhammad in London to write to Minister of Culture Sheila Kaul to reject this proposal. When that effort failed he got Lord Harewood to write to PM Indira Gandhi. Her office forwarded this letter to me and asked for my comments. In the detailed note submitted, I highlighted ICCR's EFA breakthrough. Fortunately, the PM agreed with me and replied to Lord Harewood that the decision to terminate the subsidised annual cultural tours of the UK had been taken after careful consideration of all aspects of this issue and available alternatives.

The second was with the British Council/High Commission in New Delhi. About three weeks before a British theatre group was to tour India in October 1984 with performances in New Delhi, Calcutta and Bombay, advertisements about it appeared in leading newspapers in these cities giving details of the performances and indicating they were being presented by the British Council and sponsored by United Spirits. Ironically, the first of these appeared on 2nd October, Mahatma Gandhi's birthday! So I telephoned BC Director (whose name I unfortunately cannot recall) and reminded him that the British Council is the cultural wing of the British High Commission, enjoys diplomatic status/immunities and therefore cannot avail of corporate sponsorships for its presentations. He replied that HCI London had done this during the Festival of India (FOI) in the UK earlier that year. I pointed out that it was not HCI but the UK-India FOI Committee which had done this. He nonetheless ignored my objection. So, when the next of these advertisements appeared I wrote him a letter stating what I had told him telephonically and cced it to JS (Europe West division) Daulat Singh in MEA. The latter acted on it more forcefully than I had expected. He instructed HCI, London not to issue visas to this theatre group until he issued the clearance for them. When the British High Commissioner Sir Robert Wade-Gery learnt about this from the mentioned theatre group he requested an urgent meeting with

Foreign Secretary Rasgotra. He came accompanied by his Counsellor (Culture), the BC Director. As instructed by FS, JS (EW) and I came to his office earlier with the relevant files. Sir Robert expressed great surprise and unhappiness that visas for this 'outstanding theatre group' had been blocked despite his government's unstinted support for India's FOI in UK. He alleged that ICCR had 'deliberately stalled' this theatre group's tour of India for 'unknown reasons'. FS responded that his information on this matter was quite the contrary. He told me to show Sir Robert the letter I had written to his Counsellor (Culture) two weeks earlier. The HC was greatly surprised to see this letter as his Counsellor (Culture) had neither shown nor informed him about it. He conveyed this to FS and apologized for his earlier unkind remarks about ICCR. He assured him that no corporate sponsorships would hereafter be availed of for their cultural presentations in India and requested that this theatre group's visas be issued earliest possible so that their already scheduled tour of India could take place. FS agreed to this, but as previously urged by JS (EW) and me, stated that since the United Spirts Logo had been printed on the tickets for this group's performances they would have to be replaced with new tickets without this logo. Sir Robert was taken aback by this but had no option but to agree.

As Sir Robert and his Counsellor (Culture) left FS's office and JS (EW) and I followed them we heard him tell the latter sternly that he would 'pay a heavy price' for the 'acute embarrassment he had suffered' in the Foreign Secretary's office. Three days later I learnt from a BHC Indian official that Sir Robert had cabled London for his Counsellor (Culture)'s immediate recall. He left New Delhi three weeks later but meanwhile had to handle the onerous task of getting new tickets printed and exchanging them for those previously sold at New Delhi, Calcutta and Bombay.

The third battle was with MEA and my revered mentor Foreign

Secretary Rasgotra. In the months after I took over as DG (ICCR), I found that all its foreign cultural centres, not so many at that time, were being manned either by young IFS officers or academicians. Even its two top posts of DG and DDG were being manned by IFS officers. ICCR officers/staff's chances of promotion were therefore practically nil. In view of this I insisted that all ICCR cultural centres abroad should be headed by its officers. JS (Admin Div) and FS pointed out that ICCR was funded by MEA and yet I, an IFS officer, was objecting to my junior colleagues being posted to these centres. I responded that as DG (ICCR) my prime concern was the morale and welfare of ICCR staff. Fortunately, they both appreciated my stand and yielded. From 1983 onwards ICCR's cultural centres began to be headed by its officers. This greatly enthused not only those posted abroad but also those at New Delhi, who now began to get long-hoped for promotions.

I escaped death by a 'hair's breadth' in my third year at ICCR. An Indo–US Sub Commission on Education and Culture meeting was held at University of California in Los Angeles, 18-21 June 1985. The Indian delegation was led by Mr G. Parthasarathy and included Smt Kapila Vatsyayan, Narayana Menon, Jayant Narlikar and myself. After this fruitful meeting we were to fly from LA to New York and take the Air India flight from there to New Delhi. On the previous morning Mr Parthasarathy learnt that the June 22 AI flight from New York landed at Bombay whereas the AI flight from Toronto landed in New Delhi. Keen to land in New Delhi and avoid the longer flight via Bombay he requested me to get our tickets changed from the ex-New York to the ex-Toronto AI flight. So I went to the LA AI office with our tickets and requested this change. The AI ticket salesgirl was willing to make this change but suggested that we board the Toronto–New Delhi flight in London rather than in Toronto. She pointed out that the AI flights from New York and Toronto arrive at Heathrow airport about the same time and are parked next to each other. Moving us and our baggage from one plane to the other is easily done. I promptly accepted this excellent suggestion and she reissued our tickets and also issued our boarding passes: Flight 102 New York–London and Flight 182 London– Delhi.

AI flight 102 arrived in London as scheduled. We were received by AI airport manager Derek Kyte and escorted to the AI VIP lounge. He assured us that our baggage would be offloaded from flight 102 and loaded onto flight 182 soon after it lands and that he would return to escort us to it when its boarding commenced. He came back about 30 minutes later, beckoned me from outside the lounge and when I got to him softly confided that AI Flight 182 which departed Toronto 90 minutes late had made a steady flight across the Atlantic but had 'disappeared from the radar' about 20 minutes ago, which was a cause for concern. He requested me to keep this information 'strictly confidential' and promised to return when he had 'verified factual information'. So when I re-entered the lounge the only information I conveyed to Mr Parthasarathy and other members of our group was that Flight 182 had been delayed by 90 minutes. About 20 minutes later Peter Mahta, AI Regional Manager in New York, and Derek Kyte arrived and broke the dreadful news that, AI Flight 182, the 'Kanishka', had crashed off Ireland's southwest coast an hour ago. We were all stunned, and must have been among the first few Indians to learn about this abominable terrorist act.

The 23 June 1985 Kanishka crash in which all its 329 passengers and 22 crew were killed is the worst airline disaster in civil aviation history. The bomb which triggered it was smuggled onto this plane at Toronto airport by a Canadian Khalistani group named Babbar Khalsa. It had been timed to go off 30 minutes AFTER this flight took off from London as it would then have been fully loaded. The bomb exploded 30 minutes BEFORE this flight landed at Heathrow because it departed Toronto 90 minutes later than scheduled!

Though I was providentially saved for my family and ICCR, the Kanishka crash plucked Shashi Tripathi from ICCR and sent her to Ottawa where a new post of Counsellor (Community Affairs) was created at HCI. She left ICCR in late July 1985. Her departure was a great loss and created a huge void in it. She had been the ever-smiling, motivational and monitoring presence in it who had taken great pains to streamline its administration, alienate corruption, update confidential reports and set up promotion panels. With her departure the 'potent Alan Nazareth-Shashi Tripathi managerial magic wand', which had transformed ICCR from a lethargic, low wattage cultural body into the strong arm of India's cultural diplomacy was broken, and what many old timers still describe as ICCR's 'Golden Age', came to an end.

Three months later, an unexpected family calamity led to my sudden departure from ICCR. My 17-year-old son Andy, who had been complaining of constant pain in his left knee which the usual CGHS (Central Government Health Scheme) medications had not relieved, was taken to AIIMS (All India Institute of Medical Sciences), and was diagnosed to have a malignant tumour in it. This was subsequently confirmed by Tata Memorial Hospital, Bombay. Dr Dave of AIIMS strongly recommended that Andy be taken to and treated at Sloan Kettering Hospital in New York. The only way I could do this was by being posted to an Indian Mission in the US. Fortunately, Foreign Secretary Romesh Bhandari (Mr Rasgotra had retired in January 1985 and been appointed as HC to the UK) promptly obliged by posting me as CG at CGI Chicago. A week thereafter, having hurriedly packed our belongings, closed down our D2-102 Moti Bagh House and entrusted our daughters Premila and Seema to my sister Margaret's care, Isobel, Andy and I left New Delhi for New York on 20 October (1985).

I was deeply touched that besides Margaret and senior ICCR officers who came to Palam airport see us off, the Ambassador of Colombia Nelly Turbay de Munoz also graciously did so. Some years later she retired as Colombia's Foreign Secretary.

We only had economy class tickets but the Air India Regional Manager, having learnt the reason for my sudden departure to New York, kindly upgraded all three of us to business class. This made our flight there more comfortable than we had expected but not less brimful of anxiety.

11

A Frozen Lake in Chicago and a Miracle in New York

(October 1985–September 1986/ October 1986–July 1989)

We arrived in New York on 20 October, 1985. Consul General Arun Patwardhan kindly invited us to stay at his 200 East End Avenue residence. The next morning, accompanied by his wife Suhas, Isobel, Andy and I went to Sloan Kettering Hospital where we met Dr Manjit Bains, the senior physician. He was warm and friendly; so was the ambience in the hospital, where all the walls were painted in bright colours and soothing music was softly played. This raised our spirits.

Dr Bains examined Andy and the biopsy report of Tata Memorial Hospital, Bombay. He prescribed eight weeks of chemotherapy prior to surgery, which he scheduled for 19 December.

On 23 October I flew to Chicago and took charge as CG there.

The office was well located but was small and in an old building soon to undergo renovation. Besides, we were required to vacate it by 31 December. I was fortunate in finding a slightly bigger office, in a newly constructed building on the same North Michigan Avenue. It was closer to East Randolph Street where the CG's residence was located, Grant Park, Field Museum and Lake Michigan.

I returned to New York on 18 December to be present there during Andy's surgery. This was performed by Dr Ralph Marcove, a renowned Sloane Kettering surgeon. It took about three hours. Dr Marcove informed us that Andy had stood it well, that the malignant tumour in his left knee had been completely excised and a titanium prosthesis inserted in replacement of his left knee. Isobel and I were greatly relieved to learn this. However, on the morning of the third day, he had a fever. His temperature, which at 8 a.m was 100.2°F, at noon was 102.8°F and 8 p.m. was 104.4°F. When Dr Marcove came to examine Andy at 9 p.m. I told him of our great concern and had hoped he would allay it. Instead, he also expressed concern as the fever could be due to only one of three reasons: an infection, which in view of Sloane Kettering's meticulous hygiene was quite unlikely: Influenza, but no such case has been reported in the hospital's vicinity; or Andy's body rejecting the implanted prosthesis. If the last-mentioned had caused the fever his left leg would have to be amputated to save his life. He added that he would have Andy's left leg minutely monitored for the next 24 hours and then decide on what to do. Isobel and I were greatly shocked and prayed incessantly that night to the Infant Jesus, Mother of Perpetual Succour and St Joseph to save Andy's leg and life.

That afternoon, a young man named Fred Schwartz had come to Andy's room in the paediatric ward, to distribute 'yuletide' gifts. When he learnt we were Indians he informed us that he had recently converted from Judaism to Christianity and now worked as a volunteer in Mother Teresa's Home for AIDS patients in the Bronx. We told him that we knew her from our days in Peru and that I had assisted in having her 'Home' in Lima opened in September 1973.

By an amazing and providential coincidence Mother Teresa arrived in New York that afternoon from Caracas en route to Calcutta and made a transit halt for that night at her Home for AIDS Patients in the Bronx. The following morning Fred Schwartz met her and conveyed that an Indian family whose son had undergone surgery at Sloane Kettering knew and remembered her fondly. She asked for this family's name. When he gave it as Nazareth she remembered even though 12 years had elapsed since she had met us. She came to Sloane Kettering at 11 a.m. that morning and requested the receptionist to meet the 'Nazareth patient'. As she was well known and widely revered after President Ronald Reagan had honoured her with the Presidential Medal of Freedom in June that year, the receptionist immediately telephoned the hospital Director and head nurse and informed them of this VIP visitor. They soon arrived and accompanied her to Andy's room. Isobel and Andy were stunned to see her and the others entering it. Sadly, I was not there. Having stayed awake the whole of the previous night keeping watch over Andy, I had returned to the Patwardhan home at 7a.m. for some sleep and a shower, before returning to the hospital by noon.

According to Isobel, Mother Teresa after greeting her and patting Andy on the cheeks, prayed over him intensely with her eyes closed for about three minutes, then made him recite a short prayer to Infant Jesus with her and told him 'If you have full faith and trust in Jesus and He wills it, you will soon be well'. She patted him again on his cheeks, briefly held Isobel's hands in her own, smiled at her and left.

Amazingly, by 4 p.m. that day Andy's fever began to decline; by 8 p.m. it was 102.4°F and was normal by 8 a.m. the next morning. As amazingly, when the pre-discharge from hospital medical tests were made five days later, they indicated 'absence of malignant cells'. The pathologist, Dr Bains and even Dr Marcove acknowledged this was 'unusual' as normally there were 3-5 per cent remnant malignant cells at the time of discharge because of which mild doses of chemotherapy are administered for four weeks thereafter.

Three days after Andy's discharge from Sloane Kettering Isobel brought him to Chicago. We had a modest New Year lunch at my fifth floor East Randolph Street apartment, which had a fine view of Grant Park (now called Millennium Park) and Lake Michigan.

The following morning, when we came into the front balcony we saw a strange and unusual sight. Lake Michigan appeared to be boiling for it was emanating 'steam'. As we kept gazing at it in wonder it began to assume a slight sheen which then kept becoming stronger. A neighbour then told us that the surface of the lake was now frozen. Three days later we saw many people, young and old, skating and cycling on it! This was the first time we witnessed the phenomenon of a lake in the process of being frozen.

I give hereunder highlights of the 10 months I spent in Chicago.

I was inducted as an honorary member of the historic Rotary One club (in which Rotary was born in 1905), thanks to an NRI friend, who was a Rotary One office-bearer.

I had the privilege of being received by Nobel Laureate S. Chandrasekhar, who was the Morton D. Hull Distinguished Service Professor of Theoretical Astrophysics at University of Chicago. I hosted a dinner in his honour which was attended by the Norwegian, British, French, Canadian and Japanese Consuls General. He greatly appreciated this.

I induced The Field Museum of Natural History to present the reputed Odissi dancer Sanjukta Panigrahi (who was coming to Chicago at that time) at its April 1986 fundraising gala dinner.

When my mother came to Chicago in early May 1986, among the many places I took her to on weekend sightseeing trips was an

American Indian reservation at Lac du Flambeau in Wisconsin. On discovering that I was the Consul General of India in Chicago, the chief of this reservation decided to honour me with a 'Pow Wow'. This turned out to be three hours of vigorous drumming, singing and dancing around a large campfire at which two sheep and many wild fowl were roasted and served to the guests and members of this tribe. A wide variety of whiskeys and wines (all tax free!) were liberally served. For all of us, particularly my mother and our three children, this 'pow wow' was an exciting and memorable experience.

When Zubin Mehta came to Chicago in early August 1986 to conduct the Chicago Symphony Orchestra at that year's Ravinia Festival (the oldest outdoor festival in the US) Isobel and I were invited to it and treated as his 'Honoured Guests'.

As Arun Patwardhan was completing his three-year term as CG in New York in September 1986 and Andy's quarterly monitoring at Sloane Kettering was to go on till December 1987, I requested External Affairs Minister Bali Ram Bhagat, when he visited Chicago in mid-August 1986, for a transfer to New York, which he kindly agreed to.

I decided to make the move to CGI New York by rail via Los Angeles and Washington rather than by air. En route we made two-day halts at Flagstaff (to visit the Grand Canyon), at Los Angeles (to visit Disneyland) and Washington (to view its iconic monuments and make my formal call on Ambassador K.S. Bajpai). It turned out to be a most enjoyable and memorable trip.

I took charge as CG at CGI New York on 30 September (1986). Arun Patwardhan, Suhas and their daughter Samhita left for India the same evening. Their son Rishi who was studying at Phillips Exeter Academy in New Hampshire stayed on in the US to complete his studies. As requested by his parents we gladly agreed to be his local guardians.

My first official engagement as CG in New York was to attend the installation of a Gandhi statue in George Washington Square on 2 October 1986. Among those present at this event were Manhattan Borough President David Dinkins (who four years later became Mayor of New York), Bayard Rustin (Martin Luther King associate), Kantilal Patel (sculptor of this statue) and Mohan Murjani, the wealthy NRI who had paid for it. On its conclusion I proposed to Mr Dinkins that an annual march be instituted from the UN Building to this statue on 2 October, in a symbolic global homage to the Mahatma. He commended and agreed to this proposal. The first march, organized in collaboration with PMI (Permanent Mission of India to the UN), FIA (Federation of Indian Associations) and Bharatiya Vidya Bhavan, was held on 2 October 1987. Mr David Dinkins, Ambassador Chinmaya Gharekhan, our Permanent Representative to UN, and I led it in that year and the following one. As far as I am aware this march continued to be held for at least 10 years thereafter.

In August 1987, Ambassador Gharekhan and I jointly organized a concert at the UN with participation of renowned violinists Yehudi Menuhin and L. Subramaniam, in celebration of the 40th anniversary of India's independence. Among those who attended it were Governor of Ohio Richard Celeste, New York Mayor Ed Koch and the Permanent Representatives and Consul Generals of about 30 countries, all of whom greatly appreciated it. This was the first such celebration at the UN of a member country's Independence Day.

Other highlights of my tenure as CG NY are the following:

CGI's five-page, cyclostyled, visa and passport application form, which had a 'signature or thumb impression' box on its last page was replaced with a single page, printed application form. On the back of it, essential requirements for issue of visas and passports, CGI's working hours, holidays, and telephone numbers were printed along with Air India's 'Fly to India by Air India' slogan. Because of the last-mentioned insertion Air India paid for the design/printing of these new forms.

CGI's outdated telephone exchange was replaced with a new one with many more lines. Consular section officers/staff were instructed that whenever any person was greatly upset because of a visa or passport delayed or denied he/she should be sent to me. This had a salutary effect. The upset person was pleasantly surprised to be dealt with by the CG himself and the latter learnt the root cause of his/her problem and could rectify it.

The most notable outcome of this policy came from an enraged Boston-based NRI software engineer named Rom Narayan. He had been 'kept waiting on the telephone for almost 10 minutes' just to be told his 'passport was being dealt with'. I explained to him that such delays occur because CGI's Passport and Visa (PV) section was not computerized and all its services were manually handled, which takes time. If this section was computerized his query would have been responded to within a minute. I then told him, 'You are a software engineer. Would you assist us in computerizing this section?' I was stunned when he promptly replied, 'Yes, I can and will design a software for this.' So I invited him to stay with me on his next visit to New York and when he came I took him to the PV section where Consul (PV) gave him a detailed briefing on how passport and visa applications were processed/issued and passports then returned to applicants personally or by certified mail. He made notes of what he had been told and indicated he would come back within a month with a software to meet our requirements. Three weeks later he returned and told me that he had created this software and was giving it to CGI, 'not free of cost but for US$1 and on condition that it would not be shared with any other consulate'. I thanked him very much for this, agreed to his contractual terms and presented him with a shawl.

Soon thereafter CGI hired a computer and Rom Narayan returned to install his software in it and ensure it functioned as intended. The transformation it brought about in our PV work was amazing. The applicant only needed to give his/her father's name and date of birth and in a few seconds was told whether the passport had been received/actioned and if so, the date/post office receipt number of its dispatch. This software also enabled us to tabulate the place of birth, addresses, telephone numbers and professions of all passport/visa applicants at CGI New York and thus create a valuable database about them. Its computerized PV services were formally inaugurated by Ambassador P.K. Kaul when he came to New York about a month later. A *PTI* news report about it was carried by India's leading national newspapers.

To give CGI an intellectual and cultural dimension the following steps were taken:

In collaboration with Bharatiya Vidya Bhavan, free of charge bi-weekly Sanskrit classes were started in CGI.

An India Forum was instituted and whenever an Indian VIP or renowned author came to New York, he/she was requested to speak at it and professors/researchers on India at Columbia, New York, Princeton, Rutgers and Yale universities invited to hear and interact with them.

In collaboration with Lotus Music & Dance Studio (LMDS) Bharatanatyam classes were provided at CGI on Saturdays 10 a.m.–1 p.m. Those who availed of them paid the modest fee charged by LMDS directly to it.

The *Darshan,* a monthly journal which Consul General P.P. D'Souza (Arun Patwardhan's predecessor) had launched but had ceased publication after his departure, was revived. Thirty issues of it were brought out with articles from reputed Indian and American scholars on important Indian and Indo-US issues. Its mailing list included Senators, Congressmen, Governors, university libraries and presidents of Indian community organizations in the states which CGI New York serviced.

I visited all the 12 North Eastern States in CGI jurisdiction and called on their Governors. Those of New York (Mario Cuomo), Massachusetts (Michael Dukakis) and Ohio (Richard Celeste) became good friends. The last mentioned had spent two years in India at the US Embassy in New Delhi and two of his children were born there. When I went to Columbus to make my farewell call on him in June 1989 he invited me to stay with him at State House. He later served for many years as President of Colorado College in Boulder. We are still in touch with each other.

In January 1988 I was elected president of the Society of Foreign Consuls (SFC) of New York. It is the largest consular corps in the world. It has an annual ball at which its members and their wives danced with each other until midnight, enjoyed a sumptuous dinner and went home. I proposed to its office-bearers that the 1988 Ball be made a fundraiser for Habitat for Humanity (HH) and former President Jimmy Carter, who is much involved with HH, be invited as Chief Guest. They somewhat reluctantly agreed to this proposal. The HH Director was then informed that SFC's 1988 Ball was being made a fundraiser for HH, and requested to induce ex-President Carter to attend it as Chief Guest. He responded three weeks later and indicated that former President Carter was happy that SFC was making its 1988 Ball a fundraiser for HH, and would be glad to attend it. He also informally conveyed that SFC would have to ensure that this fundraiser ball raised at least US$50,000.

Among the first steps taken by SFC office-bearers was to get NYC real estate tycoon Mr Richard LeFrak to be chairman of the Ball Committee and Ms Phylicia Rashad ('Mrs Bill Cosby' of the TV serial) to emcee the event. Thereafter VIPs I knew personally were requested to attend this ball. Those who responded favourably were Governor Richard Celeste and Mrs Celeste, Mrs Matilda Cuomo (wife of New York Governor Mario Cuomo), Princess Irene (sister of Queen Sofia of Spain and president of World in Harmony), Mr

David Dinkins, Manhattan Borough president, Mrs Gillian Sorensen, NYC Commissioner (Diplomatic/Consular Corps). President Ronald Reagan graciously sent a message which I was privileged to read out during the Ball's formal commencement ceremony.

The amount raised/donated to Habitat for Humanity through ex-President Carter was US$145,000! This and the VVIP participation in it made this the most impactful of all SFC balls until then. Two photos taken at it and the message which President Reagan sent for it are included in this book.

Prime Minister Rajiv Gandhi visited New York twice during my tenure as CG New York. The first was in early October 1987 when he transited New York en route to Boston and Washington on his first official visit to the US; the second was in June 1988 to deliver his historic address at the UN General Assembly's Third Special Session on Disarmament.

Six weeks prior to Prime Minister's latter visit his Principal Security Officer (PSO) came to New York to assess the security arrangements we had made for this visit. On the following morning, he barged into my room without even a knock on the door, and bluntly asserted that these arrangements were 'absurd'. I pointed out they had been made exactly as stipulated in the latest MEA Security Manual. He rudely countered, 'You have designated a Sikh officer as Chief Security Officer (CSO).' I was astounded but firmly stated he was the Deputy Consul General, in whose integrity and ability to handle this onerous responsibility I had full confidence. Rudely again he asked, 'Recall who assassinated Prime Minister Indira Gandhi.' This angered me and I coldly replied 'Two of her security guards.' This enraged him and he snapped 'You are being impertinent. You better appoint some other CSO immediately.' I replied 'Please give this to me in writing. If and when you do so, I will go on leave for if an able and upright Sikh Deputy Consul General cannot be trusted, a Christian Consul

General might also be a grave security risk.' On hearing this, he stormed out of my room with the same swagger with which he had entered it, muttering 'You will soon hear from MEA.' The threatened bombshell never arrived. The Prime Minister's visit was made, without a single hitch, with the same security arrangements we had made, and the same 'Sikh officer' (Pripuran Singh Haer) as CSO.

On his previous visit Prime Minister Rajiv Gandhi addressed the Harvard University Graduate Students Union and then flew to Washington. (As Boston was in CGI NY jurisdiction all arrangements for his visit and meetings there were made by us in coordination with EI Washington and the US and Massachusetts security agencies.) His most important meeting there was with Governor Michael Dukakis, (then on the campaign trail in California as Democratic Party nominee for the 1988 Presidential election). This was arranged by me and took strenuous efforts to achieve.

His Harvard address was stimulating both for intellectual content and the animated, friendly interaction between him and the students. The great admiration of him, particularly by the female students, was clearly visible.

The meeting with Governor Dukakis was notable for two reasons. He flew all the way from Los Angeles to Boston and back, five hours each way, for this 45-minute meeting with PM! Both being young and dynamic they established a good rapport and spoke about their aspirations and plans for their respective countries. If the Governor had won the presidential election he was then campaigning for, India-US relations might have warmed up earlier than they did.

Soon after this meeting, the Prime Minister flew to Washington and the Governor to Los Angeles. I had the great privilege to travel to Washington in PM's special plane. It was an exhilarating and memorable experience. The PM was completely relaxed and even bantered with the air hostesses, one of whom teased him that the 'flutter' the plane had had soon after it took off was because it was 'gasping for breath over his good looks'. On that flight it was difficult to believe he was Prime Minister of India. He was more like a renowned film star among his doting fans!

On 9 September 1988 we received the shocking news that Ambassador Arun Patwardhan, his wife Suhas and son Rishi were killed in a Vietnamese Airlines plane crash at Bangkok airport. Rishi had gone to Hanoi, where Arun was Ambassador, to spend his summer holidays. The crash occurred when the plane in which Arun and Suhas were accompanying Rishi (to see him off to New York) was caught in a thunderstorm when coming in to land at Bangkok airport.

As Arun and Suhas had been extremely supportive to us during Andy's surgery and hospitalization at Sloane Kettering in December 1985, their and Rishi's tragic deaths were emotionally shattering for Isobel and me. I organized a condolence meeting at CGI to which Consul Generals who knew them well and office-bearers of Indian Associations in New York and neighbouring states were invited. Many of them paid moving tributes to him and Suhas. When I was paying my tribute I was so emotionally overcome that I could not complete it.

In early June 1989, I received intimation about my appointment as Ambassador of India to Egypt.

In July, two Enforcement Directorate officers from New Delhi called on me and requested authentication of an 'important document', which they then handed over to me. It was the **customer copy** of a bank account opened in the First Trust Corporation Bank in St. Kitts, (a Caribbean Island) in the name of Mr Ajeya Singh and V.P. Singh. I scrutinized it and told them that I could not authenticate it for the following reasons:

1. It was a **customer copy**, which only the customers named therein could request authentication of.

2. CGI NY jurisdiction included the Virgin Islands but not St. Kitts

which was serviced by EI, Washington.

The ED officers were surprised and disappointed by my response and requested to speak to JS (PMO) from my office. They reported my unhelpful attitude to him and got him to speak to me. He (an IFS colleague!) tried to induce me to 'do the needful' as it was a small but important matter, but I firmly refused. So these ED officers had to go to EI Washington and get this document authenticated there.

In October 1989, *Arab Times* carried a news report that Ajeya Singh, son of V.P. Singh (former Finance Minister who had quit Prime Minister Rajiv Gandhi's Cabinet following the Bofors scandal), had opened a US$21-million bank account in First Trust Corporation Bank in St Kitts, in the joint names of himself and his father V.P Singh. This report was immediately lapped up by the Indian news media. Nonetheless V.P. Singh won the December 1989 National elections and became Prime Minister. A CBI enquiry was then initiated about this account. Nine months later, CBI filed criminal cases against Enforcement Director K.L. Verma, 'Godman' Chandraswami, his associate Larry J. Kolb (Adnan Kashoggi's son-in-law), and George McLean, First Trust Corporation's managing director, for falsely implicating V.P. Singh!

As we left for Cairo, Isobel, Seema and I travelled by the QE 2 from New York to Southampton, and from there by train to London, Zurich, Vienna and Athens, from where we flew to Cairo. In Vienna we spent three days with Ambassador Peter Sinai at India House. These were joyful and memorable as Peter and Rowena took us to many iconic sites of that historic city as also to Richard Strauss' *Rosenkavalier* at the Vienna Opera House.

12

In the Land of the Sphinx and Pyramids

(September 1989–August 1992)

I arrived in Cairo on 6 September 1989. India House here is a grand and imposing mansion located on the west bank of the Nile, in the heart of Cairo. It is also historic as VVIPs like Prime Minister Jawaharlal Nehru have stayed in it and President Gamal Abdel Nasser has attended meetings in it. It has always been well maintained. However, the EI Chancery building, also located on west bank of the Nile close to the Marriott Hotel, was in a dilapidated condition. Besides, its owner, Mr Mohammed Maher Abaza (Minister for Electricity in the Egyptian government) was pressing for it to be vacated and relations with him were strained.

About a month after my arrival in Cairo, I called on Minister Abaza. He was courteous but sullen. When I asked him why he was so keen on our vacating it despite Egypt's historic ties with India, he initially stated he wished to renovate and live in it but later admitted he wished to sell it. At this point I proposed that he sell it to GOI. He replied that it was unlikely to afford or be willing to pay its market value. I informed him that GOI owned some of the finest Embassy residences in many countries. I also told him GOI can and will make payment in US Dollars or British Pounds. This aroused his interest but it took three more meetings with him over the next six months before he finally agreed to sell this building to GOI and the US$1.2 million for it was mutually agreed. The sale deed was finally signed in June 1990 and the mentioned price paid to him through State Bank of India, New York. Soon thereafter this building was renovated and repainted. Many old timers could hardly recognize it as its exterior had not been repainted for over 10 years!

In early August 1990, our Ministry of Education requested us to induce Al-Azhar University (AAU) to depute 10 Arabic lecturers to India. Rather than make this request via the Egyptian Foreign Office, I decided to call on its Grand Sheikh, His Eminence Gad Al Haq. As the father of one of our Egyptian staff worked in his office this call was promptly scheduled.

When I entered the Grand Sheikh's elegant, wood panelled office I was pleasantly surprised to see a large, glass-enclosed silver sculpture of Lord Krishna and Arjuna on a four-horse chariot. So soon after His Eminence had welcomed me I commented on this exquisite sculpture and mentioned that it depicted the prime episode in India's renowned *Mahabharata* epic. He responded with an embarrassed smile, 'I do not know what it is. It was presented to me by the President of Indonesia.' I was amazed. The President of the world's largest Islamic country had presented the world's most revered Islamic cleric an exquisite silver sculpture of Lord Krishna and Arjuna! This was clear testimony of India's deep and enduring cultural impact on Indonesia and of that country's thoroughly secular outlook.

His Eminence readily agreed to our request for 10 Arabic lecturers but stated that India should reciprocate by sending to Al-Azhar 10 lecturers in the agricultural, engineering and legal fields. The latter surprised me as it was my impression that AAU was an Islamic university-cum-seminary which focused on theological teaching and research. This was the first time I learnt that it also had most other faculties of other reputed universities. I thanked His Eminence for his favourable response regarding the Arabic teachers and suggested that AAU send a delegation to India from its agricultural/engineering/legal faculties to meet their counterparts in reputed Indian universities and then decide from which of them they would like to receive lecturers. His Eminence welcomed this idea.

The latter proposal moved at a snail's pace but the AAU delegation finally visited India between 26 March and 6 April 1992. It was composed of its Vice President for Post Graduate Studies and Research and Deans of its faculties of Engineering and Islamic Law. They visited/interacted with Vice Chancellors of JNU (Jawaharlal Nehru University), Jamia Millia, AMU (Aligarh Muslim University), IARI (Indian Agricultural Research Institute), Indian Institute of Technology-Delhi, and CIEFL (Central Institute of English and Foreign Languages)/Osmania University at Hyderabad. On conclusion of this visit, an MoU was signed whereby AAU would increase its intake of scholarships for Indian students/researchers in Arabic language and Islamic studies and send Arabic lecturers to JNU, AMU and Osmania universities. The UGC (University Grants Commission) would reciprocate by sending lecturers/researchers in the Agricultural/Engineering/Legal and Advanced Computing fields. This was the first MoU that AAU had signed with UGC.

An Organisation of Islamic Cooperation (OIC) Conference of Foreign Ministers was held at Cairo, 31 July–5 August, 1990. Its prime focus was on adopting an Islamic Declaration on Universal Human Rights. Just 10 days before it was to be inaugurated I learnt from a good friend (an Egyptian diplomat who had served in India) in President Mubarak's office that Pakistan PM Benazir Bhutto (who had visited Cairo and called on President Mubarak a few weeks earlier) was pressing for Kashmir to be discussed at this conference as a Human Rights issue. I immediately requested calls on Foreign Secretary Amre Moussa. and Foreign Minister Esmat Abdel Meguid. Both of them received me and I urged them that the mentioned Pakistani move should be firmly resisted. They assured me this would be done but the latter advised that I should contact Ambassadors of OIC countries friendly to India and mobilize their support.

Because of time constraints I could only meet the Bangladeshi, Indonesian, Jordanian and Palestinian Ambassadors. So I made a detailed note on the Kashmir dispute, pertinent UN resolutions, Pakistan's non-compliance with them, and Jammu and Kashmir Constituent Assembly's endorsement of its rulers' accession to India. Sixty copies of this note were printed and delivered by EI staff to all OIC member embassies (except Pakistan). Copies of it were also delivered to the offices of the Egyptian President, Foreign Minister and Foreign Secretary and editors of leading newspapers/TV channels. Some of the last mentioned published/telecast extracts from this note.

The Saudi Foreign Minister Saud bin Faisal reacted to this by declaring at a press conference: 'If India has such a strong case on Kashmir why does it not hold a plebiscite there?' A *Gulf Times* reporter telephoned me for my reaction to this. I told him 'The Saudi Foreign Minister should practice what he preaches and ensure an election is held in his own country.' This riposte was published by that newspaper as also by the *Egyptian Gazette*.

Foreign Secretary Amre Moussa complimented me on the note I had circulated, and described it as a 'perfectly-timed ballistic strike!' He mentioned that the Pakistani Foreign Minister had ruefully told him that their Ambassador had been 'outmanoeuvred by the hyperactive Indian Ambassador'.

Six weeks later, at a Chinese embassy reception, I met the Pakistani Ambassador's wife, a charming, well-educated Baluchi lady. She had recently arrived in Cairo. So I asked her how she was enjoying Cairo, she responded with a smile, 'I am enjoying it but my husband is not, as you are constantly creating trouble for him!'

On 2 August 1990, Iraq's shocking invasion and occupation of Kuwait took place. Soon thereafter Cairo became the hub of political activity in view of Egypt's importance as the largest and most influential Arab country and the Arab League's location there. The American, British and French Ambassadors were even more active than the Kuwaiti Ambassador. It soon became clear that these four countries as also Egypt and Saudi Arabia much preferred military to diplomatic action to secure Iraq's withdrawal from Kuwait. In view of India's traditional peacemaker role, my strenuous effort was to highlight Iraq's offer to withdraw from Kuwait if certain conditions were met. I formed a like-minded group of Ambassadors of Algeria, Jordan, Malaysia, Mexico, Sudan and Yugoslavia, which came to be known as the 'Peace Plotters', which met by rotation at each other's residences every weekend to keep track of latest developments.

On 12 October 1990 at about 11 a.m., the suave, Sorbonne-educated 64-year-old Speaker of Egypt's Parliament Rifaat al-Mahgoub was assassinated by two motorcycle-borne gunmen, near the five-star Semiramis hotel. He was Egypt's second most high-ranked State official at that time and had been Speaker since 1984. The previous high-level political assassination was that of President Anwar el-Sadat on 6 October 1981. I had called on Speaker Rifaat al-Mahgoub just three weeks earlier and handed over an invitation to him from the Lok Sabha Speaker to visit India later that year. I still have the nine-inch-long silver paper knife he presented me on this occasion.

President Hosni Mubarak blamed Iraqi and Sudanese 'terrorists' for this heinous act. However, it more likely was perpetrated by Egypt's own Muslim Brotherhood which was strongly opposed to President Mubarak's close collaboration with the US/UK/France in the impending military attack on Iraq, which it saw as a fellow Muslim and Arab country.

As the Muslim Brotherhood (MB) and its affiliates, Islamic Jihad and Gamma'a al Islamiya, were well entrenched in Sudan, and that country was strongly opposed to Egypt's close collaboration with the US, Britain and France, there was much concern in Cairo at this time over rumours that Sudan and MB were planning to blow up the Aswan Dam. If that happened many Egyptian cities and most of its archaeological treasures would have been washed away by the tsunami of Nile waters released. President Mubarak therefore issued a stern warning to Sudan that any such action would result in its total destruction by Egypt.

An important interaction I had at this time was at the Egyptian Diplomatic Academy where I was invited to speak on India and the Arab World. In the concluding part of my talk I brought up the Iraq–Kuwait issue and drew attention to India's history in the eighteenth and nineteenth centuries when European powers had instigated its princely states to war with each other and then took over all of India and impoverished it. When reports of this reached other diplomatic colleagues the Iraqi ambassador was pleased and grateful, but the American, British, French and Kuwaiti Ambassadors were quite unhappy. The British Ambassador cautioned me that my stand on this sensitive issue was 'indiscreet' and could damage India's close relations with Kuwait and Egypt. He must therefore have been quite surprised that when Operation Desert Storm was launched on 17 January 1991 and Egypt broke diplomatic relations with Iraq, both countries requested India to look after their interests in the 'other' country. A First Secretary of the former Iraqi Embassy in Cairo now became

First Secretary (Iraqi Interests) in EI Cairo! When I took him with me to the Foreign Office about a month later to discuss security for Iraqi properties in Egypt, the security officer at its entrance would not permit him to enter. I therefore requested to speak to Chief of Protocol Ambassador M. Samy Sabet on telephone. Being a good friend of mine he instructed the security officer to permit both of us to enter. He was also helpful regarding the matter we had gone to see him about but requested me courteously not to bring my 'First Secretary (Iraq Affairs)' to the Foreign Office hereafter as this causes 'consternation' at various levels within it.

On 28 February 1991, the 54,000-strong Egyptian contingent in the Desert Storm war disembarked at Port Suez. When they arrived in Cairo, they were given such an exuberant welcome that most ordinary Egyptians, unaware of the hi-tech, 'shock and awe' nature of this war, must have assumed it was these troops which had liberated Kuwait! But, not only was their contribution minimal it was also little valued as it became clear later that year. In the March 6, 1991 Damascus Declaration, Egypt and Syria had offered the six Gulf Cooperation Council (GCC) countries a 'security shield' with a large military contingent in return for economic assistance but some months thereafter the latter opted for the US/British 'Shield' which was far better equipped and had a smaller military contingent. This was a big disappointment to both these countries. An even bigger disappointment for the Egyptians was that all the major reconstruction contracts were awarded by Kuwait to US and UK firms. Tom Hundley wrote about this in the *Chicago Tribune* of 7 July 1991 under the title 'Egyptians abandoned by Gulf War allies'.

When I visited Alexandria in January 1991, to call on its recently-appointed Governor, I had gone to the Graeco-Roman Museum there. Its Asst. Director Ms Mervat Seif-el-Din who guided me through it took me to the 'South Asian Skulls' section and stated they were skulls of 'Indian Buddhist monks who had come to the ancient library of Alexandria during the Ptolemaic period to teach and to learn'. This triggered the idea of organizing an India-Egypt seminar on the lines of the India–Greece seminar at Delphi I had organized in 1984 as DG (ICCR). I mentioned it to Ms Mervat Seif-el-Din as also to Mr Mostafa Abbadi, Prof. Emeritus of Greek and Roman studies at Alexandria University. They both welcomed it and offered to identify reputed Egyptian scholars to participate in it. Egypt's Minister of Culture Farouk Hosny (an Alexandrian and previously Director, Egyptian Academy of Arts at Rome), on whom I called on soon thereafter, was equally supportive. So I wrote to DG (ICCR) Veena Sikri and proposed that ICCR collaborate with Egypt's Ministry of Culture in holding this seminar at Cairo. She kindly agreed to this.

This seminar was held at the Cairo Opera House 10-12 September 1991. The Indian delegation was led by Smt Najma Heptulla and included former Foreign Secretary T.N. Kaul, Metropolitan Paulos Mar Gregorios (scholar on Indian/Greek Monastic history), M.C. Joshi, DG Archaeological Survey of India, Saryu Doshi, Editor, *Marg* Publications, Geeti Sen, Art Historian, and Ismat Mehdi, Arabic Professor at the Central Institute of English and Foreign Languages at Hyderabad.

The Egyptian delegation was led by Minister of Culture Farouk Hosny and included Mostafa Abbadi, Sahar Abdul Aziz Salem, Lecturer of Islamic History at University of Alexandria and Ms Mervat Seif-el-Din of the Graeco-Roman Museum.

The inaugural address at this seminar, which lasted three days, was delivered by Egypt's Foreign Minister Amre Moussa.

This seminar got extensive coverage in the Egyptian print media particularly *The Egyptian Gazette* which published five half-page articles on it by its popular columnist Manal Abdul Aziz. Its most enduring outcome however is the elegant coffee table book titled *India and Egypt: Influences and Interactions* which *Marg* published in 1994. It was edited by Saryu Doshi, who in her Preface inter alia wrote 'To His Excellency Alan Nazareth, Indian Ambassador to Egypt 1989–1992 our very special thanks for his characteristically original approach in emphasizing culture as an important aspect of diplomacy. It was he who conceived the idea of a conclave on historical and cultural relations between India and Egypt and with indefatigable energy and zeal brought it to fruition with the generous collaboration of Egypt's Ministry of Culture.'

In mid-September (1991), Deputy Foreign Minister Boutros Boutros-Ghali telephoned and asked whether he could 'come for a cup of tea' at India House. I promptly invited him to do so. On arrival he revealed that President Mubarak had approved his candidature for the UN Secretary-General's post, which the incumbent Mr Perez de Cuellar was vacating at the end of 1991. It was now Africa's turn to occupy it but it was a large continent of diverse cultures and had many aspirants for this post. As the majority of its states were black they wanted a 'black'. Nonetheless, his chances were fairly good as France had assured him of its support and had promised to lobby for him with Francophone countries. India was widely respected by Africa's Non-Aligned and Commonwealth countries and also had high-level contacts in the UK. He would, therefore, much appreciate my inducing India's Prime Minister to support his candidature and induce Africa's Non-Aligned/Commonwealth countries and the UK government to do so. I promised to do my best on this. Fortunately, Prime Minister Narasimha Rao knew me quite well from my DG (ICCR) days, when he was Foreign Minister/Chairman (ICCR). So I conveyed Mr Boutros-Ghali's request directly to him by CCB telegram with CCs to FM and PR, PMI New York (who was Chinmaya Gharekhan, a good friend from my CGI New York days). By a fortunate coincidence he was to chair UN Security Council meetings in October, when the next

UNSG was to be elected.

Mr Boutros-Ghali won this election. He secured 11 votes in favour, four abstentions, Nil against. President Mubarak, Foreign Minister Amre Moussa, and senior MFA officials were very appreciative of India's strong and active support for their Deputy Minister Boutros-Ghali's candidature. I hosted a dinner in his honour before he left Cairo for New York. At it, he publicly thanked GOI, and me, for the valuable support he had received from us.

In early November (1991), a new Israeli Ambassador named Efraim Dofak arrived in Cairo. In sharp contrast to his predecessor, the sullen, unsmiling Shimon Samir, he was sociable and friendly. A few days after our first casual meeting at the US embassy, his secretary telephoned to request a call by him on me. As India had no diplomatic relations with Israel at that time I told my PS to inform her that he would revert when this call was scheduled. When I next met Ambassador Dofak at a British Embassy reception, I courteously informed him that I could not receive a formal call from him because India had no diplomatic relations with Israel. He gracefully accepted this. I reported this incident to JS (WANA) in MEA and enquired why India had not yet established diplomatic relations with Israel when Egypt, the largest Arab country, has had them since March 1979. In the same letter, I requested permission to make a five-day visit to Israel, to visit the Christian sacred sites there as a 'pilgrim'. It was Addl. Secretary (AD) I.P. Khosla who responded to my letter. He indicated that establishment of diplomatic relations with Israel was under active consideration and a decision on it was likely to be taken before long. In view of this he requested me to postpone my visit to Israel.

In mid-December 1991, our greatly revered former Ambassador/High Commissioner B.K. Nehru and Mrs Fori Nehru came to Cairo and spent five days with us at India House. They were returning to India from New York, where he had chaired a meeting of the UN

Pensions Committee. He said he had come to Cairo to see 'how good an Ambassador I was!' Their visit to and stay with us was a great joy and honour for Isobel and me and we did our best to make their stay with us comfortable and memorable for them. We took them to the 'Light and Sound' show at the Pyramids, on a Nile dinner cruise and a day trip to Alexandria. We also hosted a dinner in their honour to which I invited American Ambassador Frank Wisner (whose parents were their good friends during their EI Washington days) and Mrs Wisner. They were delighted to meet each other after many years.

As the September 1991 India–Egypt Seminar (IES) had generated much interest in India's history and culture, I proposed to MEA/ICCR that India Tea Board's 'India Tea House (ITH)' at Talaat Harb Street in downtown Cairo, which had been closed for over three years but its premises not yet released, be converted into an India Cultural Centre (ICC) and inaugurated during EAM Madhav Singh Solanki's visit to Cairo in January 1992. This proposal was promptly approved in view of the mentioned visit and a special grant sanctioned for renovation/conversion of the ITH building into an ICC. As requested by me MEA also sent Mrs Ismat Mehdi (the Arabic professor who had participated in the mentioned India–Egypt Seminar) as director of this centre. Named Maulana Azad Centre for Indian Culture (MACIC), it was jointly inaugurated by EAM Solanki and Egyptian Culture Minister Farouk Hosny on 14 January 1992. An exhibition of Rabindranath Tagore's paintings and drawings was also inaugurated by them on this occasion.

Just three weeks before MACIC was inaugurated, the Cairo International Film Festival took place. Amitabh Bachchan came for its closing ceremony. The excitement and mega crowds was incredible. I hosted a reception in his honour at India House. On that day there was a half-a-km throng of young women, on both sides of the road, just to see him drive by! The security squad deployed for his 'protection' was twice as large as that for the subsequent visit of EAM!

EAM Solanki had fruitful talks with President Mubarak, Prime Minister Atef Sedki, Deputy Prime Minister Agriculture Minister Youssef Wali, Foreign Minister Amre Moussa, Foreign Trade Minister Youssri Mustafa, and Arab League Secretary General Esmat Abdel-Meguid. All of them thanked him for India's support to their Deputy Foreign Minister Boutros-Ghali in the recent UNSG election.

The lunch I hosted for EAM Solanki was attended by the ministers for foreign affairs, agriculture, commerce, electricity and culture and the Arab League Secretary General.

About this visit, F.J. Khergamvala wrote in *The Hindu* (19 January 1992) under the title 'Back to the good old days in Cairo':

> Seldom could an External Affairs Minister's visit be packed with such content and planned so meticulously.... Mr. Solanki took back with him an Egyptian commitment on cooperation in security matters. This was clearly the result of both sides seeing eye to eye on terrorism and fanaticism.... India opened the Maulana Azad Cultural Centre and there were no half measures. The Ambassador prodded, New Delhi agreed and the Vice Chancellor of Rabindra Bharati University readily responded by himself being present to display 29 originals of Rabindranath Tagore's works. The cultural centre is located in the hub of Cairo not in some millionaire's suburb. Its Director is an elegant woman Arabic scholar from Hyderabad, not some politician's nephew-turned-bureaucrat.

As I was to complete my three-year term at EI Cairo in September 1992 and Ambassador Arjun Asrani was completing his tenure at EI Tokyo about the same time I requested EAM Solanki for Tokyo as my next post, as it would be my last, and Japanese was my IFS allotted language. His response was encouraging; he indicated that Foreign

Secretary J.N. Dixit had already proposed this to him and he had heard much praise for my work at EI Cairo. I therefore felt confident my keen desire to retire as Ambassador of India to Japan would be fulfilled. Sadly, a dramatic turn of events destroyed this prospect soon thereafter.

From Cairo EAM Solanki flew to Davos for the 1992 World Economic Forum. It was a historic one as the long imprisoned and recently released Nelson Mandela was addressing it. Other VVIP participants in it were Prince Charles of UK, President F.W. De Klerk of South Africa, President Vaclav Havel of Czechoslovakia, Chinese Premier Li Peng, and Henry Kissinger, former US Secretary of State.

During this meeting, EAM Solanki reportedly drew Swiss Foreign Minister René Felber aside and told him that thorough investigations by Indian agencies into the Bofors scam had revealed no wrongdoing and therefore Swiss assistance in this matter was no longer needed. He also handed over an unsigned memo to this effect. Unfortunately for him, a copy of this memo was faxed to Chitra Subramaniam, correspondent for *The Hindu* in Geneva, by one of her contacts in the Swiss Foreign Office. The story she filed and which *The Hindu* published triggered a political uproar in India. EAM Solanki initially refused to confirm or deny this story but on 10 April (1992), when a censure motion against him was introduced in Parliament by the BJP (Bharatiya Janata Party), he submitted his resignation.

On 29 January 1992 India finally announced its decision to establish diplomatic relations with Israel. A week later I received a letter from AS (AD). It was a pleasant surprise. After thanking me for postponing my previously planned visit to Israel he not only permitted me to make this visit now but also make it an official one by looking for suitable premises for the EI Chancery and Residence there, thus enabling me to make this journey in the EI Cairo flag car!

I decided to make this visit 15-20 April along with Isobel, so that we could attend Good Friday/Easter Sunday Services in Jerusalem, which that year were on 17 and 19 April.

As we were travelling by car, Israeli Ambassador Dofak (whose call on me I now gladly accepted!) had advised that the safer road to Jerusalem was via Suez/Eilat as the road via Rafah passed through Gaza where security was unpredictable. Nonetheless, I decided to take the latter route as it was shorter and I had only five days for this visit.

Ambassador Dofak kindly had our visas issued promptly and also sent us brochures on Israel's Christian sites. He also telexed Israel's Erez border post about our arrival there by car, on 15 April afternoon.

The road from Cairo to Rafah was excellent and in its latter part quite scenic as it was alongside the 'beautiful, blue Mediterranean'. Once we entered the Gaza strip the beauty vanished and poverty and squalor was everywhere. However, the people were friendly. Those who recognized us as Indians waved out to us and shouted 'Amitabh Bachchan'! When we finally arrived at the Erez border post we faced a quite unexpected problem.

The Immigration officers were warm and friendly but after examining our passports courteously pointed out to me, that though we had Israeli visas, our passports been stamped 'valid for all countries except Israel and South Africa'. I was shocked! Neither had I noticed this when I sent our passports to Ambassador Dofak nor he when Israeli visas were issued on them. It was 4 p.m. already and the Israel Foreign and Home offices would soon be closed for the day. One of the Immigration officers then asked, 'Ambassador Nazareth, do you know Zubin Mehta?' I confirmed this and indicated that as DG (ICCR), I had handled NYPO's 1984 tour of India which he had conducted. He perked up and stated 'Only he can solve this problem now.' He added that as his elder brother was a violinist in Israel Philharmonic Orchestra he too knew Zubin. He then telephoned him, briefed him about our problem and then passed the telephone to me. Zubin expressed great surprise at my predicament, recalled that in New York it was always he who needed my 'passport assistance' but promised to speak to the Israeli Foreign Minister and call me back. He did this in 20 minutes, stated that our entry into Israel had been approved and already intimated to the Erez border post. He then invited us to the concert he was conducting the next evening at Tel Aviv's Mann Auditorium and to dinner thereafter. I gladly and gratefully accepted this invitation. Soon thereafter we proceeded to Tel Aviv after profusely thanking the immigration officer who had thought of the 'Zubin solution' to our problem.

EI Cairo had booked our accommodation at Dan Hotel. We arrived there at about 8 p.m. on 15 April. The following morning (16 April) we drove to Bethlehem and Nazareth and returned to Tel Aviv for the lunch hosted by a friend of Ambassador Dofak at an Indian restaurant who then drove me through its Embassy and residential areas and gave me coordinates of its leading real estate agents.

At 6 p.m. that evening we drove to the imposing Mann auditorium. We were received by Zubin's secretary and escorted to his box. So we had a 'ringside seat' of him conducting Israel Philharmonic Orchestra (IPO)'s rendering of Andre Hajdu's *A Rhapsody on Jewish Themes* and Haim Zukerwar's *Concerto for Violin and String orchestra*. The encore was Beethoven's *Turkish March*. It was a most enjoyable concert.

The post-concert dinner was at a nearby Indian restaurant. There were 12 people at it. Amazingly, each of them, other than Zubin, Isobel and me was born in a different country—Argentina, Brazil, France, Germany, Mexico, Morocco, Russia, UK & USA! As we returned to our hotel that night I was struck by the thought that if it were not for the mentioned error in our passports we would not have had this memorable concert and dinner!

On 17 and 19 April (Good Friday and Easter Sunday) we went to the Garden of Gethsemane, walked the 'Via Dolorosa', and went to the Church of the Holy Sepulchre for the Good Friday service. On Easter Sunday after the 9 a.m. service at the Church of the Holy Sepulchre and lunch at a charming Greek restaurant close to it, we went to the 'Wailing Wall' sacred to the Jews and to the Dome of the Rock mosque, sacred for the Muslims.

I was deeply impacted by Jerusalem's sacredness to three great religions and the thought that it could become the world's prime venue for religious pilgrimage, inter-religious harmony and universal brotherhood if Israel would give up its insistence on being a 'Jewish state' and decide to be a secular state like India.

We left Tel Aviv the following morning (20 April) and arrived in Cairo by 6 p.m. In the official mail awaiting me was a sealed envelope marked 'Top Secret'. The telegram was from the Foreign Secretary and stated that President of India had approved my appointment as Ambassador of India to Yugoslavia! He then congratulated me 'on being given this important assignment'. These six words were deeply hurtful. Between June 1991 and April 1992 former Yugoslavia had been almost totally dismembered. Bosnia, Herzegovina, Croatia, Macedonia and Slovenia had declared independence and Serbia was at war with four of them. Even the historic Dubrovnik had been bombed and devastated. At the UN in New York strenuous efforts were being made to prevent Yugoslavia's tiny rump state of Serbia and Montenegro from occupying its UNGA seat. So I wrote to Foreign Secretary Dixit and Secretary to the President P. Murari (who was a good friend from our days together at New York, 1967-69) pointing out the injustice done to me, a senior Grade I Ambassador. Mr Murari wrote to Foreign Secretary and urged a review of this appointment. The latter now proposed that I be appointed High Commissioner to Canada. However, Prime Minister Narasimha Rao disagreed and decided that I should be sent 'south of the border down Mexico way!'

I left Cairo on 7 August 1992. As my farewell to Egypt I wrote an article titled 'Egypt in Indian Eyes' and sent it to the leading newspapers. Most of them carried it in full or abridged form. The full version carried by *Al-Ahram English Weekly* in its 6-12 August issue is included among the annexures in this book.

13

'La Magica de La India' in Mexico
(September 1992–April 1994)

Except for EI Lima which I opened, EI Mexico was the smallest mission I had served in during my entire IFS career. But it had been headed by eminent colleagues in the past. It had a well-located chancery. The residence, a modern, split-level building with a large inside garden, was close to the renowned Chapultepec Park. In Mexico City's highly polluted environment this was a big boon.

Though greatly disappointed on not being appointed Ambassador to Japan, I was happy to be in Mexico, an old civilization with diverse cultures and friendly, jovial people. Besides, I had three neighbouring countries—El Salvador, Guatemala and Belize—to tend as concurrent accreditation.

As I was to retire on 30 April 1994 and had only 19 months of service left, I decided that my 'swan song' should be impactful and long remembered in Mexico.

My first public but informal event (as I had not presented my credentials) was the wreath-laying ceremony at the Gandhi statue in Chapultepec Park on 2 October. Other than EI officers and staff, members of the small Indian community, there were only five Mexicans present among whom was Prof. Graciela de La Lama, Mexico's former Ambassador to India and subsequently to Egypt. On return to Mexico she had reassumed her post as Professor of Oriental Studies at El Colegio de Mexico, which is renowned all over Latin America.

The location of the Gandhi statue here is remarkable. Almost 15 ft high, it is adjacent to the National Museum of Anthropology. All Mexican and foreigners who visit this famed Museum see this imposing statue before entering it.

On this occasion Prof. Graciela congratulated me on my appointment as Ambassador of India to Mexico, and promised me her full support for setting up an Indian Cultural Centre (ICC). Soon after I had presented my credentials, she kindly hosted an informal dinner at her residence to which she invited Miguel de la Madrid (former President of Mexico), Nobel Laureate Octavia Paz, Attorney General Jorge Carpizo and Foreign Secretary Andres Rosenthal, all good friends of hers.

I presented my credentials to President Carlos Salinas on 19 October. In his 20-minute conversation with me he spoke of his great admiration for Mahatma Gandhi and stated that Mexico had much to learn from India particularly in the fields of poverty alleviation, rural development and industrial diversification/management. I briefly informed him the steps India had taken in these fields and also mentioned Ispat International's recent acquisition of Mexico's Sicartsa steel plant at Lazaro Cardenas. He immediately perked up and stated, 'It was I who instructed that Ispat should be invited to make a bid for this plant. When it was sold to them at a lower price than we had paid for it my political opponents accused me of selling valuable national assets at "basement bargain prices". But within a year Ispat transformed this huge loss-making steel plant into a valuable revenue earning national asset by producing/exporting steel slabs to the US and some other countries. This is why I stated Mexico has much to learn from India in industrial management.' I thanked him for this and congratulated him on the PRONASOL and PROCAMPO programmes he had recently launched and stated this was the Gandhian approach to poverty alleviation and rural regeneration.

Three weeks later I was pleasantly surprised to receive an invitation from the President's office to visit some PRONASOL and PROCAMPO projects in southern Mexico, which I promptly accepted. On the day prior to this visit I was informed of the airport and time at which I should arrive there. When I got there I was stunned to learn that I was to travel to these projects not by plane but in the Presidential six-seater helicopter along with President Salinas, his Education Minister Ernesto Zedillo and the Colombian Ambassador. The helicopter was airborne by 8.30 a.m. and between 9 a.m. and 4 p.m. we visited four projects. At each of them the President and Education Minister inspected PRONASOL schools and health centres and PROCAMPO irrigation projects, interacted with rural folk, and even danced with the 'campesinos' at some of them. We had a campesino lunch at one of them. When I got back that evening I could hardly believe that I, a newly-arrived Ambassador, had spent almost eight hours in close and friendly contact with the Mexican President, his Education Minister and their citizens in remote villages. I felt deeply grateful to President Salinas for this gracious invitation and exceptional privilege.

In early February (1993), Prof. Graciela telephoned to convey that her friend Jorge Carpizo MacGregor, former Attorney General and now Minister for the Interior, had offered one of the residences confiscated by his ministry from 'drug barons' for the proposed ICC.

Noticing that I was taken aback by the latter information she clarified that this residence was not being offered to the Embassy of India but to a trust which she and some other Mexican friends to India would set up. She added that this had been done for other cultural centres including European ones. Three weeks later I was pleasantly surprised to learn from her that former President Miguel de La Madrid and Nobel Laureate Octavio Paz had agreed to join the mentioned Trust.

In late March (1993), the Directors of the TDA/HHEC (Trade Development Authority/Handicrafts and Handloom Exports Corporation of India Ltd) offices in New York, whom I knew quite well from my CG tenure there and had requested to organize an impactful India promotion in Mexico, arrived in Mexico city. FS (Com) Amarendra Khatua took them to reputed department stores and leading handicraft and textile importers. El Palacio de Hierro was the most reputed of the department stores and Mr Rodrigo Rivero Lake the biggest importer of Indian handicrafts.

El Palacio de Hierro agreed to do an 'India promotion', in collaboration with TDA/HHEC, in mid-May 1993 at their stores in Mexico City and Acapulco.

Having learnt from my DG (ICCR) days of the imperative need to build adequate mass and momentum to break through the 'culture barrier', I now wrote to the Directors of India Investment Centre, India Tourism, Air India and State Bank of India in New York to collaborate with El Palacio de Hierro's India promotion which it had aptly named 'La Magica de La India' (The Magic of India). I also wrote to Ismail Merchant to have a retrospective of his films in Mexico at this time. All of them responded favourably. Thus, before the end of April the groundwork for a major, wide-spectrum India Promotion in Mexico was well laid.

'La Magica de La India' at the El Palacio de Hierro (PH) was inaugurated in Mexico City on 15 May by former President Miguel de La Madrid and at Acapulco on 18 May by me.

Both at Mexico City and Acapulco, the PH department stores were elegantly decorated with Indian handicrafts and textiles, and every section, including jewellery and footwear, had a profusion of Indian items. Mexicans who played the sitar or had learnt Indian dancing were invited to give performances. On other days India tourism films were screened or recorded Indian music played. All this continued until 31 May.

During the same period, five Merchant Ivory films were screened at Palacio de Bellas Artes; an India Trade and Investment seminar held in collaboration with Mexico's International Business Council and a 10-day Indian food festival presented at the Sheraton Hotel. Air India held discussions with Aeroméxico about jointly marketing a Mexico-India tourist airfare in the US$1,200 range—US$600 lower than the normal US$1,800 round-trip fare. The Ashok Leyland representative met leading Mexican transport companies and secured an order for 30 Leyland 54-seater luxury buses, from Quatro Senores, an inter-state transport company. It appointed a Mexico-based NRI named Cornelius Menezes as its representative in Mexico and Central America.

The Economic Times (of India) published an *IANS* report about the 'La Magica de la India' event. It was titled 'Mexicans discover India as best option for partnerships'. Its opening para was:

> For generations Mexicans have viewed India as an exotic destination that magically juxtaposes the wisdom of the Vedas, the beauty of Taj Mahal and the tragedy of abject poverty. They did not view it as a potential trade or investment partner, at least not until Pascal Alan Nazareth came to town. In an ambitious attempt to foster closer relations between the two countries, the Indian envoy organized a month-long, multidimensional India cultural festival in Mexico City and Acapulco with a total price

> tag of nearly US$1.5 million. It was the first of its kind in Latin America.

The mentioned price tag was borne entirely by those who participated in this event. The Embassy of India's expenditure on it was only the time and effort spent in organizing it.

Meanwhile, since I was concurrently accredited as Ambassador of India to Guatemala and El Salvador and High Commissioner to Belize I visited these countries and presented my credentials there.

Guatemala is the prime locus of the ancient Mayan civilization which covered all of Central America. Its heroic civil rights leader Rigoberta Menchú Tum was awarded the 1992 Nobel Peace Prize (NPP). Some extracts from her moving acceptance speech are given hereunder as they epitomize the greatness, and tragedy of the Mayan people:

> The Maya people developed and spread geographically through some 300,000 square km; they developed a very rich civilization in the area of political organization, they were great scientists in the fields of mathematics, astronomy, agriculture, architecture and engineering; they were great artists in the fields of sculpture, painting, weaving and carving. They discovered the zero value in mathematics, at about the same time that it was discovered in India. Their astronomic forecasts based on mathematical calculations and scientific observations were amazing. They prepared a calendar more accurate than the Gregorian, and in the field of medicine they performed intra-cranial surgical operations.
>
> One of the Maya books, which escaped destruction by the conquistadores, known as *The Codex of Dresden*, contains the results of an investigation on eclipses as well a table of 69 dates, in which solar eclipse occur in a lapse of 33 years.
>
> Today, we must fight for a better world, without poverty, without racism, with peace in the Middle East and in Southeast Asia, for

> the end of the apartheid in South Africa; for stability in Nicaragua, for re-establishment of democracy in Haiti and restoration of sovereignty of Panama; because all of these constitute justice in the international situation.[1]

I had greatly looked forward to meeting Nobel Laureate Menchú during this visit to Guatemala but learnt that she lived in the US but visits Mexico occasionally as her Nobel Prize is kept in protective custody at its Museum of Indigenous Cultures. So, when she came there in October 1993 I called on her and draped an Indian shawl on her as my respectful tribute for her heroic struggle on behalf of her people.

In Guatemala I made two amazing discoveries.

Our Honorary Consul was a renowned fighter pilot who now suffered a severe lung problem which required him to be continuously on oxygen. So even when he accompanied me to my presentation of credentials to President Jorge Serrano, he had a small oxygen cylinder strapped to his back. He was warmly and respectfully greeted by the President.

In our conversation on this occasion the President informed me that one of his predecessors (1972–1978), General Carlos Arana Osorio was a great Sai Baba devotee. So, I requested him to arrange a call on him for me, which he kindly did. When I called on the former President he told me the following remarkable story:

An atheistic soldier most of his life, he was induced by his son, a long-time Sathya Sai Baba devotee, to accompany him to his Prasanthi Nilayam Ashram in Puttaparthi, Andhra Pradesh in 1985. When he had his first *darshan* of this renowned Indian saint he was 'awakened' and became his ardent devotee thereafter. On return to Guatemala he built a 'Sai Baba temple' in his mansion's spacious compound and this

1. Rigoberta Menchú Tum, Acceptance and Nobel Lecture, 10 December 1992, https://www.nobelprize.org/prizes/peace/1992/tum/lecture/

soon became the meeting place for Guatemala's numerous Sai Baba devotees.

As General Osorio was to celebrate his 50th wedding anniversary in May 1990, he and his wife travelled to Prashanthi Nilayam in January that year to request Sai Baba's blessing. He gave them his blessing and promised to be with them on their 'golden day'. When this day arrived and champagne was served to the guests at the well-attended reception, they all saw the Sai Baba's smiling face at the bottom of their glasses. General Osorio showed me the photos taken at this reception which clearly showed this amazing 'miracle'! If I had not seen it with my own eyes I would never have believed it.

General Osorio introduced me to a fellow Sai Baba devotee who was keen to import Indian three-wheelers into Guatemala. He had made a careful study of various Indian three-wheelers and decided on the one made by Kerala Automobiles as it had a reverse gear, essential for Guatemala's narrow, winding roads. I promised to assist him in this. Nine months thereafter 100 of these vehicles arrived in Guatemala and 50 of them were bought by Coca-Cola of Guatemala, which then used them with a large size Coca-Cola logo painted on them to deliver its products all over this country. It became an impactful advertisement for Indian three-wheelers, more of which were then imported into Guatemala, as also neighbouring countries.

El Salvador is the smallest, most densely populated country in Central America. It is also the only country of Central America where the Spanish were initially defeated by the indigenous Pipil and Lenca warriors. It took the Spanish nine long years to finally subjugate them.

Despite its miniscule size, El Salvador has 22 volcanos; some of which are still active. The highest, Santa Ana, is 7,800 ft high. Its most important Mayan archaeological site, the Tazumal pyramid, is close to the Santa Ana Volcano.

India's best known and much-loved icon in this country was an

Indian female elephant named Manhewla (Manjula) which El Salvador purchased in 1955 for its Parque Zoológico Nacional in San Salvador. When she died in January 2011, her body was honoured with a '*velacion*', a Salvadorian all-night funeral ceremony in which friends and relatives gather around the deceased and sing dirges.

President Alfredo Cristiani whom I presented my credentials had assumed office in June 1989. Soon thereafter he initiated efforts to end the 12-year-long civil war, in which the US-backed military junta led by Jose Napoleon Duarte had fought the Farabundo Martí National Liberation Front (FMLN) guerrillas. In which according to UN reports, the Junta's death squads had killed over 75,000 people among whom was the revered Monsignor Oscar Romero, Archbishop of San Salvador. He was assassinated on 24 March 1980, while saying Mass in his cathedral.

President Cristiani's strenuous efforts, supported by Mexico and the UN, finally bore fruit when peace accords were signed by him and FMLN leaders at Mexico's Chapultepec Castle on 16 January 1992. These accords are therefore known as 'Acuerdos de Paz de Chapultepec'.

I congratulated and lauded President Cristiani on these historic 'Acuerdos'. He reciprocated by congratulating India on its recent election as UN Security Council member and requested Indian experts in the IT and Horticultural fields and scholarships in Indian medical and engineering colleges. I promised to follow up on his requests.

El Salvador's miniscule Indian community at this time comprised three Indian Missionaries of Charity nuns and two UNDP Indian experts.

Belize (formerly British Honduras), is located at the southeastern tip of Mexico. It has an area of 8,800 sq. miles but a population of only 300,000 (in 1992) of which 4 per cent are of Indian origin.

As a member of the Commonwealth, CARICOM, CELAC,

& SICA it has more diverse international relations than any other Central American country. Besides, it is the only Central American Country where English is fluently spoken and whose head of state (the British Queen) is located outside its territory.

Belize has had four distinct Indian immigration 'packages'. The first, in 1858, were 1,000 sepoys (and their families) from the 1857 'Sepoy Mutiny'. The second were ex-indentured labourers (EIL) from Jamaica, in 1872. The third were EIL from the Bahamas, in 1884. Both these groups had worked in the mahogany forests of these countries, which having been depleted, those of British Honduras were now to be 'logged'. The high value international trade in mahogany, formerly in Spanish hands, had passed into British hands after Napoleon's invasion of Spain in 1808 and they were determined to take full advantage of it. The fourth group of Indian immigrants, mainly Sindhis, had trickled in from Canary Islands and Panama in the early 1980s.

When I presented my credentials to Governor General Dame Elmira Minita Gordon on 29 March 1993, the Indian community in Belize was approximately 7,000 strong and quite well established. The Solicitor General was Gian Chand Gandhi. He was fondly referred to as 'the capital's ultimate survivor' as he had continued in office despite four government changes. Another PIO (Person of Indian Origin), George Singh (a Christian of Sikh origin), was then a puisne Judge of Belize's Supreme Court. (Five years later he became its Chief Justice.) His son, Douglas Singh, was a leading member of United Democratic Party, which was then the ruling party. (Three years later he was appointed Minister of Public Security.) As most Indian community members were well educated—many of whom had graduated from UK and US universities—it was not surprising that some of them had risen to the highest levels of Belize's government and judiciary.

The Indian community reception in my honour was attended by Foreign Minister Dean Barrow, Solicitor General Gian Chand

Gandhi and Douglas Singh MP. Towards the end of this reception, a Sindhi lady came up to Isobel and hesitantly asked her whether she was from Bangalore and if so had taught at St. Francis Xavier Girls High School. When Isobel confirmed this she was overjoyed and revealed she was her student. She then beckoned her family members and friends to come and meet Isobel. Teacher and student had met each other in faraway Belize, after 33 long years!

I had travelled from Mexico City to Belmopan, the Belize capital, via Villahermosa, capital of Tabasco State, made a two-day stop there and called on the Governor there. On the return journey I took the road via Cancun, and made a two-day halt at Merida, where I called on the Governor, an elegant lady named Dulce Maria Sauri. She was a great admirer of India and invited us to dinner, at which we became good friends. Thereafter whenever she came to Mexico City she would visit us and have lunch or tea with us. On one occasion she invited us to dinner at the elegant Hacienda de Los Morales Restaurant at which among the other guests were Mr Louis Donaldo Colosio, (a former president of the ruling PRI party and current Minister for Social Development) and his wife Diana Laura Riojas. This was our first meeting with them and we then became friends.

In mid-September 1993, the long-awaited Indian Cultural Centre was inaugurated at the historic Chapultepec Castle. Among the VIPs present at it were: former President Miguel De La Madrid (as ICC chairman), Minister of the Interior Jorge Carpizo and Mrs Carpizo, Minister for Social Development Luis Donaldo Colosio and Mrs Colosio, Nobel Laureate Octavio Paz and Mrs Paz, former Mexican Ambassador to India Prof. Graciela de La Lama, India's Minister for Steel Mr Santosh Mohan Dev (who had come to Mexico to inaugurate Ispat Mexicana's new pelletization plant), India's former Agriculture Minister C. Subramaniam (as BVB chairman), and BVB Executive Secretary S. Ramakrishnan.

In his remarks Minister Mohan Dev stated that India and Mexico 'already bound with strands of steel were now being tied with the silken bonds of culture'. The renowned violinist T.N. Krishnan, whom BVB had kindly sent to play at this event, provided it with its grand finale.

Soon thereafter, I convened a meeting of Mexican scholars on India and proposed that a scholarly publication on historical and cultural links between Mexico and India be brought out on the lines of India and Greece and India and Egypt which ICCR had published. Prof. Graciela de La Lama, Prof. Eva Uchmany and four researchers from El Colegio de Mexico and National Autonomous University of Mexico (UNAM) attended this meeting and enthusiastically supported it. Prof. Uchmany, reputed author of books on interaction between Jewish communities in diverse countries, kindly undertook to secure scholarly articles from Mexican and Indian researchers. Prof. Graciela promised to assist her in this.

I induced Ispat Mexicana to sponsor its Spanish edition and ICCR to publish its English edition. The former was published by Mexico's Fondo de Cultura Económico in 1996 and the latter by ICCR in 2003, jointly with Macmillan India. Both these editions have the same content, 15 articles by Indian and Mexican scholars on topics ranging from concepts of space and time to artistic, agricultural, sea faring and textile traditions of India and Mexico and their political, economic and trade relations in the modern era.

In October 1993 two Indian business delegations came to Mexico. The first was led by Minister of State for External Affairs Mr Salman Khurshid and the second by Mr Hari Singh Singhania, chairman of the India chapter of the International Chamber of Commerce. These two visits and the high-level contacts established with Mexican firms in diverse fields through them aided our efforts to boost India-Mexico business and trade.

A big breakthrough which Mexico made in India at this time was the order Productora de Cospeles of San Luis Potosí secured from the GOI Mint to supply 2,250 tons of 1 Rupee, 50 paisa and 25 paisa stainless steel coins. Earlier these coins were being ordered from Germany.

As NAFTA (North American Free Trade Agreement) was to come into effect on 1 January 1994, Mexico's three Commerce and Industry federations—ANIERM, CONACEX and CEMAI—jointly organized a conference on it at Puerto Vallarta on 18 November (1993). It was titled 'Hacia Nuevos Horizontes' (Towards New Horizons). I was pleasantly surprised to be invited to speak at it on India's experience in protecting its handicraft industries despite its extensive industrialization. On arrival at the conference venue I was even more surprised that I was the only Ambassador invited to it; not even the US and Canadian Ambassadors had been invited. I later learnt that it was President Salinas who had suggested that I be invited to speak on the mentioned topic.

As I had been allotted only 20 minutes and using an interpreter would reduce this even further, I took the bold decision to speak in Spanish. The large audience included Mexico's Agriculture, Commerce, Industry and Social Development ministers. I began my talk apologizing for my rudimentary Spanish and then went on to speak about Mahatma Gandhi's adoption of the *charka* (spinning wheel) as the prime 'weapon' of India's freedom struggle and how this had revived its moribund handicraft industries which today provide employment to almost 30 million artisans and their families and earns India over US$1 billion annually in export earnings. I also mentioned the quality control and design centres and sales emporia in India and abroad, which GOI had set up to upgrade and promote India's handicrafts. I ended by stating that in poor, capital deficient countries '*el talento en el manos de nuestro pueblo is valuroso capital que tenemos utillizar al mas medida que es possible*' (The talents in our people's hands are valuable capital which need to be utilized to maximum extent possible). I received much appreciation for my talk (including from Minister Colosio) but did sense that most of those at this conference were more enamoured by the prospect of Mexico soon becoming like Canada and the US rather than the wisdom of safeguarding its traditional handicrafts!

Just three weeks later Social Development Minister Louis Colosio received the 'dedo' (nomination) from President Salinas as the PRI presidential candidate for the July 1994 presidential election.

From early October (1993) I was in regular touch with MEA about President Salinas' visit to India in December which both sides had mutually agreed on. December 8-12 had been fixed as the dates for this visit. By 30 November all its details had been finalized; even the presidential aircraft's 'call signals' had been provided by the Mexican President's office and forwarded to MEA. On 2 December, MEA requested a 'slight change' in the dates of this visit so that President Salinas could be present at the 'Education for all Summit of Nine High-Population Countries' at New Delhi on 12-16 December 1993. As President Salinas was proceeding from India to Japan and therefore could not make any change in his India visit dates I immediately dictated a telegram to MEA to convey this. Just then Ambassador Jorge Chen, Director (Asia), telephoned from the Foreign Office to inform me that the Presidential visit to India had been cancelled. The President's office had already learnt of the 'slight change in dates' request from the Mexican Ambassador in New Delhi and decided to cancel the visit to India. MEA then proposed this visit be made in March 1994 just prior to the G-15 Summit at New Delhi on 28-30 March. But in view of the major calamity which struck Mexico on 1 January 1994 this was quite impossible.

Two hours before sunrise on New Year's Day (1994) about 3,000 indigenous guerrillas, some armed with AK-47s and others with swords and axes, emerged out of the forests of Chiapas State and occupied San Cristóbal de las Casas and five other neighbouring towns. They described themselves as the Zapatista Army of National Liberation (Zapata was the leader of the 1910 indigenous peasant uprising). Their spokesman was a tall, masked, pipe smoking, tech-savvy non-indigenous middle-aged man who identified himself as Subcomandante Marcos. In his 'First Declaration from the Lacandon Jungle' he declared, 'We are the product of 500 years of struggle. Today we say enough is enough.' Almost half of Mexico's 20 million indigenous people live in Chiapas state.

As NAFTA came into effect on 1 January 1994, and cheap American corn would begin flowing into Mexico from that date and destroy their livelihoods these people had chosen this date for their uprising.

The Mexican army attacked them with full force on 3 January, and continued this for a week. Almost 150 Zapatistas were killed. When this news spread large crowds of indigenous people gathered in Mexico City squares in support of the guerrillas. The Bishop of Chiapas Samuel Ruiz, a staunch advocate of justice for indigenous farmers, mediated on their behalf with the Mexican government. A ceasefire was declared on 10 January. The ZNLA withdrew into its jungle hideouts but continued its struggle against NAFTA on social media led by Subcomandante Marcos. *The New York Times* described this uprising as 'the world's first post-modern revolution'.

The Chiapas uprising was a big political setback for President Salinas. It was also a big blow to the Mexican economy as it triggered a massive capital outflow. NAFTA which had been looked upon as a boon by Mexico's elite suddenly turned out to be a curse.

Among the steps Mexico took to mitigate its new economic woes was to promote tourist inflows/investments by taking Ambassadors based in Mexico City to its best tourist sites and urging them to publicize them in their respective countries/and through reputed tour agencies. Isobel and I were included in the group of 10 ambassadors taken to Baja California, 8-14 March (1994). We travelled by plane to Cabo San Lucas and then by luxury buses all the way to Tijuana in its far north, spending a day/night at the Concepcion, Puerto Vincente Guerrero and Ensenada tourist resorts en route. It was a very enjoyable tour, the memory of which was gravely marred by a gruesome tragedy which occurred just nine days later at Tijuana.

At about noon on 23 March, the PRI presidential candidate Luis Donaldo Colosio was assassinated in a working-class ward of this city while campaigning there. This was a great shock to most Mexicans and their friends worldwide. Drug-related killings were frequent in Mexico but political assassinations rare. The last such assassination (that of President Alvaro Obregon) had occurred in 1928. Besides, Luis Colosio as Social Development Minister had done much for working-class communities and was popular among them.

The assassin was a 24-year-old maquiladora (auto assembly) worker named Mario Aburto. He was immediately arrested but gave no credible motive for his crime. Therefore most political analysts suspected he was a paid assassin who had been instigated or paid to do this dreadful deed by a political rival, either within the PRI or the PAN party, which then ruled Baja California. This assassination hurt PRI and benefitted PAN. The former lost its seven-decade-long grip on the presidency. Though Education Minister Ernesto Zedillo (who was in President Salinas' helicopter with me in November 1992) replaced the assassinated Luis Colosio and won the July 1994 presidential election by a narrow margin, the 2000 election was won by PAN's Vicente Fox with a large majority.

As Luis Colosio and his wife Diana were good friends of ours, Isobel and I were deeply shocked and grieved by his assassination. I wrote a condolence letter to Senora Diana Colosio on behalf of both of us. She graciously and promptly acknowledged and thanked me for it. I still have this letter.

As I was to retire on 30 April 1994 I made farewell visits to Guatemala, El Salvador and Belize in the first half of April and on return to Mexico made my farewell calls on President Salinas (who expressed deep disappointment that his much-looked forward visit to India had not been made), Foreign Minister Fernando Solano, and ICC Chairman Miguel de La Madrid. Thereafter, I worked on my travel itinerary for the return to India.

Rather than take the approved route via New York and London, I decided to travel via San Francisco, Tokyo, Seoul, Beijing, Shanghai, Bangkok and New Delhi to Bangalore. I sought and secured prior approval of MEA and paid the additional cost of this itinerary over that of the approved route.

At each of these cities we stayed with IFS colleagues and visited historic sites. The entire journey took three weeks. It was a very enjoyable, culturally enriching and memorable end to my 35-year IFS career, in various parts of the world.

14

Post Retirement Joys, Tragedies, Travels and Spiritual Awakening

(May 1994–)

My post retirement years have been spent mainly in reviving and diffusing Gandhian ideals, lecturing on land and 'blue waters', savouring family joys and handling its tragedies. I have also promoted Opera in Bangalore and organized a friendship visit of five retired Indian diplomats to Pakistan. Each of these activities is being dealt with separately in this chapter.

Reviving and diffusing Gandhian Ideals

As an IFS officer, I had proudly proclaimed at every one of my foreign posts that religious tolerance is India's gift to the world and quoted its age-old maxims of *Ekam Sat* and *Vasudhaiva Kutumbakam* as proof thereof. I therefore decided to spend my retirement years mainly in promoting the Gandhian ideals of *Satya, Ahimsa, Sarva Dharma Sama Bhava* and *Sarvodaya* (truth, non-violence, equal respect for all religions and all-round uplift of everyone).

On return from Mexico, Isobel and I had arrived in New Delhi in early June 1994. She proceeded to Bangalore and I stayed on there for a week to collect my provident fund, gratuity, etc but also to meet Rajmohan Gandhi, biographer and grandson of Mahatma Gandhi, whom I had known since my DG (ICCR) days. We met at India International Centre over lunch. I shared my post retirement plans with him and requested his support. He kindly agreed to give it. In our discussion we mutually agreed that a trust would be set up to promote the above mentioned Gandhian ideals not only in India but also abroad. It would be named Sarvodaya International Trust (SIT) and its logo would be an octagon, to represent India's eight main religions (four born in India and four that came from abroad) with the *Dharma Chakra* at its centre to highlight that the moral essence of all these religions is the same. We also agreed that the following well-known Indian and foreign persons would be approached to be trustees: Ustad Amjad Ali, Mr Soli Sorabjee, Air Chief Marshal Arjan Singh, Mrinalini Sarabhai, Saryu Doshi, Bindeshwar Pathak, Princess Irene (president, World in Harmony, Madrid), Abie Nathan (Israeli Peace activist) and 'Ibu' Oka (Founder of the Gandhi Ashrams in Bali, Indonesia).

Rajmohan highlighted the need to make Gandhi 'enjoyable', particularly to the youth, and proposed an annual 'Concert for Gandhi' on his birthday. I readily agreed to this.

We decided to approach the widely respected, soon to retire, Chief Justice of India M.N. Venkatachaliah to be chairman of SIT. He kindly consented to be SIT trustee as also its chairman. This was a major breakthrough. Securing the consent of the other eminent persons we had agreed upon became fairly easy. Every one of them we approached agreed to be trustees. I had known the three foreign trustees from my DG (ICCR) days.

I must mention here Air Chief Marshal Arjan Singh's inspiring response when I called on him at his New Delhi residence in early January 1995. 'If you are inviting me to be an SIT trustee from the Sikh community my answer is no, because the day I joined the IAF I relinquished my religious identity. But, if your invitation to me is as a retired IAF officer who has great respect for Mahatma Gandhi my answer will be yes. If the world can solve its problems the Gandhian way, without violence and war, those of us in the armed forces would be the most grateful.' I promptly invited him as a retired armed forces officer and he graciously agreed.

Soon thereafter I proposed to Justice Venkatachaliah and Rajmohan Gandhi that in all SIT regional chapters that would be set up we should have retired armed forces officers. They promptly agreed to this suggestion. (Air Marshal S.J. Dastur, former chairman of HAL, was chairman of Karnataka Chapter 1998–2012; Vice Admiral John D'Silva, former Vice Chief of Naval Staff, was chairman of Goa Chapter, from 2014 until his death on 19 November 2019). Air Chief Marshal Arjan Singh was SIT vice chairman from 1995–2005; former Air Chief Marshal A.Y. Tipnis was Vice Chairman from 2006-2009; Gen N.C. Vij is its present vice chairman.)

The first meeting of SIT Board of Management was held at Sabarmati Ashram in Ahmedabad on 15-16 July 1995. A photo taken on its conclusion and released by *PTI* was carried by almost 50 newspapers all over India. A scan of it is among the photos in this book.

In the next two decades as some founder trustees passed way, new ones have been inducted as co-opted trustees. Notable among them are Mr Vladimir Tolstoy, great grandson of Count Leo Tolstoy, the late Prof. Glenn Paige, chairman, Center for Global Nonkilling, Honolulu,

Prof. Lia Diskin, director, Palais Athena, Sao Paulo, and Prof. Quanyu Shang, director, Confucius Institute at Riga, Latvia.

SIT also has an 'Honor Panel of Eminent Counsellors' among whom have been/are: Shri Baba Amte, Dr Miguel de La Madrid, Mrs Corazon Aquino, Nobel Laureates H.H. the Dalai Lama, Archbishop Desmond Tutu and Mrs Mairead Corrigan, as well as Nobel Peace Prize nominees A.T. Ariyaratne (often called 'Sri Lanka's Gandhi') and Prof. Johan Galtung.

Regional chapters, in the order in which they have been set up, are: SIT (Karnataka), SIT (Andhra Pradesh), SIT (Gujarat), SIT (Maharashtra), SIT (New Delhi), SIT (Odisha), SIT (Tamil Nadu), SIT (Kerala), SIT (Goa), SIT (J & K) and SIT (Rajasthan). In all of them the trustees belong to all the eight major religions.

SIT's annual 'Concert for Gandhi', launched in a modest way at the Gandhi statue in Bangalore on 2 October 1996, with two school choirs singing Gandhi's favourite *bhajans* and Christian hymns, has subsequently also been held at Hyderabad, Mumbai, Chennai, New Delhi, Ahmedabad, Kochi, Bhubaneshwar, Jaipur, Panjim and Jammu. In Bangalore they have moved from the Gandhi statue to Chowdiah Hall, and since 2007 to the Raj Bhavan Glass House, where they are being held in collaboration with Bangalore Doordarshan Kendra which telecasts them nationwide on its Chandana channel.

Among the renowned artists who have participated in these concerts are sarod maestro Ustad Amjad Ali Khan, violinist L. Subramaniam, Odissi dance guru Kelucharan Mohapatra and Bharatanatyam dancer Mallika Sarabhai.

Among the many corporates who have/are supporting these concerts are Confederation of Indian Industry (CII), Godrej Industries and Hotel Association of India.

A collage of news reports about SIT activities since its inception is among the inserts of this book.

The URL of SIT website is http/ www.sarvodayatrust.org

My two books on Gandhi

The first book, titled *Gandhi's Outstanding Leadership*, presents his transformation from a timid youth to a fearless leader, the spiritual and other components of his leadership and its impact on freedom fighters, Nobel laureates, spiritual activists, environmentalists, music composers and academic disciplines. Published jointly by Bharatiya Vidya Bhavan's Gandhi Centre of Science and Human Values and Sarvodaya International Trust in March 2006, it was released at Bangalore by Karnataka Governor T.N. Chaturvedi, at New Delhi by former Prime Minister I. K. Gujral and at the UN Library in New York by Under Secretary-General Shashi Tharoor.

In the 14 years thereafter, this book has been published in 12 Indian and 23 foreign languages.

Former Soviet President Mikhail Gorbachev has written the Foreword for 12 of its foreign language editions. Its text is among the annexures of this book. Besides, many of these editions have been released at prestigious venues: The Czech edition at Parliament House in Prague, Dutch edition at Leiden University in Amsterdam; French edition at UN Library in Geneva, German edition at Humboldt and Heidelberg Universities; Greek edition at National Library of Cyprus, Italian edition at Pontifical Gregorian University in the Vatican at Rome, Swedish edition at Uppsala University, Portuguese edition at National Library of Brazil at Brasilia, Romanian edition at the National Library of Romania and Russian edition at Institute of Philosophy of Russian Academy of Sciences.

Notable in the considerable praise this book has received are the following:

I particularly liked the chapter 'Gandhi as the Ideal Leadership Model'.

—A.P.J. Abdul Kalam, Former President of India

My deepest thanks and appreciation for your wonderful gift of Gandhi's Outstanding Leadership.

—Barack Obama, Former President of United States of America

Alan Nazareth has chosen an important aspect of Gandhi's personality to focus on. In his book he presents the Mahatma as an outstanding modern leader, who greatly influenced other leaders during his lifetime and has continued to do so after his death.

—Mikhail Gorbachev, Former President of the Soviet Union

I have found several passages most relevant to the present political situation in my country.

—Corazon Aquino, Former President of the Philippines

The conceptualizing of the subject, treatment of the matter, enrichment with examples, facts and documentation, representative pictures, printing and get up are exemplary. The book is really outstanding.

—N. Kasturi, president, Gandhi Literature Society, Bangalore

Alan Nazareth has a genius for setting Gandhi in his widest possible setting and making him into a contemporary figure.

—Antony Copley, author of *Mahatma Gandhi* and *Gandhi: Against the Tide* books

The book is a marvellously instructive contribution to understanding the principles, practices and significance of Gandhi's leadership for India and the World—past, present and future...

—Glenn Paige, Director, Center for Global Nonkilling, Honolulu, Hawai'i, USA

My second book is titled *Gandhi: The Soul Force Warrior: Revolutionized Revolution and Spiritualized It.* I chose this title after reading Arthur Herman's *Gandhi and Churchill: The Epic Rivalry that Destroyed an Empire and Forged our Age.*

It presents Gandhi as a revolutionary, who in a century replete with bloody revolutions triggered with class, creed and racial hatreds, launched and successfully carried through a non-violent 'soul force' revolution which has transformed India and brought down many authoritarian regimes in various parts of the world.

Its Foreword has been written by H.H. the Dalai Lama. A scan of it is among the annexures of this book. Published by Wisdom Tree, New Delhi, it was released by Gandhi's granddaughter Smt Tara Gandhi Bhattacharya at IIC New Delhi on 4 December 2018 and presented to President of India Shri Ram Nath Kovind at Rashtrapati Bhavan the following morning.

Its Spanish edition, which is titled *Gandhi: Guerrero Del Alma* has already been published by Editorial Porrúa of Mexico City.

Its French, Mandarin, Myanmarese, Polish and Serbian editions are presently on the anvil and expected to be published before the end of the year.

Lord Swraj Paul and Lord Bhikhu Parekh had kindly scheduled the release of this book at the House of Lords on 16 April 2020. Unfortunately, because of the Covid-19 pandemic, this event has been indefinitely postponed.

Lecturing globally on land and 'Blue Waters'

In early September 1994, my nephew Vivian Peres who was a Director at Ventours International Travel telephoned to enquire whether I would be interested in lecturing on cruise ships. He told me that Radisson Cruises, whose ships his travel agency serviced in Indian ports, had requested them to find a good onboard lecturer for their elite 'Song of Flower' cruise ship and send them his/her bio. So I sent him mine highlighting, as advised by him, the various prestigious universities in various countries I had lectured at.

In early January 1995 Radisson Cruises invited me to deliver eight lectures on their 'Song of Flower', 6-22 April on the Cochin to Suez sector of its Wellington–London cruise. I prepared eight lectures, four on India's civilization, history, religions and Gandhi and one each on the Arabs, Oman, Yemen and Egypt.

The 'Song of Flower' Cochin–Suez lecture cruise was my 'trial run' and since I 'made the grade' with it I was invited regularly thereafter to lecture on Radisson and subsequently on Regent, Silver Seas, Seabourn and Holland America cruise ships. Between April 1995 and December 2018, I have done 35 lecture cruises. These have taken me, north to south from Edinburg in Scotland to Wellington in New Zealand, east to west from Kobe in Japan to Rio in Brazil. The 'Song of Flower Millennium Cruise' headed for the International Date Line on December 31, 1999 so that those onboard would be among the first to view the Millennium Sunrise. I have three stunning photos of it.

Audiences at my onboard lectures were mainly Americans, British, and Australians. There quite often were Stanford, Columbia and Yale University Alumni groups, one each of whom invited me to lecture at their universities. One Aspen based onboard guest recommended me to the Aspen Institute which then invited me to three of its Executive Seminars (2000–2002).

Notable among the renowned persons I met on these cruises are Brigadier General/Ambassador John Eisenhower (son of President Eisenhower), Bruce Riedel (of CIA/Brookings Institute), Steven Bechtel Jr. (Chairman of Bechtel Corporation) and Mark Conroy (Chairman of Silver Seas Cruises).

Isobel has accompanied me on most of these cruises but Premila and Seema accompanied me on four of them. When these cruise ships were in Indian ports and women cruisers bought Indian sarees Isobel gave them saree draping demonstrations which were much appreciated.

Goodwill Visit to Pakistan

As Mahatma Gandhi had urged that India and Pakistan live as friendly neighbours I had joined the Pakistan-India Peoples Forum for Peace and Democracy (PIPFPD) soon after it was founded in 1995. I attended its third annual meeting at New Delhi in 1998 and its fifth meeting at Bangalore in April 2000. On conclusion of the latter meeting I invited the Pakistani and Indian chairmen/vice chairmen for dinner and during the cordial interaction at it, suggested a goodwill visit by retired Indian diplomats to Pakistan as such visits by MPs, lawyers and even retired generals had taken place. The Pakistani chairman I.A. Rahman pointed out that in all such visits the visitors stay with Pakistani and Indian host families, and retired Indian diplomats, long used to staying in five-star hotels, might find this difficult. I assured him that we would much prefer to stay with host families rather than in hotels. He and vice chairman Mubashir Hasan (a former Finance Minister) then indicated they would initiate action on this proposal soon after their return to Pakistan.

Three weeks later Vice Chairman Hasan emailed me that official clearance for this visit had been obtained. I then contacted former Foreign Secretary M.K. Rasgotra and requested him to lead this delegation and secure GOI clearance for its visit to Pakistan. He kindly agreed to both requests. I then induced retired IFS colleagues Salman Haider, Manorama Bhalla and C.V. Ranganathan to join this group. I emailed Mr Mubashir Hasan and conveyed the composition of our group and stated that the names of its members would be indicated only when confirmation was received that Pakistani visas would be issued to us. Mr Hasan replied, 'I cannot confirm issue of your Pakistani visas but our Foreign Minister is hosting a lunch in honour of your group. Presumably therefore visas will be issued to enable you and your colleagues to attend it!'

We flew from New Delhi to Islamabad on 31 July 2000. We were pleasantly surprised to be received at the airport by a Protocol Officer of the Pakistan Foreign Office. HCI officers and PIPFPD office-bearers were also there. Though ours was a 'private visit' organized by PIPFPD the Pakistan government had given it a semi-official status.

In view of our late arrival, the forenoon of the next day (1 August) was kept free. After lunch we were taken for a drive through Islamabad and then to India House where Acting High Commissioner Sudhir Vyas briefed us on the current state of India-Pakistan relations and hosted a dinner in our honour.

Foreign Minister Abdul Sattar's lunch in our honour was on the following day. Among those present at it were his Deputy Minister and Foreign Secretary, three former Pakistani High Commissioners to India, Acting High Commissioner Sudhir Vyas and PIPFPD chairman I.A. Rahman and vice chairman Mubashir Hasan. The conversation at this lunch was cordial and lively. When Foreign Minister Sattar enquired whether we wished to see or do anything more than what had been scheduled already I requested a visit to Taxila, as it was only 40 km away. He graciously agreed to this and instructed his Deputy Minister to arrange this.

We were taken to Taxila the following morning (3 August) and were much impressed by the meticulous care with which this pre–Islamic world heritage site was being maintained and protected.

After lunch we left for Lahore by a Daewoo luxury coach. It was a fascinating 380-km drive on a six-lane highway, much of it alongside the majestic Indus River flowing through vast expanses of lush green rice fields. We arrived in Lahore at 8 p.m. and were met by our respective hosts: General Wajahat Hasan (Retd.) (for Salman Haider); Air Marshal Zafar Chaudhry (Retd) (for C.V. Ranganathan); Ms Nusrat

Jameel (for Manorama Bhalla) and Engineer Iftikharul Haq (for me). Mr Rasgotra was hosted at the government-owned Khakani House.

During our four-day stay at Lahore all five of us received such gracious and generous hospitality that none of us felt we were in an 'enemy' country. It was not only at the Khakani guest house and our host family homes but also at the book and gift shops we were treated as 'honoured guests' in Pakistan and no payments were accepted for purchases we made.

In Lahore, we had meetings at the PIPFPD office, Pakistan Institute of International Affairs and Human Rights Commission of Pakistan (HRCP). With Mr Rasgotra's prior approval, PIPFPD also arranged a meeting with India's most vociferous critics. Mr Rasgotra's sauve and self-confident handling of these critics, often quoting Urdu or Punjabi couplets, was amazing. This meeting which began with harsh barbs against India ended on a jovial note of Punjabi camaraderie.

Dinners in our honour were hosted by former President Sardar Farooq Ahmad Khan Leghari, former Prime Minister Malik Meraj Khalid and HRCP chairperson Asma Jahangir. We were greatly honoured by all this but a greater and quite unexpected honour was in the offing.

On 6 August morning Acting High Commissioner Sudhir Vyas telephoned to inform Mr Rasgotra that General Pervez Musharraf would receive him at 2 p.m. the following day and that a business class ticket on a Lahore to Islamabad morning flight had been booked for him. He had an hour-long meeting with the General. The topics discussed and the latter's comments on various India-Pakistan issues are detailed in the nine-page annexure (pages 404–412) in Mr Rasgotra's book, *A Life in Diplomacy*. He carried a cordial message from the General to Prime Minister A.B. Vajpayee: 'I know Mr Vajpayee is a strong and wise leader who can address difficult issues. Therefore, we have expectations from him. Please convey my warm regards to him.

I am a sincere, honest and open person and wish for peace and happy future for both countries.'

Seven months later Prime Minister Vajpayee extended an invitation to General Musharraf to visit India, which he promptly accepted. Their summit meeting took place at Agra 14-16 July 2001. It progressed well and on the evening of the second day a Joint Declaration seemed fairly certain. But by noon of the following day (16 July) someone had thrown the proverbial 'spanner in the works'.

A.G. Noorani has written about this in an article titled 'The Truth about Agra' in the 16 July 2005 issue of *Frontline* magazine.

If the expected Joint Declaration had been signed it would have been a major breakthrough in India–Pakistan relations and the five retired Indian diplomats who had made their goodwill visit to Pakistan in August 2000 could have rejoiced over it as it was their visit which had triggered the July 2001 Summit meeting. By an amazing coincidence I was in Agra during this meeting, lecturing to an elite 'Journey to History's Lost cities' group of TCS expeditions (of Seattle USA). I thus had 'a ringside seat' to the high hopes this meeting initially raised and were later cruelly betrayed.

Promotion of Opera in Bangalore

Having become an opera addict during my postings as DHC in London and CG in New York where I was privileged to become friends with Zubin Mehta, I decided to promote this musical art form, in Bangalore. As I had a large collection of opera DVDs I initially began screening them to a small group of friends in my home 2005 onwards. This group gradually enlarged itself and came to include IFS colleagues Eric Gonsalves and Nirupama Rao and Indian Institute of Astrophysics Director Siraj Hasan and his wife Sultana. In November 2009 it was written about, as the 'Opera Club of Bangalore' in *Deccan*

Herald's 'Metrolife'.[1] Screenings were then made at Bangalore School of Music (BSM), Alliance Française (AF), Smriti Nandan Cultural Centre and Time and Space Art Gallery. These steadily increased the number of opera lovers in Bangalore.

The big breakthrough came when the Bangalore Club screened Verdi's '*Rigoletto*' and Puccini's '*Tosca*' in January and March, National Gallery of Modern Art (NGMA) screened Puccini's '*Madame Butterfly*' in June and Bangalore International Centre (BIC) screened Verdi's '*Othello*' in August 2019 and Saint-Saens '*Samson et Delila*' in March 2020. At all these five screenings attendance was about 100, which for opera screening in Bangalore is impressive, but it took 15 years of arduous effort to achieve it!

Honours Received

On 9 October 2007, I was presented the U Thant Peace Award by Shri Chinmoy, Founder of The Peace Meditation at the UN, in New York for my 'Lifetime of Dedication and World Service'. Among previous recipients of this award are Pope John Paul II, the Dalai Lama, Mother Teresa, Nelson Mandela, Archbishop Desmond Tutu, and Mikhail Gorbachev.

On 23 February 2015, I was awarded the Doctor of Letters (Honoris Causa) degree by the Mangalayatan Jain University, Aligarh, 'in recognition of outstanding contributions to the fields of administrative services, academics, and promotion of Gandhian values'.

Family Joys and Tragedies

Our elder daughter Premila, who had done her schooling in Lima, Yercaud (Tamil Nadu) and London, undergraduate studies at St

---

1. Jackie Pinto, 'Meeting point for opera lovers', Deccan Herald Metrolife, 22 November 2009, https://www.deccanherald.com/content/37326/meeting-point-opera-lovers.html

Stephen's College, New Delhi, graduated with a Master's degree in International Affairs from Columbia University in 1988. She then worked for seven years for the UNCTC (United Nations Centre on Transnational Corporations) and UNCTAD (United Nations Conference on Trade and Development) at New York, Cape Town, Pretoria and Laayoune (Western Sahara). She returned to India in January 1995, re-established contact with her St Stephen's collegemate Mohit Satyanand, (whom she had greatly admired as a debater and actor) and married him on 23 October 1996. The wedding reception, held on the spacious lawns of my sister Margaret Alva (then Union Minister for Parliamentary Affairs)'s No. 1, Ashoka Road residence was a grand one. Former Chief Justice of India M.N. Venkatachaliah proposed the toast. Among those present at it were the American, Japanese, Mexican, Egyptian and Peruvian Ambassadors, all good friends from my days in Cairo and Lima.

Soon after her marriage, Premila specialized in FDI research and began to do consultancies for UNCTAD, World Bank, Columbia University, and the Economist Intelligence Unit.

Premila's son, Kedar Pascal, born 15 September 1998, has grown into a fine young man, excelled at his studies right through middle/ high school and has recently graduated with an Economics degree from North Western University in Chicago. He is an outstanding drummer, fine swimmer and a keen cyclist who cycled from Zurich to Munich in June 2017.

Teamwork Arts, the impresario organization set up by Mohit in 1993, has been 'producing' Indian cultural troupes for the Edinburgh Festival as also for 'Bonjour India' at Paris, 'India on the Nile' at Cairo, 'Confluence' at Sydney, 'Sarang' at Seoul, and 'India in the Sunshine City' at Harare. It has also been 'producing' literary events, the most successful of which is the Jaipur Literature Festival, held annually at Diggi Palace Hotel. Its great success has enabled Teamwork to set up similar literary festivals at Boulder Colorado in 2017 and London in 2018.

Thirty-four years have gone by since Andy's cancer surgery and his malignancy has not recurred. For Isobel, Andy and me, this is a miracle we personally witnessed. When Mother Teresa's canonization process commenced I wrote to His Holiness Pope John Paul II and reported this miracle. My letter was acknowledged by his Nuncio in New Delhi. He thanked me for the information I had furnished but indicated that the Vatican needed details of miracles that have happened after her death!

Isobel and I celebrated our golden wedding anniversary on 1 September 2012 with Holy Mass in the morning and dinner at Taj West End Hotel in Bangalore, (which kindly provided us with a complimentary suite for that night as we had spent our wedding night there 50 years earlier and were still together!) Our 10-day golden honeymoon was spent at Lucerne in Switzerland and Salzburg in Austria.

All this has given much joy to Isobel and me but we have also had to experience heartrending sorrows.

The greatest of all our sorrows was the sudden demise of our younger daughter Seema in March 1999. She was our most talented child, excelled in her studies, painted, composed poetry and was also a Bharatanatyam dancer trained by Smt Lakshmi, daughter of the renowned Bharatanatyam dancer and Natya guru Balasaraswathi. Sadly, she was afflicted with asthma from age seven. Allopathic treatment had failed to cure it but the reputed homeopath of New Delhi Dr Jugal Kishore had succeeded in controlling it. Yet, whenever she was under mental pressure or there were dust storms, as in New Delhi and Cairo, the asthma would recur.

In Cairo in 1990 she had written the following poem about her asthma travails:

While dust unveils itself delicately,
Asthma precipitates
Through narrowing tubes;
Needle-like whiskers
Shout through when
Lungs are laid down. Unawares
And violent sneezes
Are bombarded
On shivering, trembling nostrils.

After she graduated from Jesus and Mary College in New Delhi in 1996, with a First Class BA (Economics Honours) degree I wanted to send her to Columbia or Yale for further studies. But, she refused stating she wished to be a journalist.

About three months after graduation she was appointed a 'Staff Writer' by *Business Standard* in New Delhi. As she fared quite well here, she was transferred to the important Mumbai office. She was fortunate in getting a room in the sea-facing Working Women's Hostel at Colaba. However, the daily one-hour bus ride to/from her hostel to the *BS* office at Worli through Mumbai's high pollution traffic brought back her asthma.

In mid-February 1999, I told her to apply for two weeks leave and accompany me on my Phuket to Mumbai lecture cruise in early March. The clean, invigorating air, good food, and freedom from journalist deadlines brought her much relief from her asthma. Sadly, (as we later learnt) soon after she disembarked on 18 March morning and went to the *BS* office, she was required to work on an important article and submit it within 24 hours. So she worked overtime that day and told her colleagues she would come to office by 9 a.m. the next day to complete it. Since she had not arrived even by 11 a.m. and their telephone calls to her were not answered, they requested the hostel warden to ascertain why this was so. The warden went to her room and when, despite repeated knocks her door, it was not opened, she had it forced open and was shocked to find Seema's lifeless body on the balcony of her room. The mental pressure of having to complete her important article before noon the next day must have brought on a severe asthma attack and taken her to the balcony for her last gasps of air.

Isobel had arrived in Mumbai on 18 March morning. She boarded the cruise ship after Seema disembarked. It departed for Muscat at 6 p.m. that day. At about 7 a.m. on 20 March, the cruise director came to our suite and gave us a telegram from my sister Margaret Alva in New Delhi. It stated that Seema had suffered a severe asthmatic attack, was in ICU of a Mumbai hospital, and we should return to Mumbai immediately. Isobel and I were stunned and feared the worst but still hoped and prayed this might not be so. The cruise ship arrived at Muscat the following morning. Our Ambassador in Muscat, to whom Margaret had spoken to, had already booked our tickets to Mumbai and sent an Embassy vehicle to the port to take us to the airport. We arrived in Mumbai at 3 p.m., and were taken from the airport to Leela Penta Hotel where Margaret, Muriel (Isobel's elder sister), Premila and Mohit were awaiting us. After initially giving us the same narrative as in Margaret's telegram and serving us with sedative-laced cups of tea, Margaret broke the heartbreaking news of Seema's demise. I must have swooned or gone into a deep sedative-induced slumber as I do not recall anything thereafter until awakened at 7 a.m. next day and told we were to fly to Bangalore by the 11 a.m. Indian Airlines flight with the coffin containing Seema's body. Meanwhile, Isobel had stoically accompanied Margaret, Muriel and Premila to the hospital morgue to view Seema's body, already dressed for her funeral.

At the well-attended funeral ceremony at St Francis Xavier Cathedral, Isobel calmly read out her farewell message to Seema. It moved many to tears. Its opening and concluding paras were as under:

> Seema, our most beloved and precious child, the Creator, who gave you to us 24 years ago, has taken you back to His bosom as He felt you were too good, too pure, and too fragile for this rough harsh world. He has taken you to protect you from anymore earthly suffering, physical, mental or emotional. He chose to take you on the feast of St Joseph, the patron of Christian families and workers. Therefore, St Joseph will lead you into Garden of Eden on his special day, to free you from any more 'deadlines'...
> Dad is too crushed to personally express his feelings but endorses wholeheartedly all the sentiments contained herein. You were his greatest joy and pride, particularly since you began to write in the *Business Standard* and your articles appeared on its front page. May the fragrance of your beautiful life be ever with us.

Even sadder for Isobel and me was Seema's burial at the Hosur Road Catholic cemetery. We had looked forward to the joy of celebrating her wedding but had to experience instead the excruciating sorrow of seeing her coffin being lowered into a grave.

For almost three months after Seema's demise I was in a stupor. When I finally emerged from it I decided to sublimate my sorrow in the following ways:

- By bringing out a well-designed elegiac brochure about Seema, with some of her poems and the most notable tributes paid to her;
- Instituting an award for young journalists in her name in collaboration with *Business Standard*;
- Creating a scholarship in her name for the best Economics Honours Graduate of Jesus and Mary College, New Delhi, where she had graduated from; and
- Setting up an Endowment for the Girl Child in her name.

The elegiac brochure was released on her first death anniversary. On its front inside page was a Tagore poem titled 'Come and take your seat in the bosom of the Limitless my child'. Its back inside page carried her cousin Giselle Mehta's poetic tribute to her:

> A Rose bud on the family tree
> Bloomed not to wither, but to fall,
> Into the lap of Eternity.
>
> Positioned in pride of place
> With freshest blush of youth adorned
> She attained a transcendental grace
> Beyond confine of earthly bourne
> The sunshine of a life so brief
> Illumines the dark and endless night
> Of those benumbed with pain and grief
> Till they likewise merge with the Light.
>
> Death where is your fatal sting
> The Rose is attended by Eternal Spring.

The award for young journalists was titled 'Business Standard Seema Nazareth Award for Excellence in Print Journalism'. It was initially open to journalists below age 25 but this age limit was later raised to 30.

The first BSSN Award was presented by President K.R. Narayanan at Rashtrapati Bhavan on 21 February 2000 (Seema's 25th birth anniversary).

The subsequent annual awards have all been presented by VVIPs who included a Vice President, two former Chief Justices of India, three Cabinet ministers, an IAF Marshal and a great grandson of Count Leo Tolstoy! Most BSSN Award winners (21 by now) have done well for themselves. Some now work for newspapers/journals in Singapore, Hong Kong, London and Toronto.

The Seema Nazareth Endowment for the Girl Child (SNEGC) was

registered on her first death anniversary. Justice M.N. Venkatachaliah and my mother E.L. Nazareth signed its Deed as witnesses. Its opening paragraph carries a Seema quote (written at age 11) 'God created me because He wanted me, Seema Nazareth, to be on this earth and make others happy. God did not have to create me. He wanted to. That makes me feel special.'

SNEGC annually gives scholarships/financial assistance to poor, outstanding girl students/institutions which provide education and vocational training to them. Some of these Seema Nazareth scholars have done very well for themselves. One now works at Ernst & Young; one in *Time* Magazine's back office, one in ANZ Bank and one as Asst Professor of Pedagogy at Azim Premji University. All of them stay in regular touch with Isobel and me and are like daughters to us. We lost a much-loved daughter and now have 12 of them!

In July 2005, my mother passed away. She would have been 90 on 13 December that year and her five children were planning a big celebration for it. Sadly, the hernia on her lower left abdomen got strangulated in mid-June and she had to undergo emergency surgery. Though the chances of her survival were considered slim, to our joyful surprise, she came through it. On regaining consciousness, she piquantly commented, 'St Peter had opened wide the gates of Heaven for me, but I gave him the slip!' She made a steady recovery and was discharged from hospital three weeks later. But on 10 July morning, soon after having a bowl of porridge she brought it all up and breathed her last. It was a painful shock for all of us.

On 31 May 2014, my three sisters and I were struck by a more painful and traumatic tragedy. We, along with our younger brother John, were at Raj Bhavan Jaipur for Margaret and Niranjan Alva's golden wedding celebration. Margaret was then Governor of Rajasthan. On 23 May afternoon we all attended an elephant polo match about 30 miles from Jaipur. A sumptuous dinner was served thereafter. For the return journey my sisters and I returned in cars. John and his wife Meena decided to return by bus along with the extended family teenagers. There was much singing and gaiety en route. When they finally reached Raj Bhavan, and John was getting out of the bus he slipped and fell backwards. His head struck the concrete driveway and he instantly went into a coma from which he never recovered despite the best medical treatment in Jaipur being given to him. Early on 31 May morning he breathed his last. In the intervening period, Margaret's meticulously planned golden wedding celebration was disrupted and its public reception which the Chief Minister and other VIPS were to attend, had to be cancelled.

This tragedy cast a deep pall of depression on all of the family members who had come to Jaipur for Margaret's golden wedding celebration. It was not only intensely painful to me but also affected me at a deeper level as John was 12 years younger than me, was brimful of energy and 'Joie de vivre'.

I was struck by the evanescence of life; that it was like a flickering flame on a candle, beautiful and bright but ephemeral and easily extinguished. It made me aware as never before of the intrinsic value of life, that it needs to be carefully nurtured and lived meaningfully and that every new day is a precious gift. This triggered the keen desire in me to know more about the Creator and the purpose and nature of His or Her immense and highly complex creation. My earlier reading of Dr S. Radhakrishnan's *Eastern Religions and Western Thought*, Arnold Toynbee's *An Historian's Approach to Religion* and Mahatma Gandhi's *Views on Hindu Dharma* facilitated my journey into this esoteric realm. I now began to read other books : Fritjof Capra's *Tao of Physics,* Michael Talbot's *Mysticism and the New Physics*, Paul Davies' *The Cosmic Blueprint*, Andrew Newberg and Eugene d'Aquili's *Why God won't go Away: Brain Science and the Biology of Belief*, and Francis Collins' *The Language of God.*

All these ancient wisdom and modern scientific discoveries have convinced me thoroughly that all of creation, whether animate or inanimate, are manifestations of the Creator, of His infinite intelligence and energy, His supreme all-pervading consciousness and cosmic master plan. God is not the many images that are made of Him/Her and worshipped, but the eternal, Cosmic Energy ('*Maha Shakti*') which pervades and sustains the entire universe, in which every object, movement and activity, whether it is the sun that shines, the cloud that rains, the flower that blooms, the bird that sings or the child that is conceived, is a manifestation of this Energy. In January 2017 I composed a 'Prayer to the Divine Spirit' embodying these thoughts. This has been my 'morning prayer' ever since. It is as under:

> Eternal and Almighty Divine Spirit
> I firmly believe that thou, the Creator of the whole Universe
> With its millions of stars and hundreds of galaxies
> And the exact laws and balance of forces
> That keep them all in their proper orbits
> Are here within me, as the Divine Spark of Life and Energy;
> That it is Thou who makes my heart to beat,
> My lungs to breathe and the blood to flow
> Through every part of me, every moment of the day.
> I beseech thee to fill my soul, my mind and my heart
> With thy Divine Presence,
> To cleanse them of all impurity, hatred, fears and resentments
> To enlighten my mind, strengthen my will and self-confidence
> And assist me in resisting all temptations
> So that I will always be a good reflection of
> Your Divine Presence within me.
> Bless me and protect me Eternal and Almighty Divine Spirit.

I pray not only for myself but also for my beloved country India, the Mother Civilization which has produced more sages and holy men, and over the centuries has culturally enriched more of the world, than any other country. I feel privileged to have been born on its soil and blessed to have had ample opportunities to serve its interests and stand up for its millennial values in various parts of the world, and the honour of being its High Commissioner/Ambassador in five African and four Latin American countries. I wish to repay to it as best I can all that it has generously provided me in physical, mental and spiritual sustenance. I pray that its age old maxims *Satyamev Jayate* (Truth alone triumphs), *Ekam Sat Vipra Bahudha Vadanti* (The Truth is One, but has many names) and *Udaracharitanam tu Vasudhaiva Kutumbakam* (For the enlightened, all of humanity is one family) will always be its guiding light and national ethos.

Annexure 1

Observer article on Isobel dated 29 January 1978

YOU goes in diplomatic circles

Mix with the history - makers

IS Embassy life all caviar, champagne and servants ? What compensates for the restrictions, duties and separations ? How does it affect the children ? Is coming home like coming down to earth ? STELLA BINGHAM asked three 'diplomatic wives' about their life and work.

THE OBSERVER REVIEW : SUNDAY 29 JANUARY 1978

Nobby Clark

ISOBEL NAZARETH'S husband became the Indian deputy High Commissioner last October. They live in an official residence in Hampstead and their two elder children are at school here, though they intend to send them to boarding school in India when they next move.

'London is a difficult posting because of the size of the Commission. In the past we have had personal contact with all the staff. Here we have more responsibility. The High Commissioner is unfortunately a widower so I have many duties that would normally fall to the High Commissioner's wife. London is the halfway house for people on their way to New York. Sometimes I feel I'm a restaurateur and hotelier, but it's nice to see old friends.

The Nazareths's first post 15 years ago was Japan. 'There I was more a honeymooner than a diplomatic wife. In Burma our responsibilities grew but we were mixing mainly with the diplomatic community because the Government was strict about nationals mixing with foreigners.' They were sent next to Peru to set up the Indian Embassy. 'Socialising was hard, but I look a course in Spanish and that was appreciated.'

After a spell at the consulate in New York they went home to Delhi before coming to London in 1976. 'In the beginning there was a certain amount of glamour, and on the whole I think it's an enjoyable life. Very often the events we are watching at close quarter are history being made and the people we meet are historymakers.'

Annexure 2

Lord Mountbatten's letter to me of 28 December 1978

BROADLANDS,
ROMSEY,
HAMPSHIRE.
SO5 9ZD.

TELEPHONE
ROMSEY (0794) 518333

28th December, 1978

Dear Nazareth,

I am writing to thank you both very much indeed for your kind card for the New Year. It has been a pleasure working with you as acting High Commissioner both at the Nehru Trustees Meeting and at the Rajaji Centenary Celebrations.

I send to you both my very best wishes for 1979.

Yours ever

Mountbatten of Burma

Annexure 3

Mrs Zubin Mehta's letter to me of 28 October 1985

October 28, 1985

Mr. P.A. Nazareth
The Indian Council for Cultural Relations
Azad Bhavan, New Delhi
India

Dear Mr. Nazareth,

Zubin and I remember with clarity your extensive gifting of both ourselves and the orchestra. These welcoming aspects were more than material, and it is that factor--the abstract--which I address.

Your broad embrace of all of this group was astonishing, and the extra standards supplied for the trip to Agra were quite remarkable. Please remember that we hold you in memory with deep affection as surely do all the members of the New York Philharmonic Orchestra.

We loved being in New Delhi, and would welcome you to New York should you ever call. Please do determine whether we are in town through the Philharmonic. We would love to invite you to join us in whatever we are doing.

Most sincerely,

Nancy

Nancy Mehta
(Mrs. Zubin Mehta)

NM:ja

New York Philharmonic Telephone Number: (212) 580-8700

Annexure 4

US President Ronald Reagan's Message for the 1988 Society of Foreign Consuls Ball in New York City

---

THE WHITE HOUSE

WASHINGTON

November 16, 1988

It gives me great pleasure to send greetings to President Carter and to everyone attending the Consular Ball sponsored by the Society of Foreign Consuls in New York.

The members of your Society are charged with the important responsibility of furthering mutually beneficial relations between your respective nations and the United States in such important areas as commercial relations, tourism, and cultural exchanges. Your success helps create a more prosperous and peaceful world, and we're grateful for your efforts.

On this occasion, you pay tribute to the work of HABITAT FOR HUMANITY, an organization that does great good in seeking to provide every family with a decent home. HABITAT volunteers build affordable housing in more than 280 communities in North America and 59 locations abroad. Your support of HABITAT is commendable and in the best tradition of your Society.

Nancy and I wish you all a most memorable evening. God bless you.

Ronald Reagan

Annexure 5

My 'Egypt in Indian Eyes' article in *Al-Ahram* Weekly of 6-12 August 1992

Egypt in Indian eyes

As he prepares to move to his new posting in Mexico **P A Nazareth**, India's ambassador in Cairo for the past three years, writes of his feelings towards India's age-old sister — Egypt

After three happy and challenging years in Egypt, my official Mission in Egypt is nearing completion and the date for my departure approaches, I am often in a reflective mood these days and try to assess what it is in Egypt which has made such a deep impact on me.

In my 33 years in the Indian Foreign Service I have travelled all over the world, and lived in many countries as far apart as Japan, Ghana and Peru. Yet nowhere else as in Egypt have I seen a civilization so ancient, built on such a grand scale, in the face of such environmental odds, and so well preserved.

Nowhere else, does a river so vital to life and civilisation, so bravely challenge the burning desert, endlessly giving its precious waters to sustain the constant cycle of birth, death and regeneration, and yet remain ever brimful, tranquil and serene.

Nowhere else, does a three hundred kilometre stretch of river host so much of history and well preserved monuments, spanning over three millions, as between Luxor and Aswan.

Nowhere else, as in Egypt, does history have to be viewed in millenia rather than in centuries, decades or years. Layer upon layer of history, each distinct and yet each an integral part of an organic whole, are visible, like the rings in the trunk of a giant Redwood tree, each showing distinctly the additional girth the tree has acquired, but not the ravages it has encountered in the process.

Egypt for me is a magnificent tapestry of different strands of history, culture and values, from ancient Nubian and Pharonic, to Greco-Roman, Christian, Islamic and modern periods, mingled occasionally with embroidery of influences, ideas and practises, from Assyria, Persia, India, China and other ancient civilisations, and all woven into a beautiful artwork that imperceptibly changes and enlarges itself and yet retains its original format.

Egypt for me is the Pyramids, Karnak, Siwa, the towering figure of Ramses II, the beauty of Nefertiti and Cleopatra, Alexandria, St. Catherine, the Suez Canal, the majestic Nile with sailboats on it, Cairo with its thousand mosques and numerous churches, the music of AbdelWahab, the voice of Um Kalthoum, the poetry of Ahmed Shawky and the novels of Naguib Mahfouz.

Egypt for me is the land where people have thought and felt deeply, and placed high importance as much on national unity as on religion and after life, where people have stood up bravely against aggression, where the Mongol onslaught was stopped and a Tripartite attack frustrated, where the first Peace Treaty was made and great risks taken for peace in more recent times, where great ideas of Arab and African freedom and unity were conceived and concretised and from where emerged one of the great and charismatic founders of the non-alignment movement.

Egypt for me is the land which with its long and unbroken history, the wide variety of the cultural influences it has absorbed and harmonised, its unity in diversity, and in its Pharaonic religion, comes closest to India, and its conception of the Cosmos.

But more than anything else, Egypt for me is a land of handsome, friendly, amiable and ever smiling people, with a self-confident and philosophical view of life, which their long, grand and unbroken history has naturally endowed them with.

May Egypt progress and prosper, and its wonderful people be smiling always. May they also always cherish their historical and cultural twin sister, and comrade in the struggle for international peace, freedom and justice, INDIA.

Annexure 6

US President Barack Obama's letter to me of 31 July 2009

THE WHITE HOUSE

WASHINGTON

July 31, 2009

His Excellency P. A. Nazareth
Regency Alandon, 3A
No. 2 Ware Road
Bangalore 560 005
INDIA

Dear Mr. Nazareth:

I would like to extend my deepest thanks and appreciation for your kind gift. Thank you for *Gandhi's Outstanding Leadership.*

As our two nations work to address the new and complex challenges facing our world, I am hopeful about what our countries can accomplish together.

Again, thank you for the wonderful gift.

Sincerely,

Annexure 7

Prime Minister Manmohan Singh's Message for the launch of the Mandarin Edition of my *Gandhi's Outstanding Leadership* book

सत्यमेव जयते

प्रधान मंत्री

Prime Minister

MESSAGE

I am glad to learn that the well-acclaimed book, "Gandhi's Outstanding Leadership", written by Shri P.A. Nazareth and brought out by Sarvodaya International Trust, is now going to be available in Chinese.

Mahatma Gandhi's life and philosophy, while a product of the socio-cultural milieu of India's struggle for independence, have abiding and universal relevance for the world and remain undiminished by the passage of time. The values of compassion and courage, simplicity and sustainability and justice and equity that he personified are timeless. His leadership of India's independence struggle is a testimony to the power of truth and non-violence in the pursuit of progress and change.

Several decades after the Mahatma's passing, his vision and principles continue to inspire people and promote research into the contemporary meanings of Gandhi's message. This book by Shri Nazareth is yet another reflection of Gandhiji's universal appeal. Its popularity is evident in its several translations in many languages.

I am confident that the Chinese version of the book will bring the Father of our Nation and the ideals that he stood for closer to more than a billion people in China and help forge deeper understanding between our two great nations.

Manmohan Singh

(Manmohan Singh)

New Delhi
5 March, 2013

Annexure 8

President Pranab Mukherjee's Message for the launch of the Russian Edition of my *Gandhi's Outstanding Leadership* book

राष्ट्रपति
भारत गणतंत्र
PRESIDENT
REPUBLIC OF INDIA

MESSAGE

I am very happy to contribute a message for the Russian edition of the book 'Gandhi's Outstanding Leadership' authored by former Ambassador of India Pascal Alan Nazareth. I understand the book is being published by the Institute of the Russian Academy of Sciences with a foreword from the Russian Foreign Minister, Mr. Sergey Lavrov. It was originally published by the Sarvodaya International Trust in 2006 and has already come out in ten Indian and five foreign languages.

Mahatma Gandhi is greatly revered not only in India but all over the world. In the contemporary scenario, he has emerged as the foremost beacon of hope for a new humanity that would be motivated by truth, love, non-violent conflict resolution and universal brotherhood. Martin Luther King had rightly observed "If humanity is to progress, Gandhi is inescapable. We may ignore him at our own peril".

I am confident that this Russian edition of Ambassador Nazareth's book will be well received and will help create deeper understanding of the Mahatma's ideals and strategies strengthening thereby the close bonds of mutual respect and friendship between the Indian and Russian peoples.

(Pranab Mukherjee)

New Delhi
September 8, 2014

Annexure 9

HH The Dalai Lama's Foreword for my *Gandhi: The Soul Force Warrior* book

THE DALAI LAMA

FOREWORD

Ambassador Nazareth's book 'Gandhi's Outstanding Leadership' published in 2006 is part of his effort to spread the message of Gandhi-ji. Judging by the number of languages in which the book has been translated, it has been topical and well received. I am glad that the Ambassador has written a sequel to this book.

Ever since I was growing up in Tibet, Mahatma Gandhi has been a source of inspiration to me and he symbolized nonviolence. I was deeply inspired by his adoption of non-violence in India's struggle for freedom while at the same time having no hatred towards the British people, and I have put this into practice in my own efforts to restore the fundamental human rights and freedoms of the Tibetan people. In addition, I admired the simplicity and discipline of Gandhi-ji's way of life.

Gandhi-ji showed to the world the power of the ancient Indian message of ahimsa or non-violence. Non-violence means more than the mere absence of violence. It is something more positive, more meaningful; for the true expression of non-violence is compassion. Some people seem to think that compassion is just a passive emotional response, rather than a rational stimulus to action. But to experience genuine compassion is to develop a feeling of closeness to others, as Gandhi-ji did, combined with a sense of responsibility for their welfare. His great achievement was to show through his own example that non-violence can be implemented effectively not only in the political arena, but also in our day-to-day life.

I hope that this book by Ambassador Nazareth will contribute in spreading and strengthening the important message that the long term interests of peoples and countries can be realized through the pursuit of truth and non-violence, and the practice of compassion and humanitarian service.

November 23, 2015

Annexure 10

Former Soviet President Mikhail Gorbachev's Foreword for 12 European language editions of my *Gandhi's Outstanding Leadership* book

FOREWORD

Mohandas Karamchand Gandhi is known throughout the world as the Mahatma ("the Great soul"). He is one of the most remarkable thinkers of the 20th century. There are a lot of books, articles, scientific studies and movies dedicated to him. It would seem that nothing more could be added to the already well formed image of this great figure. However, the ' Gandhi's Outstanding Leadership' book authored by the Indian diplomat Pascal Alan Nazareth has aroused much global interest. It has been published already in 11 Indian languages and in 9 foreign languages (including a Russian edition in 2014). The number of foreign language editions keeps growing as the German, Italian, Hungarian and Dutch ones are soon to come out. What is the secret of such success?

The fact of the matter is that Gandhi's spiritual heritage not only continues to arouse interest but it becomes ever more pertinent. We live in a world where many old threats to humanity's existence still exist and more challenging and formidable ones have been added to them. People are anxiously looking for a way out of this critical situation.One of the most promising ways of doing so has been indicated by Mahatma Gandhi : humanity should forsake violence.

Alan Nazareth has chosen an important aspect of Gandhi's personality to focus on. Even the many who recognize Gandhi as an outstanding figure still consider him to be only a thinker, almost "a dreamer". In his book, the author presents Mahatma Gandhi as an outstanding modern leader, who greatly influenced other leaders during his lifetime and has continued to do so after his death. Here I would like to give a specific example from my own experience. Being head of the Soviet government, I paid considerable attention to relations with India. I had established close and fruitful relations with the then Prime Minister of India Rajiv Gandhi. Rajiv's views on the modern world were much in accord with mine. Both of us, as political leaders of our countries, considered Mahatma Gandhi's ideas of non-violent conflict resolution very pertinent. After wide ranging and deep discussions between us and expert advice from both sides, the historic Delhi Declaration on the Principles of a Nuclear Weapon Free and Non-Violent World was formulated and signed on November

27, 1986. In it we proclaimed a number of principles for establishing world peace. These are : highest importance should be placed on human life; non-violence should be the foundation of human society; the political and economic independence of every state should be recognized and respected; the "balance of terror" strategy should be replaced by a comprehensive international security pact.

The Delhi Declaration is an outstanding document, the significance of which goes far beyond the confines of the historical context in which it was signed. It clearly shows the impact of Mahatma Gandhi's spiritual heritage. However, the idea of non-violence is also deeply rooted in the Russian tradition.

Leo Tolstoy's writings had a great impact on the youthful Gandhi who read and pondered over them deeply. The great Russian poet Tyutchev, in his poem "Two Unities" has written : "Unity can only be welded by iron and blood some oracles have said. Well, try welding it with love and see which lasts the longer." Even though these lines were written many years ago and in quite a different scenario, its profound message still remains true "

Alan Nazareth's book contains many impactful Gandhi's quotes as well as opinions about him expressed by famous thinkers, leaders, cultural personalities and others from various spheres of global society. Among the many photographs in his book I was glad to see one of the revered Indian spiritual master Sri Chinmoy, who founded and directed the 'Peace Meditations Centre" at the UN Headquarters in New York for many years. He awarded the prestigious U Thant Peace Award to Mr. Nazareth in 2007.

I knew Sri Chinmoy personally, and he also awarded me with the U Thant Award in the mid 1990s. I stayed in touch with him until till his passing away in 2007. I will forever remember his words "World-peace can be achieved when the power of love replaces the love of power".

Mahatma Gandhi died a martyr's death; he became a victim of the violence which he detested so much. But his life and his ideas give firm assurance to all people of good will that violence has no future and non-violence will ultimately triumph.

Mikhail Gorbachev

Index

Adi Jayanti, 38
Africa, 10, 90, 100, 105, 121, 141, 152–53, 192, 196–97, 207
Ambassador of India, 72, 74, 100, 113, 140, 159, 182, 196, 199, 202, 206
Ambassador's Club: The Indian Diplomat at Large, The, 95
AOG (Aircraft on Ground) indents, 110, 114

Bangladesh, 51, 90, 99–102, 106
Basmati rice exports, 107
Belize, 201, 206, 209–11, 217
Bihar, 16, 22–23

Bofors scandal, 183
Boy's Prayer, A, 2
Brazil, 198, 222, 225
Buddhism and National Cultures Conference, 155, 160
Burma, 41, 43–45, 47–52, 55–57, 71

Cairo, 97–98, 183–84, 186–91, 193–99, 231–32
CDA, 33, 45–47, 49, 55, 72, 78, 135
Central Bureau of Investigation (CBI), 68–69, 83, 183
Chakravyuha, 158
Chandragupta Maurya, 38
Chief of Protocol (COP), 97–98, 130, 134, 139, 146
Chile, 74, 92, 94
China, 11, 29, 33, 36, 86, 158–59, 164
CIA, 94, 152, 225
Commonwealth, 19, 100, 120–21, 124, 128, 192, 209
Concerto for Violin and String Orchestra, 198
Consul General of India (CGI), 5, 57–59, 61–64, 66, 68, 70, 72, 83, 113, 169, 171–72, 175–78, 180–82, 192, 204, 229
Cosmic Blueprint, The, 238
Costa Rica, 62–63, 65–70, 72, 82
Coups, 12, 43–44, 75, 95, 106, 131–33, 141–43, 146, 148–49, 151–52
Cultural events, 141, 155
Cultural tours, 164–65

Deputy High Commissioner (DHC), 14, 40, 113, 119, 123, 129–30, 134, 153, 164, 229
Desai, Morarji, 38, 119–20, 125, 130
Diplomacy, 14, 20, 153–54, 169, 192
Diplomatic missions, 31, 83

Eastern Religions and Western Thought, 238
East European Countries, 44
EBD, 99, 101, 102, 106
ECAFE (UN Economic Commission for Asia and the Far East), 100
Egypt, 182, 184, 188–94, 199–200, 202, 212, 225
El Salvador, 201, 206, 208–09, 217
Embassy of India (EI), 26–28, 30, 33, 36, 38–40, 43, 45–50, 57, 64, 68, 72, 76–79, 82, 87, 89, 91–93, 97, 101, 109, 129, 131, 138, 142, 159, 164, 181, 183–84, 187, 190, 194–96, 198, 201–02, 204, 206
Embassy Residence (IER), 122–23, 131, 139
Europe, 99, 164–65

European Festivals Association (EFA), 164–65
Executions, 133–34, 138, 143, 146, 148, 150
EXIM bank credit, 140
Extradition case, 69, 82–83

Festival of India (FOI), 163, 165–66
France, 74, 83, 93, 129, 142, 189, 192, 198
Fuji, 35, 39, 85

Gandhi, Indira, Indian Prime Minister, 11, 47, 49–51, 72, 99, 106, 118–19, 126–28, 153, 154, 161, 165, 180
assassinated, 161, 180
Gandhi, Mahatma, 66, 112, 165, 202, 213, 219–20, 223, 226, 238
Gandhi, Rajiv, Prime Minister, 92, 161–62, 180–81, 183
Gandhi's Outstanding Leadership, 32, 40, 222–23
Gandhi statue, 176, 202, 221
Germany, Federal Republic of, 40, 88, 139, 198, 213
Ghana, 129–33, 136, 138–41, 144–50, 152
  Armed Forces Revolutionary Council (AFRC), 132–35, 137–38
  Flagstaff House, 131–32, 139, 147
  Tata buses for, 140, 144, 147
  Gleneagles Declaration, 121
Government of India (GOI), 11, 13, 19, 24, 26, 45, 68–69, 78, 83, 87, 89, 91, 97, 106, 126, 134, 144, 164, 185, 193, 213, 226
Guatemala, 201, 206–08, 217
Guerrillas, 151, 209, 214–15

Habitat for Humanity (HH), 179
Hailee, 40–42
HAL (Hindustan Aeronautics Ltd), 114, 116, 126, 147, 220
Haute Volta, 140–42, 149, 152
High Commission of India (HCI), 14, 40, 49, 77, 100, 109–15, 117–26, 128–30, 132, 134–35, 140, 164–66, 169, 193, 199, 206, 227–28, 240
Historian's Approach to Religion, An, 238
Hong Kong, 25, 35, 236
Honorary Consul of India, 79

IAF indents, 116
Inca Land, 86
India and Egypt: Influences and Interactions, 191, 192
India *and Greece—Connections and Parallels*, 158
India–Bangladesh Ganga Waters Sharing Treaty, 102
India–Bangladesh Joint Rivers Commission (JRC), 101
India–Bangladesh Treaty of Friendship, Cooperation and Peace, 100
India House, 36, 42, 49–50, 112, 123, 125, 129, 159, 183–84, 192–94, 227
Indian Community, 31, 46–48, 87, 93–94, 118, 122, 125, 128, 142, 178, 202, 209–10
Indian Council for Cultural Relations (ICCR), 153–55, 157–67, 169, 191–92, 194, 197, 204, 212, 219–20
Indian Cultural Centre (ICC), 194, 202–03, 211, 217
Indian diplomats, 20, 27, 134, 187, 218, 226, 229
Indian Film Export Promotion, 80
India–Pakistan, 57, 229
  ceasefire, 57
  relations, 229
  war, 57
India's Shipping Development Fund, 37, 59
Indo–US Joint Commission on Economic, Commercial, Scientific, Technological, Educational and Cultural Cooperation, 102
Indo–US Sub Commission on Education and Culture, 167
Israel, 55, 193, 196–99
ITPO (India Trade Promotion Organisation), 136

Jaguar Fighter Aircraft deal, 124, 126
Japan, 24, 26, 29–30, 32–33, 36, 39–41, 84–85, 196, 201, 214, 225
Jewellery crisis, 45–47, 49

Kanishka plane crash, 168
Kashmir dispute, 187
Kuwait, 107, 188–90

Language of God, The, 238
Latin America, 72, 76, 78, 80, 89, 153, 202, 206
Liberia, 130, 140–41, 143–44, 146, 150–52
Life in Diplomacy, A, 228
Lifted Up, 152
Lima International Trade Fair (LITF), 78–80
Lost City of the Incas, 86

Machu Picchu, a Citadel of the Incas, 86
Mahatma Gandhi Society, San Jose, 66
McMahon Line, 36
Mexico, 63, 65, 93, 158, 188, 198–99, 201–05, 207, 209, 211–17, 219, 224
Military attaché, 31, 48
Military coup, 75, 106, 131, 152
Ministry of Commerce (MoC), 10, 76–77, 79–80, 89, 105–07, 109, 163–64
Ministry of Defence (MoD), 31, 116–18
Ministry of External Affairs (MEA), 13, 15, 22, 24, 33, 45–47, 56–57, 60, 63, 68, 76–77, 83, 87, 97, 99, 104–06, 115, 117–18, 138, 146, 149, 165–67, 180–81, 193–94, 214, 217
Ministry of Home Affairs (MHA), 107
Missionaries of Charity Home (MCH), 90–91, 95
Modern Ghana, 150
Monrovia, 140–43
Morocco, 198
Mother Teresa, 89–91, 95–96, 150, 172–73, 230, 232

NAFTA (North American Free Trade Agreement), 213, 215
NAM, 155–56
Narasimha Rao, Indian Prime Minister, 162, 192, 199
Narayanan, K.R., Indian President, 236
National Academy of Administration, 17, 19–20
Nazareth, Pascal Alan
as Acting High Commissioner (AHC), 123–25
as Ambassador of India, 140, 182, 199, 202, 206
as a member of Foreign Minister Y. B. Chavan's delegation, 104
as Consul General (CG), 5, 70, 171, 175, 180
as Consul (Passports/Visas), 58
as Deputy High Commissioner (DHC), 14, 40, 130, 134
as DG (ICCR), 153–54, 161, 163–64, 167, 191–92, 197, 204, 219–20
as Director (EBD), 99, 106
as Director (West Asia & North Africa), Ministry of Commerce, 10
as High Commissioner of India (HCI), 129–30, 140, 206
as India's Charge D' Affaires in Peru, 75
as Japanese language officer, EI Tokyo, 40
choice of the IFS, 14–15
disciplinary actions, 117
'District Training' (DT), 22–23
family joys and tragedies, 230
goodwill visit to Pakistan, 226, 229
honours received, 230
lectures, 225
led delegations, 107
marriage, 34
passed Japanese language exam, 34
promotion of opera in Bangalore, 229
rationalization of the issue of licenses for import, 105
studies, 3–6
study of Japanese Kanji, 28, 32
Supply Wing in High Commission of India London, 109–10, 113–18

visit to Machu Picchu, 74, 85–86, 105
Nehru, Jawaharlal, Indian Prime Minister, 3, 13–14, 32, 37, 47, 61, 68, 83, 122, 184
New York Philharmonic Orchestra (NYPO), 153, 159–60, 197
Non-violence, 161, 219

Operation Desert Storm, 189–90
Orsova, 34, 40

Paintings and drawings, 36–37, 159, 194
Pakistan, 56–57, 87, 107, 187, 218, 226–29
army's surrender to Indian army, 87
military moves in Kutch and Kashmir, 56
Pakistan-India Peoples Forum for Peace and Democracy (PIPFPD), 226–28
Peru, 72, 74–76, 80–82, 84–85, 87, 89–91, 93, 96–98, 101, 105, 173
PMI (Permanent Mission of India to the UN), 72, 77, 100, 176, 192
Poetry, 92, 153, 155, 232
Prague Spring uprising, 72

Radhakrishnan, Dr S., 32, 47
Rahman, Sheikh Mujibur, Prime Minister, 87, 99, 106
Relations
Bangladesh–India, 99
cultural, 192
economic, 99
historical, 192
India–Burma, 48–49
India–China, 36, 158
India–Egypt, 192
India–Ghana, 146, 148
India–Mexico, 212
India–Pakistan, 229
India–US, 178, 181
Revolution, 147–48, 150, 215, 224
Rome, 58, 89, 91, 103, 129, 191, 222

Sarvodaya International Trust (SIT), 219–22
Savoy: The Charm of a Great Hotel, 111
Scotland, 121, 225
Shastri, Lal Bahadur, Indian Prime Minister, 49, 56–57
Shipping Corporation of India (SCI), 84, 145–46
Silver Jubilee of Queen Elizabeth's reign, 121
Society of Foreign Consuls (SFC), 179–80
South Africa, 90, 121, 196–97, 207
Soviet Union, 44, 163, 223
Spain, 84, 86, 179, 210

Tata buses, 140, 144, 147–49
Theatre, 54, 82, 153, 155, 158, 165–66

UK, 60, 83, 100, 119, 121–24, 126, 128, 139, 155, 163–66, 169, 189–90, 192, 196, 198, 210
UNCTAD, 89, 91–92, 94, 231
UNCTC (United Nations Centre on Transnational Corporations), 231
Union Public Service Commission (UPSC), 7, 9–10, 13, 18
Personality Interview, 7, 9–10, 13
United Nations (UN), 58, 70, 75, 100, 138, 151, 176, 180, 187, 192–93, 199, 209, 222, 230
United Nations Security Council (UNSC), 72, 192, 209
USA, 33–34, 36, 51, 57, 59–60, 62, 65–66, 68–70, 72, 78, 85–86, 93–94, 100, 102–03, 113, 141, 151–52, 155, 163, 167, 169, 175, 178–81, 185, 189–90, 193, 196, 198, 203, 207, 209–10, 213–14, 223, 229

Views on Hindu Dharma, 238
Virginity Test Crisis, 113, 128

When I Fell from the Sky: The True Story of One Woman's Miraculous Survival, 88
WHO, 55, 90
World Bank, 5, 93, 151, 231